LEGENDS OF MODERNITY

LEGENDS OF MODERNITY

ESSAYS AND LETTERS

FROM OCCUPIED POLAND,

1942–1943

Czeslaw Milosz

Translated from the Polish by Madeline G. Levine

Introduction by Jaroslaw Anders

FARRAR STRAUS GIROUX / *New York*

Farrar, Straus and Giroux

19 Union Square West, New York 10003

Distributed in Canada by Douglas & McIntyre Ltd.

Printed in the United States of America

Originally published in 1996 by Wydawnictwo Literackie, Poland,

as *Legendy nowoczesności*

Published in the United States by Farrar, Straus and Giroux

First American edition, 2005

Library of Congress Cataloging-in-Publication Data

Milosz, Czeslaw.

[Legendy nowoczesności. English.]

Legends of modernity : essays and letters from occupied Poland,

1942–1943 / Czeslaw Milosz ; translated from the Polish by Madeline G.

Levine.— 1st American ed.

  p. cm.

ISBN-13: 978-0-374-18499-5

ISBN-10: 0-374-18499-2

  1. Milosz, Czeslaw—Correspondence. 2. Andrzejewski, Jerzy, 1909– —
Correspondence. 3. Authors, Polish—20th century—Correspondence.
4. Milosz, Czeslaw—Translations into English. I. Andrzejewski,
Jerzy, 1909– II. Levine, Madeline G. III. Title.

PG7158.M553L4413 2005

891.8′58709—dc22

2005040950

Designed by Dorothy Schmiderer Baker

www.fsgbooks.com

1   3   5   7   9   10   8   6   4   2

Contents

LETTER ESSAYS OF JERZY ANDRZEJEWSKI

AND CZESLAW MILOSZ

Introduction

by Jaroslaw Anders

In his autobiography *Native Realm*, Czeslaw Milosz describes the strange mixture of terror and relief he experienced with the outbreak of World War II. "That long-dreaded fulfill-ment," he writes, "has freed us from the self-reassuring lies, illusions, subterfuges; the opaque has become transparent." Familiar forms of collective life collapsed overnight. The debates over ideologies and political doctrines came down to a display of unthinkable brute force. At last, modern man was able to behold his total, unashamed nakedness.

It was a horrifying view that called for intellectual mobilization, a return to the source, revisiting some of the most fundamental questions about human nature, history, and morality, to dissect the extreme ideologies that ushered in the totalitarian era. That was, indeed, the project that occupied Milosz during his amazingly productive wartime years. The result was the series of cystalline essays and letters collected in this volume—an urgent voice from the past that sounds strikingly relevant today.

The outbreak of World War II found Czeslaw Milosz in Warsaw. The twenty-eight-year-old Polish-Lithuanian poet, the author of the well-received early volumes *A Poem on Frozen Time* and *Three Winters*, was working at that time as a broadcaster for the Polish State Radio. After Poland's capitulation he crossed the Polish-Romanian border, then headed east to the city of his youth, Wilno (today Vilnius), just in time to see it overtaken by Soviet troops under a secret clause of the Soviet-German nonaggression pact. A few months later he clandestinely returned to Nazi-occupied Warsaw, where he remained until the early days of the Warsaw Uprising of August 1944. For a time, he held work papers as a laborer, carting cases of books between library buildings, with the exceptional privilege of reading them as well. He was active in the cultural arm of the Polish anti-Nazi resistance, publishing underground works and literary anthologies. At the same time, he continued his own literary efforts, writing poetry, translating T. S. Eliot's "The Waste Land," and working on the essays collected in this volume.

The decision to brave several well-guarded wartime borders, risking death or deportation to a concentration camp, was made partly for personal reasons—Milosz wanted to be close to his wife, Janina—but also because he sensed that the Soviet occupation, though externally less atrocious than the Nazi one, could prove both more durable and more devastating to the human spirit. In one of the essays in this volume, "Wartime Experience," he returns indirectly to those seemingly erratic relocations in the first year of the war. Using the literary prototype of Pierre Bezukhov from Leo Tolstoy's *War and Peace*, he says that civilians faced with the sudden eruption of a military conflict succumb to a frenetic, hallucinatory state in which they want to be everywhere and with everyone, to remain involved, to participate in the general drama while realizing that much of what man can undertake matters very little in a world where "everything collapses; everything seems artificial and ephemeral [and] the cruelty of human beings . . . is identical in its results with the cruelty of nature."

For the young poet the war was a physical and moral shock, but not an intellectual shock. A sharp observer of his times, he knew that interwar Europe was a pile of kindling waiting for a spark. The economic deprivation of millions, the rise of bloodthirsty ideologies, outbreaks of national and racial hatred—all spoke of a social and spiritual crisis at the very heart of European civilization. In an early poem, "Artificer," written in Wilno in 1931, Milosz depicts a dark deity walking the earth with a fist raised to the sky and crushing human dwellings: "pensive, he looks at the honey seeping from those huge honeycombs: / throbs of pianos, children's cries, the thud of a head banging against the floor. / This is the only landscape able to make him feel."*

The sense of Europe's spiritual crisis, and his own crisis of faith, launched Milosz's lifelong preoccupation with religious and metaphysical subjects. While taking a law degree at Stefan Batory University in Wilno, he devoted much time to the study of the scholastic philosophy of Saint Thomas Aquinas, still considered the intellectual foundation of the Roman Catholic faith. Based on the Aristotelian system, the Thomist doctrine strove to resolve many of the contradictions caused by implanting Christian dogma into the classical cultural soil—to reconcile faith with reason, intuition with logic, the world of ideas with the physical world, the uniqueness of the human soul with the communal aspects of life.

For centuries, the philosophy of Saint Thomas was the bedrock of a relatively unified, coherent worldview. But with the coming of the modern era this formidable edifice began to crumble. The result was an unprecedented period of creativity and innovation—the great, exciting adventure of the human mind—but also of intellectual vertigo, a cacophony of divergent truths man has never encountered before. The hitherto

---

*Translated by Milosz and Robert Hass in Czeslaw Milosz, *New and Collected Poems: 1931–2001*, New York: Ecco Press, 2002, p. 3.

integrated areas of reflection—metaphysics, physics, ethics, the study of the human mind and the study of the human polis—broke up into separate, often contending "disciplines." The breakdown also released a swarm of extreme ideas previously held back by the intricate system of scholastic checks and balances. Pure rationalism began to vie with unfettered irrationalism; the romantic celebration of the individual competed with the naturalistic notion of the human anthill; nature was worshipped as a new deity or denounced as a monstrosity. More often than not those extremes met in odd, sinister configurations, such as twentieth-century totalitarian ideologies that managed to combine rationalism and irrationalism, the search for an earthly paradise with the ultimate contempt for man.

As did many of his contemporaries, Milosz entered the years of World War II convinced that modern man, more free than ever in history, is also condemned to wander among ruins, to create and discard new "legends" about himself, to fall into traps set by his own mind. The outbreak of a new European conflict and the unspeakable Nazi brutalities seemed to him the culmination of a centuries-long spiritual drift that finally brought civilization over the edge. Milosz's wartime essays and letter essays exchanged with his friend the Catholic writer Jerzy Andrzejewski (1909–1983) are his earliest attempts to survey this landscape of desolation in a direct and systematic way. His goal is to dissect the "legends" of modernity and see if a new kind of reality can be found among the shadows and phantasms of the modern mind. Calm, erudite, relentlessly honest and self-knowing, and eventually hope-inspiring, they also establish the main themes of Milosz's future literary work: the theological mystery of evil, the apparent contradiction between man's natural instincts and his spiritual aspirations, the unending struggle between intellect and imagination, and the impact obscure philosophical and artistic ideas have on the history of people and nations.

Milosz's exploration begins on Robinson Crusoe's island, where he sees an expression of Rousseau's myth of the natural goodness of man and a glorification of the individual liberated from the demands of culture and society. In both the classical and pre-modern Christian view, man's path to perfection or "salvation" led through the community. Placed outside his civilization or religious kinship, man meant very little. With the advent of what Milosz calls "Protestant-merchant morality," man attempts to encounter both the world and God individually, without an intermediary. The human soul becomes its own government and its own church. Milosz points out that Rousseau's romantic ideal of a "noble savage" paved the way for liberal individualism and the capitalist cult of self-sufficiency and served as the ideological justification of the "tenacious, blind energy" of innumerable conquerors, colonizers, and industrialists who were the early incarnations of the modern superman.

In the novels of Balzac, Milosz explores a seemingly opposite myth of "the Monster City," a soulless organism that destroys and devours the individual. In this human anthill people only seem to make reasoned, moral choices. In fact, they obey biological rules of adaptation, camouflage, and survival. Although man retains some of his spiritual aspirations, society is a purely naturalistic, Darwinian entity. It teaches man that "the basic element of existence is evil and struggle, that throughout time, both nature and the human race, which is only one part of nature, have been a battlefield."

In the essay on Stendhal, Milosz shows how a clash between the naturalistic concept of "the Monster City" and the romantic ideal of a powerful, self-creating individual gives birth to a new hero of *ressentiment* who dares to challenge the monster by exercising his unconstrained, morally unfettered Will—in his view the only thing that separates him from the blind, enslaved masses. Stendhal's Julian Sorel is a gifted, ambitious man full of "envy, anger, longing for what is beyond his reach," who sees absolutely no reason to behave in an ethical way. "This rebel, observing that both religion and morality are only and exclusively a human creation and that the world is a world of evil, feels justified in declaring war on the cowardly, worthless mass, which erects its own gods, its own fetishes . . . and orders him, too, to believe."

If Stendhal's heroes defy morality in order to achieve a particular goal—usually a social or financial position they think they rightly deserve—the liberated Will soon becomes an end in itself. The hero of André Gide's *Les Caves du Vatican* (*Lafcadio's Adventures*) commits purely gratuitous acts of immorality—his Will desires and worships only itself. André Gide ("that depraved man," Milosz calls him) was a follower of Friedrich Nietzsche, whose celebration of instinct and of the blind, unbridled "life force" Milosz sees as one of the underpinnings of Nazi ideology.

It may be surprising to find the American pragmatist philosopher William James in the company of Nietzsche and Gide. The author of *The Varieties of Religious Experience* had a great influence on Milosz and his generation. The Polish poet remembers a sense of liberation when he first came in contact with James's work. "It taught that there is no other truth than the truth of human desires and aspirations, and that what contributes to internal clarity and goodness requires no other test." But during the war Milosz came to the conclusion that philosophical pragmatism leads to the same irrationalism, moral relativism, and the elevation of "myth" over objective "truth" that in his view had led to the breakdown of European civilization.

Reason and rationalism are for Milosz perhaps the most ambivalent concepts with which he struggled throughout his life. On one hand, the cult of the irrational, instinctive, subconscious in man, while promising liberation and creativity, seems to deliver only slavery and destruction. On the other hand, the "scientific" reason that occupies itself with the visible world has a tendency to reduce man to the level of nature. When it turns its analytical lens toward man's interior, it inevitably stumbles upon layers of darkness and mystery. In both cases it resembles a snake swallowing its own tail: "Intellect arrived at the condemnation of intellect, which was greeted with a howl of joy by proponents of the superman. For nothing guarantees such freedom as the rupture of trust in rationally ascertainable truth."

For Milosz the issue also had a personal dimension. Although intellectually inclined toward rationalism, he admitted to being a natural intuitionist. In this way he resembled his Wilno professor Marian Zdziechowski (1861–1938), to whom he devoted one of his wartime essays, as well as one of his late poems from the volume *This* (2000). A literary critic, an authority on Slavic cultures, and a philosopher, Zdziechowski was the spiritual patron of the "Żagary" poetic group co-founded by young Milosz in Wilno. He believed that the world approached rationally excludes the possibility of God. Nature is pure disorder, and it does not point at anything larger than itself. But faced with the choice between faith and reason, Zdziechowski chose faith. He posited that God is a miracle and can be approached only irrationally. God dwelled neither in the world nor outside the world, but in the hearts of men.

Zdziechowski's vision was very close to that of Milosz himself. In Milosz's numerous poems and essays he ponders the essential irrationality of God and the power of religious intuition. He seems to suggest that at least in the area of religion, irrationalism can be some kind of solution. And yet he feels that by leaving the domain of reason man steps onto a very unstable, dangerous ground. "Is it not too risky a proposition," he writes in the essay on Zdziechowski, "to rescue religion by reference to feelings emerging from the darkness that is every human soul?" Our intuition has a knack for deceiving us, he says. What we take for the voice of God may well turn out to be the whisper of the devil.

The hero of the essay "The Boundaries of Art" is Polish playwright, novelist, and philosopher Stanisław Ignacy Witkiewicz, who was one of the most interesting and enigmatic personalities of the interwar era. Like José Ortega y Gasset, Witkiewicz feared the political and cultural triumph of the masses that in his view would put an end to all higher aspirations of humanity. He believed that art, the human spirit's last line of defense, must protect its autonomy by turning away from traditional human concerns and strive for "pure form." It must become maximally irrational, individualistic, and offensive to common tastes. Milosz views Witkiewicz as a tragic artist-hero typical of his times. (He committed suicide in the first weeks of the war upon learning that the Soviets had invaded Poland from the east.) But the author considers Witkiewicz's approach to art decadent and unsound. Milosz questions the modern, self-conscious search for a pure aesthetic experience as a substitute for religious rapture—artificial excitations of the soul mistaken for transcendence. For Milosz, true art always aspires to something larger than itself—a kind of wisdom, understanding—and creates beauty almost by chance.

The letter essays included in this volume testify to the intensity of intellectual life in wartime Poland. During the winter of 1942–1943 Czeslaw Milosz conducted this written exchange with another writer of his generation, Jerzy Andrzejewski. Before the war, Andrzejewski moved in the circle of young Polish Catholic conservative-nationalist intellectuals. After the war he joined the Communist Party and became one of the "official" literary voices of the new regime. In the late 1960s Andrzejewski broke with the communists and became an icon of the Polish dissident movements. He is best known as the author of *Ashes and Diamonds*, a novel about the first days of communist rule in Poland. (It was turned into a movie classic by the Polish director Andrzej Wajda.) Milosz and Andrzejewski parted ways soon after the war, and Andrzejewski appears as Alpha, the Moralist in Milosz's *Captive Mind*—the Christian writer who succumbs to historical determinism and makes a pact with the devil. Though the exiled Milosz was banned in communist Poland and viciously attacked by its literary establishment (until he was awarded the Nobel Prize in 1980), the two men maintained their friendship, and Andrzejewski may have secretly visited Milosz in France in the late 1950s. During the war, Milosz and Andrzejewski were close friends working together for the Polish cultural underground. In the "letters," exchanged in Warsaw's clandestine literary pubs, they debate the apparent bankruptcy of all political ideas of the century and the atrophy of religious imagination even among modern believers. It is Andrzejewski who raises the issue of "the dematerialization of such concepts as heaven, hell, the immortal soul, and grace." But the peculiar relationship between belief and imagination frequently arises in Milosz's poetry and essays.

In these early essays the poet also explores the relationship between the world of ideas and the world of historical events. Without ignoring history's tremendous inertia, Milosz gives clear precedence to ideas over historical processes. It is the thinking man that sets history in motion, not the other way around. That is why Milosz speaks with special loathing about political doctrines and philosophical theories that claim action should precede reflection or deny ideas any role in the visible world. Moral responsibility of thinkers and artists is the main subject of many of Milosz's poems, such as "A Treatise on Poetry" or "Child of Europe," and his best-known books of essays—*The Captive Mind, Native Realm,* and *Emperor of the Earth.* In his essay on Nietzsche and Gide entitled "Absolute Freedom" Milosz says that the antihuman doctrine of Nazism, "the sword that found its way into the hands of madmen," was in effect forged by the works of antirational, romantic philosophers, "who destroyed faith in the gravity of thought."

Despite his metaphysical fascinations and his moralist fervor, the Milosz of the wartime essays is already aware that the old feeling of unity between the material world and the human spirit, between reason and imagination, between history and transcendence, has been taken away from man, possibly forever, and that striving to reconstruct that unity from the heap of broken fragments is both futile and dangerous. Though intellectually at odds with modernity, he seems to accept modernity's chief message: not everything adds up; some contradications will never be reconciled; some gaps are not meant to be closed. The best we can do is to treat matters of the spirit with respect, to put thought before action, ideals before ideologies, wisdom before artifice, and to practice "systematic doubting that might be capable of unearthing the few values worthy of rescue and development." In a letter written in the last years of the war, the young writer mapped out, in touchingly modest terms, what would become his epic intellectual journey of the next sixty years: "I am satisfied with sketching contradictions; a stroll through the garden where 'pro' and 'contra' grow side by side suffices for me."

ESSAYS FROM THE

OCCUPATION

Preface

This book is not a collection of essays about various writers, although it might seem like one. In fact, each of these figures is studied from only one particular angle and is no more than a pretext. This work was certainly not intended to provide more or less accurate literary portraits.

The book was planned as a unified whole, and the same concerns are repeated in each of its chapters, refracted each time in a different prism. Had it been written as well as its author wished it to be, in a simple, clear, accessible manner, what connects the chapters would have been more apparent. However, it was written at a time when most people did not see the world as simple, clear, and accessible, and because such times are not particularly conducive to good writing, it is not shameful to balance the book's deficits now, at least partially, with the help of a preface.

History's violent leap and the sense that there is much to be done evoke a desire to be rid of old habits and illusions. Whoever has the ambition to take an active role in change as a new, creative man must attempt to recognize and explain the phenomena that shock him. Burdened by obsolete methods of thought and style, his attempts will be in vain ten times in a row. On the eleventh try, he will achieve what he aimed for.

What number attempt these essays are, the author, obviously, does not know.

The basic theme, threaded through numerous digressions, is an attempt to clear the field of convictions about man's natural impulses and also about the natural conditions of his life—not without the hope that by destroying the legends he creates about himself, it will be possible to locate the surest footing. The chapter about Daniel Defoe is aimed against belief in natural goodness outside of civilization. The chapter about Balzac describes the evil spell cast by civilization conceived of as an automatic process subject to laws of natural evolution. The chapters about Stendhal and André Gide grapple with the position of an individual who identified the laws of nature with the laws of human society and, taking this further, arrived at a cult of power. The chapter about William James criticizes the acceptance of fictions and legends as a normal condition that we cannot move beyond. The fragment from Tolstoy's *War and Peace* is used as an example of disillusionment with civilization and the miseries connected with this disillusionment. Marian Zdziechowski makes his appearance as a specimen of religion founded on the innate demands of the heart. The rather long sketch about Stanisław Ignacy Witkiewicz shines a light on metaphysical theories of art.

Awareness of the ties linking the various fields of human activity makes it easy to notice the political undertone of these literary observations. Looked at in this way, they are transformed into observations from the period of historical dialectics. What stands out in them is a critical stance against nationalism, a negative appraisal of recently fashionable "myths," a question mark over the future of religion, and a defense of realism in art, as well as the intention to subject art to the overarching ideas that shape the collective. Certain *i*'s are not dotted. In some cases there is more irresolution than certainty. In this sense, the book is an expression of dark times in which any thorough accomplishment is a virtually impossible task. The book's value, then, is based instead on its being something of an intellectual memoir.

Warsaw, January 1944

The Legend of the Island

I knew an old woman who would slowly raise her hands to her temples in difficult moments and say, "Oh, if only I could be on an unpopulated island and have nothing to do with people, just escape, escape to somewhere far away." I always pictured her standing in front of a window outside of which the autumn trees are swaying and the lake is like a shimmering white spot. Her words did not echo against a background of city traffic; it was impossible to ascribe them to a distaste for the crowds filling the streets, factories, and cafés. All around was pure country, woods, a roadless expanse. The people from whom she wished to flee were her closest relatives, a cook, the sawmill's old watchman.

Recalling this image, I think about all the men and women who, with a similar gesture and similar words, have expressed a longing for total isolation—about the generations that cultivated the legend of the island. An island without people! Given concrete form in *Robinson Crusoe* and thus conveyed from hand to hand as a Christmas present. As the first book about the world, it was one of those symbols acquired in childhood whose language was used by grown-ups to name their complicated experiences. An island without people is a legend, and like every legend, its contents are richer than the events that gave birth to it, that created the external skeleton for its development. Certain objects, thanks to their "underground" ties with features of human nature, acquire an almost magical power over man; they enter the vernacular lexicon as terms useful as names for hidden desires. To say "island" is to say at the same time "separation from the rest of the world by a barrier that is difficult to penetrate, yet one that is transparent, a brilliant blue, and does not offer a barrier to sight." "Island" signifies the safety of its inhabitants from the battles, quarrels, and wars of the rest of humanity. This absence of a threat, so fundamental to every legend of happiness, whether it be the biblical paradise or the "golden age" that has been transmitted outside of history, beginning with Ovid's *Metamorphoses*, is the essential feature of the island as it figures in the child's imagination (no teachers or parents can reach us there—a favorite daydream in class), just as it figures in the imagination of various epochs ("the fortunate islands," the island of Utopia).

One may also assume that the island leads us into a different understanding of time than the time in which we normally live. Man conceives of time with the help of spatial images (time flows, a "segment" of time, a large "block" of time); he sees time as a fluid hovering above the earth. Cutting an island off from the mainland and surrounding it with the blue of the sea, he is inclined, by dint of many strange and beautiful errors, to sever its time from mainland time, to give it a different time, just as he gives it different laws and privileges from those on the mainland. The action of time on man, his aging, is a sensitive issue, where the youth of the people around him reminds him at every step of the number of years he has lived. Islanders of the legend are among people just like themselves; they form a single generation, and time loses its venom. A stay on Calypso, the island of nymphs, brings the gift of eternal life or the eternal peace of death. When processions of lovers frozen in a gesture of farewell (Watteau's *De-*

parture for Cythera) snake along the shore among tall feathery trees and debark from a green port, eternal happiness awaits them on the island of love. Prospero in Shakespeare's *The Tempest* is, in a sense, the lord of time—for the gift of summoning and quieting tempests, which is possessed by this hero of the most "islandic" work in the history of the theater, is, in the final analysis, the gift of changing and regulating time and its atmosphere. This is no doubt also the reason why Robinson, after so many years on his island, has not aged, but leaves the island full of energy and enthusiasm for further voyages.

An absence of inhabitants adds one more feature to these general characteristics of the island: it has flora and fauna, but a human footprint in the sand is an unheard-of phenomenon, sufficient to send one into shock. On an uninhabited island, whoever visits and takes possession of it encounters the world with no assistance and no intermediary; he is alone, all ties with society sundered. His deeds no longer have any resonance among beings who resemble him; the causes and consequences of his behavior lie solely within him. In its condemnation of the hero to life in isolation, the legend of Robinson Crusoe is different from the island legends of the past. It contains both an attempt at submitting man's nature to close analysis, so that he can demonstrate who he really is when the garments of custom and convenience that adorn him fall away, and the weakly expressed conviction that in isolation, when he frees himself from the evil influences of the crowd, man is capable of extracting from within himself virtues that until then have been suppressed, buried under bad habits—in other words, the contrast between a single individual and collective life, a feeble outline of Rousseau's theory of man as naturally good. The old woman yearning for an uninhabited island appears to believe that the source of evil lies somewhere outside her, in her surroundings. And although she does not take her own words seriously, they help her to express that enveloping of oneself within oneself, that familiar escape into the depths of one's being, when we see how the mechanism of interpersonal relations creates evil without creating either perpetrators or victims: all are simultaneously perpetrators and victims.

It should be clear from what has been stated here that, treated in this way, *Robinson Crusoe* expands to fit the dimensions of a phenomenon whose meaning significantly transcends both the English novelist's intentions and its own literary and artistic qualities. It is evidence, a spool on which the thread of one of our contemporary myths is wound. A Christian book, but already with a faint tinge of doubt about the goodness of this world, a grimace of bitterness whose consequences will be felt only in the nineteenth century. A Christian book: Robinson is cast away onto an island that is, for him, an island of penance and renewal. Saved by the hand of Providence from the ocean depths while his entire crew perishes, he regains consciousness on unfamiliar ground. His first gesture is to curse fate and to despair. Searching within himself, however, he discovers the cause of his present condition—his own sinfulness. The accident takes on the appearance of a just sentence and, at the same time, of kindly protection. It was by God's decree that he found himself on the island. God's protection sent him the tools he needed in the hull of the shattered vessel, not even forgetting a bit of grain, which he carelessly spilled, but, guided by the hand of God, spilled onto a place where it could grow and ripen. Deprived of the moral help of other men, having only the Bible as the sole rock upon which he can build, he elaborates on his own an entire system of good and evil and comes to understand his own guilt, a guilt defined precisely according to the principles of a Protestant-merchant morality; he had sinned by disobeying his parents and by craving profits he had not labored to earn. Translated into the language of ethical precepts, this means that man has an innate ability to distinguish between good and evil, and is religious by nature. All that need be done is to tear him away from collective errors and collective defects, and he will become pure, in the full brilliance of his immaculate majesty.

For this change to occur, however, an extraordinary intervention is required, a violent shock such as the breaking up of the ship carrying Robinson and his comrades, a rupture with civilization. Does this not mean that civilization is contaminated? Does this not contain a discreet but sufficiently clear condemnation of civilization's gifts?

This is where we come up against the flaw in the traditional Christian image of the world. The paths toward perfection of the individual that are indicated by Catholicism were strictly communal; the communal institution of the Church depended on collective prayer, on participation in the sacraments. The most pessimistic of Catholic philosophers, Saint Augustine, did not hesitate to recognize the Church as the sole effective instrument for the rebirth of the human individual and of all humankind. "In Catholicism, pessimistic elements are not tempered by the optimism of hope, but the optimism of faith in the Church is directly opposed to the pessimistic affirmation of evil, that is to say, of flawed human nature; the Church and the Church hierarchy are one; the Church, mediating between man and God, is the bestower of grace, the inerrant guide leading mankind out of the darkness of sin and damnation."[1]

Robinson, instead of turning feral and falling into a condition of dull-wittedness, is reborn morally in a virgin wilderness that had never before been disturbed by more than some cannibal's footsteps. From the Catholic point of view, he is nonhuman; he achieves heights accessible only to eremites adorned with the halos of saints. The story of Robinson Crusoe could not have arisen among cultures and peoples inclined to consider the individual as a part of the whole, regardless of whether those cultures are religiously, or secularly, communal.[2]

The task of digging an abyss between civilized society and the noble individual fell to writers of a Protestant spirit, who were, to a far greater degree than Catholic writers, obsessed with their moralizing mission and who sought within man himself the innate foundations of a good life, foundations that did not depend on any institutions. In this struggle, a race of indefatigable conquerors, colonizers, and sailors seemed to provide one more weapon in defense of these thinkers' belief that man, lost in the wilderness, in the company of wild animals and wild tribes, loses nothing of his moral worth—that on the contrary, only in those circumstances does he achieve it. Thanks to this belief, a farmer in a plaid shirt saying his evening prayers on the doorstep of a cabin he has built with his own hands in the woods beside the Mississippi or Missouri River could feel pure and noble as he made do without confessor or preacher. Beside him, gleaming in the setting sun, his rifle leans against a bench carved out of a tree trunk. He has used it to eliminate more than one Indian in self-defense or while participating in a raid against the original inhabitants of the land he has acquired by force.

Tenacious, blind energy required an illusion that would justify and purify it. After all, Robinson Crusoe, creating *ab novo* a system of moral precepts, deriving them solely from his own soul, creates the very same conventional morality of the milieu from which he came, which is reason enough for us to doubt the existence of a seed of virtue, capable, like Japanese paper plants, of growing and producing flowers in a tightly corked bottle. Robinson Crusoe's pangs of conscience are the pangs of conscience of a merchant family's prodigal son. He is a Christian Buddenbrook, returning by some miraculous dispensation to the path of grim duty. He is one of the many characters, so popular in bourgeois novels, in which the child-monster, the child-freak who upsets his family, is a frequent if not constant motif. The sin of such a freak consists, above all, in his deplet-

ing the property accumulated through the labor of generations. The estate passes into the hands of the young people, and all that the parents worry about is the ability of their
heirs to preserve and increase their inheritance, whether it be
money, property, or a name held in regard by their neighbors.
The prodigal son, different in his preferences and tempera-
ment from the other members of the clan, a cuckoo chick
dreaming of forbidden flights, is a true misfortune for a stable,
sober-minded family line.

Exaggerated fear of this sort of catastrophe suggests to the
burgher class the unequivocal rejection of all passions in life
that are capable of turning the heir's attention away from a
career prescribed by custom. The burgher class detects in every
independent woman who is neither a wife nor a mother, nor
a marriageable girl, a demon lying in wait for the chance to
ensnare and ruin their sons. This class detects in art (in eighty
out of a hundred cases the freak is an artist) the sign of imma-
turity, a sickness prolonged beyond the permissible bounds of
childishness. Alcohol, cards, women, art, and an urge to keep
changing his place of abode—that is a combination of mad-
nesses that no self-respecting burgher drama can do without.
Robinson Crusoe, above whom the voice of a puritanical God
seems to thunder, "You did not obey your father and your
mother, so you will obey your own dog's skin" (at least, that is
what a puritanical God would have said had he been familiar
with Polish proverbs), is the scourged prodigal son, deprived at
last, in the most perfect way, of all temptations.

"Eternal man" in the abstract, drained of the color that the
social organism imposes on him, is astonishingly similar to a
shopkeeper who works behind the counter in the gloomy out-
skirts of the city and hands over all his pitiful earnings to his
mother. Robinson's model endurance, his years on end spent
doing business errands, his gift for calculation (for example,
seeking a place to erect his tent, he first enumerates four con-

ditions that the place must meet and only then begins to survey the ground), his common sense, all conspire to make him
into an ideal—but an ideal from a certain historical period and
a certain tradition. The operation of revealing the true nature
of man, undertaken in order to edify the reader, is not successful. Nonetheless, in this entrusting of the hero to the elements,
a certain centrifugal aspiration of this civilization emerges, an
urge to flee its environs, a search for new continents whose
conquering will allow men to expand horizontally, to simplify,
and to make younger—for how long?—whatever it is in this
civilization that inhibits his ability to grow higher and to put
down roots.

That is how the weariness of the gaze directed at the social
creation appears, in which one can discern only the dark sides.
Defoe, hounded by believers, selling himself to political par-
ties, betraying for mere pennies the press secrets of his col-
leagues, had to flee to an unpopulated island in his desire to
rescue his model Christian. Thus arose the first portrait in the
long gallery of noble savages, the unspoiled children of nature.
Eighteenth-century literature would find the heroine of a
novel in Virginie, a maiden from the wilderness who could
barely read and write. She commands the simple folk of the
Huron Indians tribe to marvel naively at the crimes of the
Christian-monarchist system. What an eloquent sight Napoleon is: the ruler of a continent, a tyrant who made use of
every injustice on his road to power, who reveled in reading the
sentimental, maudlin adventures of Paul and Virginie, those
lovers "unspoiled" by civilization, in a novel written by that
unfeeling, greedy, conniving Bernardin de Saint-Pierre, a master of intrigue in literary circles, who, just like his imperial
reader, knew very well the secrets of the hunt in the human
jungle. That is what is known as blindfolding oneself with a
scarf painted with exotic flowers, yearning for deception at any
price so that, though those who surround us and we ourselves

are really like criminals, somewhere far away, beyond the reach of scepter and gold, there are just people, capable of enthusiasm and of tears.

Robinson Crusoe is not yet sentimental. That element, which, once it is mixed into a way of life, begins its destructive work of greater and greater intensification—of increasing the dose of emotions to include sadism and absolute coldness—is utterly foreign to him. Practical, sober, with the characteristics of an entrepreneur and a bookkeeper, he might rather arouse amazement with his lack of feeling. His attitude toward those closest to him is always correct, but no more than that. His description of the death of his most faithful servant and friend, Friday, is a model of concision: "We had a very good Voyage to the *Brasils*, and arriv'd in the *Bay de Todos los Santos*, or *All-Saints Bay*, in about Twenty-two Days after." Near the Lesser Antilles their ship was surrounded by a great many Indian boats. "I made Friday go out upon the deck, and call out aloud to them in his language, to know what they meant. Whether they understood him or not, that I knew not; but as soon as he had called to them, six of them, who were in the foremost or nighest boat to us, turned their canoes from us, and stooping down, showed us their naked backs; whether this was a defiance or challenge we knew not, or whether it was done in mere contempt, or as a signal to the rest; but immediately Friday cried out they were going to shoot, and, unhappily for him, poor fellow, they let fly about three hundred of their arrows, and to my inexpressible grief, killed poor Friday, no other man being in their sight." His master did not shed a single tear over this poor body, which had once enclosed such an obedient and devoted soul.

This simplicity of soul, this somewhat wooden didacticism, which measures the goods of feelings by the yard rather than the heart, lost its applicability as time passed and ceased to be the truth about man, just like the sentimental tale about happiness in nature's virginal bosom created by the pre-Romantics. Later generations observed that the individual human being, even if he has put an expanse of ocean between himself and the turbulent cities, carries the entire weight of civilization like his shell; he is an ambassador from that civilization, and everywhere he sets his foot, the blaring of trumpets and roar of gunshots reverberate, profit and exploitation reign; and therefore, seeking the golden fleece of virtue in far-off journeys is of no avail. *Robinson Crusoe* was exiled to the nursery and continued to live there, since the novel encompasses in itself the myth of the island, the myth of flight and change. Soon there was no room on the maps for an uninhabited island. The sea, with its steamships, lost the charm of an unconquered border between one reality and another. The island shrank to an ideal, unimaginable point, to despondent fantasies.

The formula of escape is "to begin life anew." As soon as masses of people begin to repeat it consciously and unconsciously, one can say with great approximation to truth that the social barometer is registering a dangerously high pressure. To begin life anew as "I" or to begin life anew as a collective? In the legend of the island, "I" is still at the center—existence not as a species but as a specific creature. Whereas a Catholic—similarly concerned with the individual—advised one to conquer one's own passions, the inhabitant of a fantasy island has, through the very fact of his isolation, the hope of insuring the blossoming of some as yet barely discerned qualities that are obscured in the daily hustle and bustle. Subduing his desires is no longer a necessity for the island man; alone with a stern and merciful God who resembles the director of a large firm, he does not discover any drives in himself other than the drive to goodness. The island of penance is at the same time the island of grace.

Robinson Crusoe looks at the world anthropocentrically. It

never occurs to him to explore the relationship between himself and an animal, a plant, or an insect—he will not even notice the kinship between himself and the Carribean savage. A thief or a savage can pretend to some degree of equality only once he has converted. Under the roof of the heavens in which a patriarchal God hovers, in the great edifice given to the just man for his exclusive use and exploitation, everything that grows from the soil, flies in the air, swims in the water, every beast of the forest and every barbarian who resembles him is a means for multiplying the fame and power of the being whose strength derives from a pact made with the ruler of the heavens. The only surprising aspect is the ingenious organization of the edifice: from the sun, which warms and spreads joy, to the stars, which point the way for sailors, and even including the tiniest plant, everywhere one can see the hand that made sure that the just man who can truly utilize the things of this earth should lack for nothing. The enthusiasm of the homeowner taking possession of his house: "Then all this is for me? Did you go to so much trouble, Lord, in your concern for me? You deserve my gratitude, obedience, and thanks."

But what will happen to this well-ordered home when the moment of truth arrives, a brief flash of sympathy and solidarity with everything that could have been only an instrument, but that feels and suffers? The hawk tearing apart a bird—that's me. The bird torn apart by the hawk—that's me. The mortal battles of ants are the battles of human armies. In the mutual devouring of bacteria, in serpents lying in ambush among the subtropical vines, in the act of love of praying mantises—strange insects, among whom the female, much larger and better armed, devours the male at the time of copulation—everywhere there is the same current of that mysterious and unknown something that is called life, to which man is subject even though he struggles mightily to escape from the rule of elementary laws.

Everywhere there is coldness and cruelty, the struggle of all against all. Then, even walling oneself off from the spectacle of human depravity will not be enough to preserve one's faith in one's own superiority and one's own refined fairness. Robinson Crusoe, strolling around on his island, might have stopped in front of a spider's nest, listened to the drowsy buzzing of a tortured fly, and perhaps one of those thoughts that contribute to the birth of heresy and create philosophical revolutions might have occurred to him. "If the same law of life governs me and the spider, perhaps I am not as good as I think I am, even when I am fulfilling the commandments of God's law. Evil resides deep inside me beneath the surface of things I know about myself, and perhaps my reason betrays me by adorning the blind workings of instinct with bright and cheerful colors. I no longer know if evil may not be my deeper, truer substance."

From whatever side one looks, then, waves of doubt wash over the islet on which this unique experiment was supposed to take place: observation of the atom of humanity, a study undertaken in order to demonstrate by example the truth of a preconceived belief in innate goodness and innate religion.

The Legend of the Monster City

In the preface to *La comédie humaine*, Balzac sums up the goal of his work in a few words: "The original idea of a human comedy came to me like a dream, like one of those impossible projects which one cherishes and which one allows to fly away: a chimera that smiles, that shows its feminine face and then unfurls its wings, returning to the fantastic heavens. But the chimera, like many chimeras, evolves into reality; it has its demands and its tyranny which one must accede to. This idea originated in a comparison of the human world and the animal world."

He describes his awareness of the *oneness* of the *structure* of all living organisms, the oneness of the principle that explains the life of all creatures from protozoa to two-legged vertebrates: "There is only one animal. The Creator used only one and the same pattern for all the beings he put together. An animal is a principle that receives its external form or, to put it more concisely, its differences of form, in the conditions where it was obliged to develop. Zoological species derive from these differences." Balzac cites Geoffroy Saint-Hilaire but sees in the past an expression of the same striving for a permanent principle in Swedenborg's chains of being, Leibniz's monads, Buffon's organic molecules. Geoffroy Saint-Hilaire and his master, his friend Lamarck (whom Balzac does not mention); these, after all, are the fathers of evolutionary thought—that most powerful direction in the history of contemporary thought that, if the monuments of nineteenth-century culture vanished and knowledge of it alone were preserved, would be sufficient for distant future epochs to make a diagnosis, and most likely, it would not be far off the mark. It may well be that Balzac's continual freshness derives from his inserting his own work into this forward-moving current, from his awareness of the most vital, still germinating ideas of his time. Let us return to his assertions, however:

> Overwhelmed by this system before it was the subject of debates, I noticed that in this regard society is similar to nature. Does not society make of man, as required by the milieu in which his activity unfolds, as many types of people as there are species in zoology? The differences between a soldier, a laborer, an administrator, a lawyer, a loafer, a scholar, a statesman, a merchant, a sailor, a poor man, and a priest are, though more difficult to grasp, no less significant than the differences that separate the wolf, the lion, the eagle, the raven, the shark, the manatee, the sheep, etc. Thus there exist and will continue to exist for all time social species, just as there exist zoological species. If Buffon created a splendid work, attempting to present the entirety of zoology in his book, should it not be possible to encompass society in a similar work?

This is not an escape from civilization into a land of magical transformation, and it is not a dream of purity accessible only to the visions of dreamers. It is useless to dash off to distant parts of the globe, useless to assign to me or to you independence from the laws governing the living in general—in the name of a divine dispensation. We are face-to-face with the enormity of evil, but curiosity is our weapon. Heroes in snug pantaloons and dark overcoats, we hide behind cold observation, which provides the best disguise for our yearning hearts, our inflamed imagination. Everything around us is new, unknown. The powerful development of industry, the authority of anonymous money, discoveries multiplying, the roar of printing presses, new forces, new enchantments: the press, the stock market, dividends. Fortunes rise in the course of a single day; one ill-conceived step tumbles potentates into the depths of hell, and here, hell is poverty. Grim passions, greed, venality, legalized thefts and murders, legalized trade in women, informers, police agents, omnipotent criminals, ministerial careers, young people coming to Paris with their pathetic bundles in search of fame, artists in garrets, coats of arms and titles for sale. The poor wandering alongside the Seine, the Seine in the glow of the gaslights, carrying away the bodies of failed gamblers. The ogling of ladies in the Tuileries, parades of carriages on the Champs-Élysées . . .

That is the terrain to be studied by the social naturalist, the zoo in which pairs of all species on earth are gathered. The observer requires a strictly defined field of observation in which processes take place intensely and can be grasped in quickened tempo. That is why the naturalist raises bacteria in a petri dish. A great modern city, with its feverish activity, with its rejection of the brakes that men have no time for here, is a living specimen that simply begs for a microscope. The speeded-up tempo arises from the very fact of living in a throng: a month goes by, a year, and already I am surrounded by new fames, new careers, new conquerors whom I encountered just yesterday in student dining halls. Poor girls in darned stockings blossom in the course of a week and turn into lionesses. Their proud gaze no longer recognizes yesterday's acquaintances. Refined ladies touched by unhappiness forget to set out roses, to pin artificial braids into their hair, and to lace up their corsets: old age is suddenly revealed as if by the touch of a wand. In a settled, orderly existence, when people constantly interact with a small circle of people they know well, change takes place imperceptibly from day to day; because I meet the same people every day, I am unable to notice their transformations, to feel shock, to reflect on transience, to ask myself, "And what about you? What kind are you? Are you making equally profitable use of your life?"

Where the layers intermingle, where new forces are forever swimming up from the depths, and where, in turn, former oligarchs sink to the ranks of the proletariat; where one must constantly become accustomed to seeing new faces and their images obscure the faces of friends, separating the friends seen today from those seen the day before yesterday—there the rush to transformism and the interest in transformism are understandable. Balzac is fascinated by the surfacing of the same people in ever newer guises. Lucien de Rubempré appears on the Paris stage as a provincial, badly dressed, ill-mannered, suffering the torments of shyness. A year passes, and there is Lucien, a famous journalist, one of the top pens in Paris, the lover of beautiful actresses, a fickle poet, glittering in the crowd of golden youth. Then comes a violent, seemingly irreversible fall. And unexpectedly Lucien is again in the spotlight, this time as a cold dandy, a cunning diplomat, in the ambiguous role of protégé of Prince Carlos Herrera, an escaped galley slave. Lucien, profiting from Esther's prostitution, calculatingly feigning love for Clothilde de Grandlieu, graciously deploying his charms, also calculated, against Comtesse de Sériza. Rastignac the poor student, and Rastignac one of the most dangerous, most influential bachelors in Paris. Mme de Bargeton the provincial beauty, and Mme de Bargeton as the wife of a prefect, directing the delicate machinery of aristocratic salons.

The various forms of the same people, depending on the circle in which they find themselves, encourage us to seek a single law, a key to their metamorphosis. We may at least as-

sume that the sight of the turbulent, mobile societies of victorious capitalism determined not only Balzac's "naturalistic"
approach but also the very phenomenon of the scientific revolution that Lamarck and Geoffroy Saint-Hilaire initiated and
Darwin and Spencer developed further. Noticing how the human individual continually changes his costumes yet does not
lose his identity, participating in a show in which the actor
runs out from the wings wearing makeup and dressed in a
mysterious wardrobe, the mind begins to home in on hidden
transitional links; it reaches beyond the decorations of art to
the point where the crystallized, hardened covering begins.
Transferring this habit to the realm of animal species, the
mind overturns the system based on differences among species
that were said to have remained immutable since the day of
creation. In the fins of a fish it sees unformed wings; it discovers in the human skeleton a vestigial tail; it ascribes the
giraffe's long neck to its feeding on the leaves of tall trees,
and the hummingbird's colorful plumage to its frequenting
of brightly colored exotic flowers. In the social realm, certain
physical and spiritual characteristics of individuals lose their
inevitability, are dislodged from under the hand of the God
who dispatched them; they are now the result of a profession,
of belonging to a stratum, if not a class, of the means of struggling for existence.

A great multitude—where the divisions between castes
have crumbled and where the only motor is money—forces
the individual to increase the pressure on himself of the multitude's fluids, the multitude's magnetisms. The individual
then seeks ways to save himself from disintegration, seeks any
confirmation at all of his own separateness and—this is an indispensable condition—of his own superiority. The position of
the observer then becomes a tower that assures him victory.
The observer, smiling benignly at the picture of mindless
desires and mindless efforts, is like a child standing over an

anthill. He inserts a stick and is delighted with the insects' chaotic scurrying. The crazier the actions of his victims, the more they lead to total infatuation and are obviously futile, the greater the imaginary power of the observer of the masses. This is probably the source of Balzac's cruelty, his delight in descriptions of aberrations, blind drives, and eccentric habits: An old miser, moved as much by the sight of gold as others would be by the sight of a beloved woman. A poor parish priest from the provinces, who imagined that he would inherit the prelate's furniture, dies, thwarted by the vicar in whom similar ambitions were aroused. A modern King Lear, this time a flour merchant, who sells all his property in order to pay off the debts of his wealthy daughters, mistaking their selfishness for love. Is it necessary to give more examples? Here is the cruelty of the situation: a propitious resolution always comes five minutes too late. As if fulfilling the Aristotelian conditions for tragedy, pity and dread emanate from the bourgeois epopee.

Rising above the anthill, it is easy to be mistaken; it is easy to minimize the significance of the fates of particular ants and to entertain oneself with statistics of incidents, general conclusions, the construction of universal laws of the species. Then man becomes only an illustration of a hypothesis; his individual life reveals to us from among his secrets only what confirms this hypothesis. In order to follow the path of one ant, to discover its tortuous path through the forest of grass blades and the boulders of gravel, one needs to be a visionary. A visionary makes everything he touches important, unique, unrepeatable; in relation to his own persona he is by turns a genial giant and a Lilliputian lifting his gaze in order to take in the monumental body that is growing, unexpectedly, to the superhuman dimensions of a hero. He is capable of assigning equal significance to fantasy and to reality, because he knows that fantasy is as real as can be, and reality as fantastic as can be.[1]

The great modern city is conducive to a certain type of vision. Here are the streets, squares, buildings. The crowd storms into omnibuses, fills the arcades of the Palais Royal. Pedestrians exchange glances; a face disappears, vanishes into the tangle of arms, hats, exclamations, smiles, curses. The mind labors for a moment: Where did that man go? What unknown human reservoir swallowed him up? Is he happy? What does the woman he loved or will love look like? What will his death be like and what shape will his mouth assume for the last time? This vision is a vision of a prolonged moment; it is a small clump of snow that rolls along and grows into a great white ball. It rests on short glances back into the past and into the future. Without being aware of it, the inhabitant of the city creates in the course of a single day a large number of such creative compositions. And precisely for this reason he is inclined to view the city mythologically, populating it with creatures of his own imagination who are endowed with fabulous power and fabulous emotional exuberance. The more impoverished his own life, the stronger is his faith in the mysterious, inaccessible center, in—if one may put it this way—the absolute of the city. Tourists traveling to the great capitals naively pursue this elusive spirit in nightspots and suspicious neighborhoods. Part of this myth is the feeling that the daytime, the surface city, is not *it*, that somewhere beneath the cover of the quotidian, the *real* city exists, boisterous and crazy, about which the local inhabitant who prowls the streets can provide information and reveal it to others. But the local inhabitant believes just as blindly in a land of urban enchantments—he believes, and that's all there is to it, because he will never be able to find it. The den of the city is created from inflated fantasies about people who disappear from view, about their hoarded goods, their battles, their successes and failures. In just the same way, hunters, never able to come upon the bones of animals who have died from natural causes, create a legend about an animal cemetery concealed in the heart of the wilderness, where elephants, lions, and bears go when they sense their imminent death. People always mythologize the absent, it seems; just think of the way history is turned into legends and falsehoods, the beautification and bronzing of creators of the past. A great number of the absent, the unknown—and that describes the city—must by that same principle assume fantastic outlines.

Roger Caillois, studying manifestations of collective myths in literature, drew attention to this in an interesting essay.[2] "It seems acceptable to assert," he writes, "that there exists a phantasmagorical representation of Paris and, speaking more generally, of the great city, which exerts such a powerful hold on the imagination that the matter of its authenticity has never been raised; borrowed in all its details from a book, it is still sufficiently universal as to create part of the collective intellectual atmosphere and to exert a certain restraining influence." Paris appears immutably as the "Babylon of our times," an ocean of crime and intoxication, whose waves close over the head of any daredevil who breaks through to the spells locked behind its fiery gates, on which can be seen Dante's inscription as on the gates of hell.

"O Paris, Paris! You are a true Babylon, the true battlefield of the intelligentsia, a true temple in which evil has its cult and its priests, and I believe that the breath of the archangel of darkness flows ceaselessly over you, like breezes over the abyss of the seas. O motionless storm, stony ocean, I want to be the black eagle among your irate waves, who mocks the thunder and sleeps, smiling, in the hurricane, having spread its wings; I want to be a genius of evil, a vulture of the sea, of the most treacherous and stormy sea, the sea where human desires cluster and roil."[3]

Acquaintance with Balzac permits one to grasp this peculiar process: *La comédie humaine* is, as it were, a collection of stories about people who meet and pass by, a reconstruction of the fates of guests amusing themselves at a feast given by the protector of some Coralia or Floryna. Their story begins the moment they cross the threshold of the hospitable home, the novelist's glance bidding them farewell, and disappear into the rocky mountains, the oceans and tempests of Paris. The myth of the great city grows, becomes even more powerful during the course of the century, and Balzac is only a pretty, ostentatious ring in a long chain of authors, from Eugène Sue to Jules Romains and the Anglo-American detective novel. Perhaps one should pursue the traces of this myth in Polish literature and ascertain how it functioned in Mickiewicz and Norwid, for example. In the period of its formation this same myth was accepted by the public, to whose unconscious aspirations it responded; it encountered more or less sharp attacks by the critics. Let us recall that at that time, being concerned with contemporary life and providing realistic descriptions of it was considered an affront to the dignity of art. It was all right in cheap romances, but was not particularly decent for the self-respecting artist. It was only with great difficulty that the allure of modern gesture, movement, costume, and urban landscapes broke through the masquerade of theatrical costumes and no less theatrical landscapes. The curious reader would find in the magazine *Illustration* from around 1850 infuriated critical attacks on Courbet, who was not spared abusive epithets for having painted his pictures in a "brutal" fashion, which is to say for introducing into painting a black frock coat, vest, and top hat. Speaking of this slow penetration of the city into the sphere of art, we arrive directly at Baudelaire. It was he who, many decades before the explosion of urbanism, heatedly defended the right of the artist to the temporary, transitory, unenduring, to the representation of fashion, custom, changing streetscapes, the café, the cabaret. It was he who in his essays on aesthetics managed to write an encomium to the observer, an encomium to the city crowd, akin, perhaps, to Whitman's hymns:

"He who loves life that penetrates everything enters into the crowd as into a gigantic collector of electricity. One may also compare him to a mirror as immense as the crowd, to a kaleidoscope endowed with consciousness, which discovers complex life behind every movement and the edgy charm of all the elements of that life." "He moves out! He observes the rushing river of vitality, so dignified and so splendid. He marvels at the eternal beauty and the astonishing harmony of life in the capitals, harmony so providentially maintained in the hubbub of human freedom. He follows the landscapes of the great city, landscapes of stone caressed by smoke or scourged by the sun's blows. He derives pleasure from the beautiful carriages, the proud horses, the glittering freshness of the grooms, the lackeys' adeptness, the posture of women moving like waves, of pretty children, happy that they are alive and well dressed; in a word, he derives pleasure from life, which fills the universe." "But evening is approaching. It is a wondrous, uncertain hour when the curtains of heaven are drawn, when cities light up. Gas stains the crimson of the sunset. Whether honorable or contemptible, wise or mad, people say to themselves, 'There it is, the day is over!' Wise men and good-for-nothings think about pleasure, and everyone rushes to his chosen place to drain the goblet of forgetfulness." "He remains to the end wherever light can blaze, wherever poetry can resound, life can swarm, music can thump, wherever some passion can pose for his eye, wherever natural man and artificial man will appear in their bizarre beauty, wherever the sun illuminates the violent pleasures of the *untamed beast*!" "The artist is a prince who delights in his incognito."[4]

How strangely these quotes reflect the *curiosity* that is the source of the urban myth and simultaneously the motor of

Balzac's creative work! Curiosity as a principle, even as a norm of behavior in response to the world. An anecdote about Balzac, relayed by Baudelaire, presents us with one more commentator. The poet of "Parisian spleen," thanks to a kinship he felt, frequently turned to reflections on the author of *The Divine Comedy*. Standing in front of a painting representing a melancholy winter landscape with cottages and peasants on a road, Balzac looked for a long time at a cottage from whose chimney a thin wisp of smoke was emerging, and suddenly exclaimed, "How beautiful that is! But what are the people doing in that cottage? What are they thinking? What troubles do they have? Was the harvest good? They probably have to pay rent!" Is this not a good example of the curiosity that seizes upon the smallest detail, weaves an entire story from it, and at the same time, by the very act of creating that story, gives the artist the freedom he would seek in vain in daily life?

The observer is a ruler. An ordinary passerby, while he draws conclusions and contrives stories for every pair of eyes and every mouth observed in a bus, is free. He dominates by the power of the story he himself has created. It may well be that the enchantment of the cinema inheres precisely in this. During the course of a couple of hours, human lives are played out before the viewer, revealing to him all the secrets of *the particular*, given to him as his property, stimulating him to weave a net of daydreams out of every detail; every detail opens perspectives onto the past and future of a house, an object, a person. In contrast to the theater—which uses conventional fictions and where the individuals who are acting make it clear that they are actors, dressed up for only a moment, soon to take their bows and wait to be applauded for the roles they played—film, at least in its present stage of development, assuages our curiosity about other people's lives, realizes the fantastic notion of cutting open apartment houses in order to see what is inside them. It is a cap of invisibility that permits the viewer to freely follow a detective into some dive in a port, to rise into the air with a flier, to participate in crime. When the lights come on, the sequel plays out in his imagination: he strolls with Charlie Chaplin as he disappears down an empty highway into the depths of the screen; he is already thinking up future incarnations, or he places on Broadway a romantic drama that has never yet been seen, pasted together of scraps of his own and others' love affairs.

There is a profound bond between film and the myth of the monster city, the city as Leviathan. Film, responding to a need that can be defined as the visual exploitation of reality, accepts the mission of giving concrete shape to this myth that inheres in the collective consciousness. This mission used to be fulfilled by the novel, and theater has attempted, though in vain, to approximate it. The novel has ceased to be an adequate instrument for this, however. As our knowledge about man has become more complex, the word, weighted down by a system of psychological, sociological, and political concepts, slowly loses its capacity for description of the outside world that would give the illusion of *objective* reality. It is no accident that the continuation and completion of *La comédie humaine* (Proust's *À la recherche du temps perdu* is without a doubt just such a work) takes place in the sphere of refined internal perceptions and employs plot to a vanishing degree, yet plot is, after all, an act of faith in the concrete, in the objective truth of external phenomena. The numerous causes that can be adduced do not alter the fact that the word is pulling away from the objects surrounding us and that it serves, rather, to express emotional states or to create constructs that are not dependent on reality, as is happening in contemporary poetry, where we are in a different reality, a reality of self-sufficient conjectures. In film, on the other hand, realism is still not a hollow sound.

It is possible that under the influence of social reconstruction the word and film will assume other tasks, but only if they return to a lower rung of culture can they retreat from the outer limit of complexity that was reached some time ago.

By assuming the position of observer, man enriches his life, which has been impoverished by being harnessed to the treadmill of differentiated production; however, like it or not, he thus represents a certain morality. This morality flows from the conscious or unconscious conviction that the basic element of existence is evil and struggle, that throughout time, both nature and the human race, which is only one part of nature, have been a battlefield. My sole role and commandment is to preserve myself. To preserve myself either by acquiring power or money (like Balzac's heroes) or by creating the power of imagination, similar to the power of a god who looks at the struggling of mortals from on high, from a great distance. Balzac's epoch is an epoch of the romantic ideal, but it is precisely the incommensurability between the ideal and reality that deepens the severity of his evaluation and must lead to pessimism. The ideal dissipates; not nourished by any food, it floats away to some inaccessible heights and gradually disappears, leaving behind the books of yearning poets who suffer from the "sickness of life." Goodness and nobility are already pure supposition in Balzac, a phenomenon devoid of a body; furthermore, they are almost always connected with weakness. He is incapable of constructing noble characters; he neither wishes to, nor do they interest him, except insofar as he endows them with eccentricity, monomania, ugliness, and degradation, and weaves around them a web of sordid intrigues that lead inexorably to defeat. The people come and go, but objects, political forms, the sum of evil always remains the same: "With regard to society, I certainly do not share a belief in endless progress; I believe in the progress of man himself." Ah, so. But if we take a good look at this confession, it turns out that it is a banality that conceals a different content. People of Balzac's type are at the intersection of two great trends in history. The first is an increasingly strong tendency to consider man as one of the animal species, a tendency that leads ultimately to drawing up laws appropriate only to that species and to seeking a collective morality. The other trend, in retreat now, is religious: individual morality based on the unchanging Ten Commandments, which will continue to manifest their vibrant power as long as the bond that connects the deity with man remains a bond between the deity and a people, tribe, humanity—in a word, as long as it determines the forms of social and political life. The trial and bankruptcy of morality based exclusively on an "inner voice," on "innate goodness," is a symptom of the weakening of the bond between the collective and that superior element of life that resides in the heavens; it is the relocation of that element into the heart of each person. As this disintegration progresses, the entire metaphysical side of Christian morality is eclipsed, and only its canons remain. After all, the history of religiosity over the last hundred years is the history of the ever greater "immanentization" (if I may use this unappealing word) of religion. Visions of heaven, hell, punishment, salvation, have less and less power to restrain deeds; on the contrary, the *human*, temporal usefulness of Christianity is emphasized. "Catholicism, because it is a universal system for the eradication of evil tendencies in man, is the most important element of social harmony," Balzac claims, pronouncing one of the countless sentences of this sort that have been repeated again and again in this century. Therefore "the progress of man himself," based neither on social transformation nor on an otherworldly power, appears to be a pale, conventional generalization, a concession to opinion which, then as now, demanded similar slogans. What remains in all their glory are passion, curiosity, the drive to power, and the vortex of the capitalist Leviathan city, in which isolated individuals struggle against isolated individuals and dream about other isolated individuals.

Warsaw, 1942

The Legend of the Will

During the period when in human consciousness the legend of
the monster collective arises—the monster organism in whose
entrails, as in the entrails of the whale, contemporary Jonahs
must live—a previously never encountered character appears,
a character who will make a great career in history. His adventures are at one and the same time the adventures of capitalist
democracy and the stitching on the reverse, evil side—one of
those antitheses that ripen to fulfillment. This character is a
powerful man, filled with a deep-seated resentment against
society for the injustices he has experienced, possessed by a
yearning for power and authority, the will to take revenge at
any cost, by fair means or foul. His personality is suffused with
ressentiment, that complex feeling composed of envy, anger,
longing for what is beyond his reach, and an artificially created
contempt for the values he holds in secret from himself, but
which he cannot attain.

For such a character to have been born, the conditions had
to be favorable for the development of *ressentiment*. First and
foremost, a social mechanism had to be constructed in such
a way that at every step, man stumbles over insurmountable
obstacles to the realization of his aspirations, so that his
aspirations are continuously impeded. Where money decides
everything—where with money one can have everything, be-

ginning with love and ending with a title—a perfect foundation for this situation is created. Possession of money is, by the nature of the system, the privilege of the few. The rest are sentenced to constraint, to poverty inflicted on them by an impersonal force, with the added hell of observing the unhampered life of the handful of the chosen. The force is impersonal; no one is responsible, and thus the anger, if it awakens in the underprivileged, is aimed not so much against those who possess fortunes as against the very essence of that binding law and morality.

But that is not the whole of it. In order for *ressentiment* to develop, a man must consider himself just as good, just as worthy as the one who arouses his envy, who acquired wealth and status not because he is better, but through inexplicable accident or through rapaciousness. The foundation for *ressentiment* is laid by placing an equal sign between one's own irrelevant virtues and the often lesser virtues of the mighty of this world. In a strict caste system, where the boundaries between one caste and another are impermeable, where, as was the case in the Middle Ages, one's caste is determined by one's birth and a man knows that he will remain within his own caste throughout his life, *ressentiment* can develop only in relation to people of one's own position (for example, a merchant can feel *ressentiment* in his relations with other merchants), whereas when the principle of equality dominates in relation to the highest authority, the authority of money, deep-seated resentment spills out over society in general, touches upon laws and customs, which the individual is inclined to treat as an invention, a clever discovery applied by an impersonal collective in order to constrain the passions and desires of a "strong man."[1] Anonymous humanity becomes a mafia lying in wait to bring me down. So: struggle, struggle without observing any rules of the game, since the other side isn't observing them, either; struggle using the selfsame deceitful methods, paying lip service to ethics, humility, devotion to the general good. And here's the paradox: an era that begins by seeking the cornerstone of morality in the social organism, instead of in revealed religion or natural religion, at the same time produces the type of the rebel that at some point, armed with modern technology, will make his mark on the pages of history. This rebel, observing that both religion and morality are only and exclusively human creations and that the world is a world of evil, feels justified in declaring war on the cowardly, worthless mass, which erects its own gods, its own fetishes, believes in these fetishes and orders him, too, to believe in them. He is not quite the same as an ordinary criminal, for the criminal enters into battle openly and builds no theories to justify his deeds. In conducting his battle, the criminal does not contradict generally held values; they lie outside his sphere of action. But the individual who is filled with resentment is never liberated by his deeds; there always remains a depth that cannot be plumbed, and, despite everything, social inhibitions are still important to him, so that he is always living in a fog of lies and feeling that he is taking only half measures. Furthermore, a reversal of the hierarchy of values takes place in him; he labors unceasingly at discovering the true (or so he believes) springs of all noble deeds and virtues, assigning to them the significance of a *means* of struggle for existence and depriving them of their independent meaning. Exaltation at his own perceptiveness and strength follows upon this. He alone sees things as they are; he alone is not deceived, whereas the rest wear the yoke of stupid, purely conventional laws and commandments. The more his own degradation seems to him to be a fate that no one can be blamed for, the more powerfully his thoughts and actions unconsciously aim at converting fate into a conspiracy and chance into the actions of hostile powers. If "the romantic consciousness of the limitless desires of the soul and its limited means must, by its very nature, be more or less pessimistic and must lead straight to absolute pessimism,"[2] then one can just as easily turn this around and say that pessimism, such as that which flows from a sense of one's own lack of power and the injustice done to oneself, gives birth to limitless desire. If I had this, if I had that, then I could show what I'm worth—such are often the thoughts of those who have no opportunity to take the measure of their talents in practice.

In *The Red and the Black*, Stendhal gave a living form to the figure we have been speaking of. This is probably one of the most consistently individualistic novels. There is just a single hero, and the entire plot is filled with his struggle against society or, to be more precise—and this is essential for *ressentiment*—against an *image* of society that is reflected in his psyche, filled as it is with grievances. Julien Sorel is the son of a peasant. He acquired some education thanks to the library of a retired surgeon, a major in the army. The books from this man's library and classes taught by Sorel's pastor are the only sources of knowledge for this lively, brilliantly capable mind. And that is the first knot, the beginning of countless complications. The condition of his origins is fulfilled. Today we know that the milieus that are most likely to produce these ambitious "despisers" are the transitional groups between the middle class and the peasantry, or the middle class and the proletariat—in general, all borderline classes. Someone who has broken away from the way of life of his own class and has not yet acquired the habits of another class that is "higher" in the capitalist structure is a restless element, fluid, submitting with difficulty to the rigors of this or that code of ethics.

Julien Sorel is totally consumed by ambition. Ambition substitutes for all feelings in him; he has no other feelings than those that flow from his sated or, more often, wounded ambition. He is seeking a means of escaping from his little provincial town to the wide world; he dreams of the heights of dignity, privilege, importance, power. There are two quick means for poor, ambitious men like him: the army and a priest's cassock. The army route is closed; it is the period of the Bourbon restoration, and the time has passed when tens of thousands of similar Sorels crossed the battlefields of Europe, mesmerized by the name of Napoleon. The emperor gave them what society did not want to give: glory, a hero's laurels, a career, money. In exchange he demanded a cheap thing— blood. Therefore there is no limit to Julien's adoration of Napoleon; he adores him with the adoration that only a plebeian can feel for another plebeian who has achieved his goal and made himself into a living model to be imitated by the socially rejected dreamers of a great deed. For Julien, Napoleon is the myth of the victory of a strong man over the monstrous collective. Prior to every difficult decision, Julien escapes into the forests and rocky cliffs surrounding his native town. There, seeing before him the enormous valley, the clear expanse where hawks are circling, he gives himself up to thoughts about his own fate. "Julien's eye mechanically followed the bird of prey; he was struck by its calm and powerful movements; he envied it its power, he envied it its solitude. This was Napoleon's destiny. Would the day come when it would be his?" For Julien, every conversation with people is a battle, and he expends no less energy on minor maneuvers intended to open his path to a career than did his leader while drafting his plans for toppling states and peoples. A clerical position—let us not forget that the novel is set in the period when the clergy ruled in France, that under the Bourbons, the clergy were all-powerful and ruled the country, that every nomination of a parish priest or a bishop was also a political act—for the son of a peasant, a clerical position, as Julien correctly understands, would be a ladder he could climb to that hawklike power. He plans his campaign. He must start on the lowest rung. With feigned piety and humility he worms his way into the old parish priest's favor. He learns the entire New Testament by heart, in Latin, and says that he feels a calling. His later efforts are more difficult; he decides to wear a mask of hypocrisy and not to betray himself to anyone by the slightest word or gesture. He is lonely, as only a man can be who has no respite, even for a moment, from carrying his secret. His days are like the days of a soldier subjected to the strictest discipline, albeit a self-imposed discipline. At night he undertakes a moral accounting: Did I neglect any precautions? Did I repress my feelings sufficiently? Did some facial expression reveal my true emotions? At certain set hours he has to appear to pass a church by chance, enter it, and pretend to be lost in prayer. At particular moments he must lower his eyes or squeeze out a tear. No rest, no freedom. Sorel is a titan of the will. "Woe to him who stands out." To conceal in his heart his hatred, his faith in his own difference, his superiority, and to behave like everyone else, but *consciously*, to lie even about the most minute details, this is his commandment. A dreadful battle rages in his heart, a battle against weakness, against each of its manifestations. Love, devotion, trust, faith are all weaknesses. Delight, pleasure, relaxation, gaiety, are all weaknesses. He is an ascetic of the will, a connoisseur of a stern ethics, the ethics of one's duty to oneself. Until finally his will loses the goal it was supposed to serve and becomes a goal in itself, and exercising it becomes the highest commandment.

Julien becomes the tutor for the children of M. de Rênal, the mayor. The children's mother, the beautiful Mme de Rênal, falls in love with Julien. Resolutely adhering to his policy of feigning gratitude, religiosity, dignity, Julien hates her because she is rich and beautiful, because she can be the trap that life places before his steadfastness, because he could love her and find in her a supporter. He is inexperienced; he has had no contact with women. But precisely because he fears and hates her, he determines to conquer her in order to demonstrate to himself that he is capable of even the most difficult test. The seduction of Mme de Rênal is an exercise, the first great deed that he must succeed at in order to convince himself he has what it takes for further heroic deeds. On a summer night, under the linden trees, when the women sitting with him on a bench lapse into daydreams, he is cold, sober, though his terror provokes in him storms unknown to the weak, who follow their impulses, their whims, and can easily abandon intentions that add to their anguish. Under the influence of his internal efforts, his voice begins to tremble, and Mme de Rênal mistakes this for a sign of tenderness. Julien cannot decide. Finally, filled with loathing for his own cowardice, he tells himself, "At precisely the moment when the clock strikes ten, I will carry out what I decided to do, or else I will go back to my room and shoot myself." And he rouses himself to the deed. He touches her hand, strokes her hand; the hand does not move away. It has begun. When he steals into Mme de Rênal's room, he does not experience any moral scruples, only lust, fear of being compromised, and, even stronger than fear, the command: Forward, no matter what happens. I must show myself that I am not a coward. After spending the night with a woman who is in love with him, the joy he feels is the joy of having fulfilled a duty to himself.

This is the plan of action of a "strong man": to demonstrate to himself his own freedom, his own limitless possibilities. Human deeds are determined by a chain of causes. Above me hangs the fatality of the social machine, but I, I am free, and I am free to do whatever I undertake, conquering my own insignificance, my fear, my emotions. In Dostoevsky's *Crime and Punishment*, Raskolnikov has similar thoughts and wages a similar battle with himself before murdering the old pawnbroker. In *Demons*, Kirillov commits suicide in order to prove that only he can choose to preserve or to take his own life, that this does not depend on other men or on God. When the process of separating the motivations for action from their social under-pinnings moves to its next stage—when what was supposed to be a training exercise for the assumption of power becomes a self-sufficient value—we get the figure of Lafcadio from Gide's *Les caves du Vatican.* Lafcadio grabs an old woman he has never seen before and throws her off a speeding train. There is no purpose to this; the crime does not bring him the slightest profit. He does this to convince himself that an *acte gratuit* is possible, an act independent of any determining fac-tors, the highest confirmation of man's absolute freedom. This act descends into a framework of interconnected phenomena like a bolt from the blue; it does not derive from that frame-work. In all these cases, we are dealing with the deification of the will, and in all of these cases, an *obsession with necessity* is concealed at their base: Living within the social monster, I am always aware of the necessity of my position. I am constantly dependent on other people; I rub up against them; I am tum-bled about like a stone in a rushing stream. Stifled revulsion explodes into rebellion against necessity, seeks out the illusion, at least, of freedom. It is not the fact of doing battle itself that is essential for these characters, but rather that in the course of things, the battle loses any utilitarian justification. It is trans-formed into a struggle with the phantoms of one's own imagi-nation; the one who does battle sees in his own nature the elements he must smother because they are the collaborators with the social monster, the forward guard deployed by a col-lective means of sensibility in order to attack the strong man from within. "Human" feelings like pity, empathy, or kindness appear to be dangerous drugs.

Nonetheless, all of Stendhal's sympathy and all of the reader's sympathy are on the side of the hero. He represents a higher, richer, more perfect type. There is no human sensation that is alien to him. He is capable of loving intensely and truly, of weeping out of pity and hatred for the wrongdoer when he hears a song about prison. He is capable of praying, of feeling remorse for his sins, even though he thinks of religion as a collection of sophistic formulas, one of the countless lies told by human beings. But let us be clear: all these are *states* that are no more meaningful than physiological states. He towers above them; the states change, but he remains unchanging. He is a subject who takes on various selves in turn, but he continues, independently, alongside them. No belief, no thought contains him; he is aware that both beliefs and thoughts flow through him; he pays attention to them in the way one pays attention to one's own pulse, to the beating of one's heart. He is beyond good and evil, beyond truth and falsehood. The one thing that is worthy and of value is to observe oneself and others clearly, not to deceive oneself. But here too we are subject to nature, to the build of our body, to our momentary reflexes. When Julien, condemned to death, delivers his bitter tirade in his prison cell and repeats that there is no natural law other than a lion's strength and the demands of a being who feels hunger and cold, that there is nothing but *wanting*, Stendhal does not miss the opportunity to comment ironically, "This philosophy might have been sound, but its nature prepared him to yearn for death."

It is not, then, as straightforward a matter as one might think. Overturning the hierarchy of values is not a matter of calling things bad that have been considered good until now, or bad things good. Here, the very life force is opposed to all moral values; they become secondary, of little import. To live, to be powerful—such a slogan is substituted in place of the broken Ten Commandments. To live, to be powerful—that is, to contain within oneself all the greatness and all the humiliation of life on earth, to safeguard and create oneself just to spite everything. So Stendhal's philosophy is not, as one might suppose, a gloomy and hopeless philosophy. On the contrary, exalting the passions, believing that man can and must be happy when he sates his passions, the author of *The Charter-house of Parma* assigns all blame to the collective, which shackles the individual. Man himself is as innocent as any animal. The engine of his activity is the drive to achieve happiness, and there are as many types of happiness as there are psycho-physical organisms. To give people the opportunity to achieve their own happiness is no different from leading them into conditions where they can allow themselves, with impunity, to commit crimes and to do good, whereas today, Stendhal might have said, both the one and the other are a dangerous luxury, and nations are ruled by hypocritical half crimes and half virtues. That is the reason for Stendhal's cult of epochs that were turbulent, stormy, tumultuous, when there were no limits at all, no brakes for magnificent Dionysian personalities. His cult of Renaissance Italy, sixteenth-century France, Napoleon. Nietzsche, Stendhal's fervent admirer (he called Stendhal "my dead friend"), similarly sought in the past a counterweight to his own worthless times. That he considered Cesare Borgia a higher type of hero than Parsifal sheds light on the direction his historical fantasies took.[3]

Now we come to a curious matter: the "powerful man" condemns contemporary civilization in the name of ancient civilizations, which supposedly gave people greater happiness and were supposedly founded on principles that are closer to human nature. In just the same way, after the war years of 1914–18, the growth of catastrophism, almost universal among German thinkers, and the proclamation of "returns to the Middle Ages" are, above all, the protest of people who deny the possibility that civilization can evolve. Although "returns to the Middle Ages" often use an entirely different language than "the powerful man" and are governed more by concern for precisely those qualities that both Stendhal and Nietzsche attacked, their background is comparable. Whether it be Berdyayev's vision of medieval harmony, Stendhal's vision of a murderous, decadent Rome under Pope Alexander VI, or Nietzsche's Dionysian Greece, everywhere there is the same inclination to entertain a purely legendary understanding of history, to create a legend about a *lost fatherland* of the spirit, to ascribe to oneself a noble genealogy that should, at least partially, compensate one for having to live among the stupid, contemptible masses. It is a way of convincing oneself that our demands are not unfounded, because once upon a time they had already been satisfied, because it was possible to achieve something by relying on them.

Stendhal, who predicted that he would be understood half a century after his death, appeared to know that his characters would leave the pages of his novel and begin to wander among the living. He knew that not only was he offering a picture of his own age, but he was the first to understand a certain way of looking at man—not by deceiving himself, as Balzac did, with artificially grafted praise of goodness. This analytical way of observing, pseudoscientific and pseudo-objective, became a universal attribute half a century after Stendhal's death, and today we employ it as a matter of course, without noticing that it is only one of many possible methods. But it is precisely this distortion of objectivity, the exaggeration of the conflict between the individual and the collective, that accounts for Stendhal's exceptional position and his influence on Nietzsche. Arming his heroes with a whole range of brilliant talents, making them handsome, seductive, impressionable, while at the same time denigrating their milieu, he manipulated them in a way that was too clearly marked by bitterness and *ressentiment*.

One of France's second-rate critics, evaluating Balzac, Stendhal, and Flaubert from a didactic-moral point of view, concluded that they are "bad teachers." This is both shallow and naive; to demand that literature that grows from soil jolted by internal explosions should play a constructive, healing role is the same as to want a boiling kettle to emit angelic music instead of the hiss of pressurized steam. Nonetheless, the judgment of ordinary, insignificant people, for whom the excellent writer had such contempt, often hits the mark with its cruel succinctness. Stendhal, says the critic, made his "I" into the center of the world. His megalomania took the form of hatred, because people naturally did not grow tall enough to be measured by his own standards. In his own eyes, he was a superior being who, precisely because of his superiority, had to offend and scandalize his fellow man. And he gave tit for tat, with hatred and contempt.

Let us add that he was really a superior man. His rare, perceptive judgment, his lack of any submission to literary fashions, his revulsion at the charlatanism of contemporary romantics, his cold, analytical mind—all these are by no means minor qualities in someone who knows that he is, in addition, gifted with immense talent. The matter of Stendhal's national defection (he considered himself spiritually a Milanese, not a Frenchman) demonstrates how much effort he invested in extracting himself from the authority of others' opinions, how painstakingly he selected his privileged position, a position on the sidelines. To be a foreigner in one's own country, to be, despite everything, a foreigner in one's adopted country, is to be able to say at all times that the tribunal of local opinion is inappropriate; it is to extricate oneself with the help of a formal subterfuge, without telling the judges to their face that one considers them too petty and too unintelligent.

Let us return, however, to that strange, touching individual—Julien Sorel. Julien perishes in his battle with society because he is unable to maintain the role of a cool and calculating gambler. His nature is given to the grand gesture; it is subject to violent passions. If Balzac's "cold-blooded cad" Rastignac and his "cold-blooded cad" Vautrin rise to the highest positions in society, this is only because Balzac does not lend his heroes his full support, whereas Julien Sorel is Stendhal's alter ego and is furnished with those qualities that determined the author's lack of success during his lifetime. There is no room for such characteristics in the so-called deluded mass of dwarfs. Because Julien Sorel's struggle was foreordained to fail, *The Red and the Black* is a tragic work. In the beginning of the novel there is a scene in which Julien, kneeling in church, spies a scrap of newspaper lying on the floor. He can make out the following words: "The details of the execution and the final moments of Ludwik Jenrel, execution carried out in Besançon, on . . ." On the reverse could be seen the first words of a headline. THE FIRST STEP. "Who could have placed this paper here?" said Julien. "Poor fellow," he added with a sigh, "his name ends just like mine . . . ," and he crumpled the paper. As Julien left the church, it seemed to him that he saw blood near the stoup. The holy water in it had overflowed, and a reflection from the draperies covering the windows made it look like blood. Suddenly Julien was ashamed of his hidden terror. "That's all I need—to be a coward!" he told himself. "To arms!"

Fate's mysterious warning was not in vain. Julien was free in each of his actions. He followed only his own desire so that the circle closed, the crime he committed took place nowhere else but in a church, and the newspapers carried notices similar to the one he had found on the scrap of paper flung down by an unknown hand. Because a type of predestination governs men, "the freer man is, the truer he is to himself, and he is forever beginning anew the selfsame life."[4] Is it Greek Ananke, Providence, chance, luck? Always, an evil power turns human efforts inside out, particularly when it would seem that the final victory has been achieved. Balzac says something similar through the lips of Vautrin: "Just at the very moment when one holds the winning card with four aces in hand, a candle suddenly falls over, the cards catch fire, or the gambler has an apoplectic fit!" "You have freedom of choice," destiny seems to say with a smirk, "but remember, no matter which road you choose, you will always stumble over me." Perhaps the attraction of freedom does not depend, then, on the final result. The pleasure of the struggle, the spreading of one's wings, the wide expanse of azure are sufficient reward for the strong. Freedom is a form of happiness. The intoxication that Nietzsche celebrated is an intoxication with struggle itself, with life itself, including, as well, with defeat.

Nietzsche's role in the formation of totalitarianism in Europe cannot be denied. It would not be wise, however, to seek spiritual predecessors, to deduce mutual influences, and, reading Balzac, Stendhal, or Carlyle, to draw conclusions about an inheritance handed down from one generation to another. The superman was born at the moment when the textile plants of Lyon began to resound with the pounding of machinery, when Manchester started emitting smoke, and when the value recorded on the Paris stock exchange as seven leaped in a couple of years to two hundred. In the barometer of literature, the column of mercury shuddered violently and surged upward, marked by lines with famous names. One can observe the ever new forms assumed by the "powerful man," measure him by the measure of the words pronounced in the meantime by beings brought to life through the imagination of writers. The powerful man's fate becomes complicated, splits into two; new types and new species arise. What shores does he aim for? When will he cast off the burden of hatred and sit down among people with a smile on his face, their equal, no longer pained by social leveling? He is condemned to wander for a long time yet, and we do not know when his adventures will end.

Nietzsche crying out, *"Pereat veritas, fiat vita"*—let truth die, let life begin—cast a spell that explains nearly the entire intellectual ferment of the past century. It is one of those magical utterances, one of those utterances that, like a spotlight, illuminate the labyrinths of spiritual crises. An era arrived when truth became an instrument and was ordered to slavishly obey the highest god, *the deed*, an era when truth was chained to the heavy, armor-plated mass of the deed. Then everything that is useful, everything that whips people and rouses them to do battle, that enrages and multiplies power, is called truth. That such an era has arrived and that there are countries that have yearned to resolve in one way and not another the dilemma expressed in Nietzsche's cry is, obviously, neither the virtue nor the fault of that naive harbinger of "joyous knowledge." He himself, even though he was in revolt, felt the weight of the evil of his times. He fought against Christianity, arguing that the Christian religion derives from *ressentiment* and that it is a religion of slaves. For him, the Christian virtues were qualities that the enslaved and debased Jewish nation had, of necessity, to possess—qualities that were elevated to the level of merits. Submissiveness, forgiveness of injuries one has suffered, love of one's fellow man, responding to evil with good deeds, were just such qualities that Christians had dressed up with an otherworldly glow. The weak, the broken, the feeble in mind and heart could hope that their indolence, incompetence, and submissiveness in the struggle would receive a heavenly reward after death.

Nothing so unmasks a struggling individual as his creation for his own use of a suitable opponent. Don Quixote, by mistaking windmills for giants, filled in the main chapter in his biography. Nietzsche attacked Christianity because he believed that Christianity bears the responsibility for the state of things whereby the anonymous crowd renounces joy and power and orders the vigorous, precious individual to renounce them, too. Did he not notice that the crowd was already made up of supermen just like him, just as abused and filled with hatred? That Christianity had retreated like the tide running out, leaving behind crabs scrabbling in a panic on the sand? Was he never visited by the suspicion that he himself had become a victim of *ressentiment*? Perhaps he simply did not want to know.

"Pereat veritas, fiat vita." The full sense of that saying depends on the meaning we ascribe to *"vita."* For sarcastic Stendhal, the word "life" was equivalent to the word "happiness." For Nietzsche it took on the appearance of violent, blind force. At times it approximates skepticism and hedonism among connoisseurs; then again it is aflame with fiery belief, explodes with hatred. There is nothing of the skeptic in Nietzsche, André Gide remarks. Only "those brains in which skepticism arouses the most profound revulsion, or in which skepticism, like a new form of belief, pushing love into hatred, preserves the entire fervor of faith" can understand Nietzsche. It is possible that this type of worshipper of life turned out to be the most dangerous for the West. Like the avengers of Julien Sorel, linking disdain for the truth with creative fervor and a destructive fury, they set out to do battle with the world.

Absolute Freedom

"Whenever I reread Nietzsche, the pen just drops from my hand, to such an extent do I think that everything that I have to say he has already said before me and better than I could ever manage." These are the words of André Gide.[1] Probably no figure in the literature of the past few decades reflects so faithfully the changeable currents of the age, its contradictions and anxiety, as does Gide. He is not a sympathetic figure. The scion of a wealthy bourgeois family, a Protestant raised on the Bible who then used the Gospels in order to attack Christian morality, an advocate of the most extreme individualism, and also, in a later period of his life, a pseudo-Communist. But it is not his changeability that causes the lack of trust that we feel in relation to him. Gide, as he himself admits, never had to work hard to earn his daily bread; the image of human poverty occurred to him only in his maturity, when, as an observer but not a participant, he became aware of the suffering of beings similar to him. The frankness of his writings, which there is no reason to doubt, only intensifies the repellent impression aroused by the humanitarianism of the privileged, a humanitarianism that empathizes from above. Gide, who is absolutely frank and terrified of lying, expresses—perhaps precisely because of that aspect of his character—the lies of the civilization of which he is a representative.

The diaries of his journey to the Congo are exceedingly repulsive reading. I cannot believe that a reader who knows what hard work costs and who has earned his daily bread amid struggle and humiliations could read the books without embarrassment. The motif of "descending to earth," of fraternity with those who suffer, which keeps returning in Gide, offers proof that Gide understood his own weakness, but I doubt he foresaw that the future would treat his humanitarianism as a peculiar, exotic document of an incomprehensible way of feeling. Carried in a palanquin by Negroes, running around Negro villages with a green butterfly net in pursuit of rare insect species, loaded down with volumes of the French classics—what a portrait of a traveling French bourgeois, what a symbol of total ignorance of the affairs of this world and of the incompetence of French colonial policy! From his palanquin he observes the life of the local people, discovers administrative excesses, laments over them, has the courage to denounce them unequivocally. His *Journey to the Congo* exposes him to strident attacks by French capitalists. Nonetheless, the corner of the curtain that he manages to lift only awakens anxiety and a suspicion that even worse things were hidden from the eyes of the naive tourist whom the governor and colonial bureaucrats had surrounded with the most attentive care. In *The Heart of Darkness*, Joseph Conrad looked at the Congo with the eyes of a sailor, with the eyes of a workingman, and what he saw was Hell. What the humanitarian, fainting from his literary perceptions, failed to achieve, the writer who was characterized by a certain aristocratic demeanor and conservatism managed to accomplish. Gide toured the Soviet Union just as he had the Congo. Deprived of experiences that can be had only by living in primitive conditions, worrying about acquiring basic necessities, and performing heavy labor, he relied on long conversations to reach the simplest, most obvious of conclusions, while other uncomplicated matters remained as inaccessible to him as to an inhabitant of Mars traveling around on Earth. His enthusiasms and disillusionments are the enthusiasms and disillusionments of an old woman from a charitable society—and just as refined, lofty, and devoid of any knowledge of daily life. In addition, the style of his works is sweet, supple, somehow misty, not manly. It is said that when Conrad received a copy of Gide's translation of *Typhoon*, he fell into a rage, hurled the book to the floor, and stomped on it. This shouldn't surprise anyone. A tragic writer, a stern and direct man, Conrad might well become enraged when he saw his own sentences clothed in a garment of artistic, saccharine *fioriture*. It is not yet known how future generations will judge Gide's complete oeuvre. Someone once said maliciously that he is "an ass, who had the courage to say everything that he thought." There's truth in that; the value of Gide's oeuvre lies above all in the superbly formed tool of language and in the frankness with which he captured on the run the most hidden thoughts. A seismograph of the intellectual currents of his age, a restless writer, quick on the uptake, he experienced universal changes as changes in his own person. That is why no attempt at probing the problems of this period can be successful without citing Gide.

The development of Gide's creative work coincides with the years of intensifying antirationalistic tendencies. The points that demarcated this antirationalist campaign were the growing popularity of Nietzsche, Europe's discovery of Dostoevsky, the appearance of Bergson, and, finally, the activity of William James. Gide claims that he professed Nietzscheanism even before he became acquainted with the German philosopher's works. This is an example of that simultaneity in which certain currents appear in a culture and give birth to spiritual affinities between people who do not know one another. Elsewhere Gide defines what he considers to be Nietzsche's greatest contribution to European thought. We are free to assume that this is also his own slogan, since he admits to such a strong spiritual bond with his teacher. "It is the question: *What is man capable of? What is a single individual capable of?'* This question is accompanied by a terrible fear that man could be something else, something greater, that he could be more: that he has stopped abjectly at the first stage, unconcerned about his ultimate fulfillment."[2]

What does this mean? It means that the goal of an individual's activity is not outside him or beyond his earthly calling, as in Christianity, but that he is his own goal. That no moral rule, no intellectual construct can or should have total power over him. Since rules and constructs arise from him, he creates them himself in accordance with his own might. Gide's creative path becomes understandable in the light of this conviction. He issued many warnings that one should not look for consistency in his writings, that on the contrary, they illustrate the zigzag line of a mind that is constantly forming itself anew. The final goal toward which he aspires is not some unchanging truth. He wants to depict man in the fullest, and according to him, to depict man is to depict the contradictions, the ferment of his changing ideas, conditions, and desires. Here an important discovery is expressed, achieved in the period directly preceding the great world cataclysms. This discovery, it is true, was long known to philosophy, but it has only now become universally known, become the mark of an era. It is the recognition of the *derivativeness* of ideas. Nietzsche raged against Platonism, which is what he called every manifestation of respect for an unchanging idea that existed, as it were, in and of itself, apart from human beings. Furthermore, reason as an instrument of the will, which cunningly employs reason, that "puppet on a string," to achieve its own goals, loses its ultimate esteem. The new apostles no longer appeal to reason, and it is not reason that they summon as the highest judge of earthly and superterrestrial affairs. The new ruler is the will—"the will of might" (Nietzsche), "the will of belief" (James)—the basic element not of cognition, but of action. Gide, building upon Nietzsche's question "What can man do?" proceeds as an observer of human actions. Ideas interest him only insofar as they correspond to certain positions; his concern is directed entirely to representing faithfully the links between action and an idea created by action. Ideas, however, and thus that side of man which can be described intellectually, are at most a minuscule part of the whole. The truest parts of the human soul are the oceans of will and passion, the mysterious X, which sometimes is expressed in spontaneous responses, gestures, seemingly meaningless words. A distortion of life occurs when the veneer of beliefs and viewpoints becomes too confining, when the internal X increases but man is incapable of smashing his chains. Free growth, free life means forever casting off one's old skin like a snake and assuming a new one; it means not being afraid of contradicting oneself. No price is too high to pay for unconstrained flowering, physical strength, vitality. He who is satisfied with the first beliefs he acquired— even though a voice inside him cries out, demanding new truths that can liberate his "I" or his X for new victories and new experiences—"remains pathetically at the first stage, unconcerned about his ultimate fulfillment."

I have a suspicion that the Negro laborers in French enterprises in the Congo, whom Gide observed as he was carried in his palanquin, might have had something to say about this. It is an ugly and demagogic thing to measure a writer by the contrast between his works and reality. But those laborers were working in conditions identical with the conditions under which prisoners labored in Europe's concentration camps in the fifth decade of this century. Europe experienced for itself the roundups, the slap in the face by an interrogator, suffocation in jam-packed barracks, death under the heel of a criminal of a higher race. And Europe learned that these words are true: "By their deeds you shall know them." Therefore, Europe is now and must be severe. It has the right to hurl the harshest accusations against writers like Gide.

Gide is a depraved writer. We have to understand the use of this adjective. It makes no sense to apply it to writers of the past, to people and issues that time has covered with blue mist. But using it is justified when we are speaking about people and matters that are close to us in time, contemporary, or just barely past, when a passionate tone is an expression of our yearning, our battle for a better tomorrow. Gide's depravity does not reside in his homosexuality, in the sensual atmosphere of his books. But who cares about that? His depravity rests on his having draped a cloak of beauty around the most poisonous and destructive intellectual currents, which prepared a world-wide cataclysm. Gide's writing is the angelic, kindly smile of the devil as he pointed out the forbidden apple and said you will be like gods once you have known good and evil. When the ominous reminder of history was approaching from all directions, writers like Gide instructed us to revel in complicating our notions of culture, understood as something completely detached from real phenomena, from human work and ordinary earthly effort. Breaking with "Platonism," with the traditional understanding of good and evil, transferring the center of gravity to the substratum of ideas, these writers simultaneously reduced that substratum to the inner powers of the individual human being, performing pious dances before this "holy of holies" in anticipation of a revelation, bah, even of salvation for humanity. These promises that a splendid flowering of mankind will somehow take place automatically, once the powers hidden in man are revealed and he achieves the maximum freedom, belong among fabrications that have an exceptionally short life span. Today we are more inclined to believe that these hidden powers are demons and phantoms, that if they are recklessly liberated from the fetters of reason, they will succeed in devastating the earth and bringing it to ruin. We would rather say, "Be careful with 'free will,' with 'the unconscious,' with 'intuition,' " because we have seen how Nietzsche's and Gide's hero arose, trusting in his "inner voice," how he spouted the slogans of "enthusiasm" and "might" . . . and we know what came of that.

The fascist movements were prepared by the long labor of charlatans of thought, confounders of conscience. Perhaps, in order to have a good understanding of the role of such figures as Gide, we need to reach for qualitatively worse figures, representatives of literary irrationalism who were endowed with lesser talents. The beauty of the word, the artistic value of exceptional writers, always preserves the capacity to mislead and frequently deflects attention from the deeper ties between their work and the ugly ills of the age. Second-rate writers who turn ideas into loose change reveal themselves much more easily; they are not protected by the cadence of their sentences and the colorfulness of their images. A valuable document in this connection is Giovanni Papini's *From Man to God*, a collection of polemical articles and essays written at a time when the influence of James and Nietzsche intersected in Italy not long before the eruption of Futurism, with its idolizing of "the leap and the fist," and shortly before the years when Marinetti, the future official bard of Fascism, offended the public with his roars in honor of energy and brutality and called for the destruction of museums. Papini proclaims the imminent arrival of the man-God, the transformation of man into God:

> Among the divine attributes to which man aspires the first is omnipotence, which all the others may lead to also. To want to become a man-God presumes, therefore, an aspiration to achieve the greatest possible amount of direct power over people and things . . .
>
> Satisfaction of only some desires can only result in an in-

crease in the remaining desires; extinguishing all desires is practically impossible, so there is no solution other than satisfying all of them . . .

The preparation of the man-God is a practical task.

The above declaration could be treated humorously were it not for the fact that it is a perfect fit with the intellectual atmosphere of the age, mirroring paradoxically the fundamental tone of that time, that nostalgia for power which, for the time being, still remained in the sphere of artistic and literary contemplation. Similarly, Gide in his book about Dostoevsky lingers with delight over a fragment from *Demons*:

> "He who teaches people that they are good will facilitate the fulfilment of the world."
> "The one who did this was crucified."
> "He will come, and his name will be 'man-God.' "
> "God-man?"
> "Man-God; there's a difference."

Papini is not embarrassed. Reading him, we get the impression that we are looking at a crooked mirror held up for us by a monkeylike nasty hand:

> If we want a new civilization to arise, which is not just a provisional one, then our most important task will be to develop romanticism to the highest effort. A romantic insurrection will lead to the triumph of emotionality, of instinct, of the deed; it is the revenge of greatness over unity.
> Romanticism led to two results: a) the nakedness of man, who has been stripped of all those things that sprang up around him, *in order to stem the flow of life, which renews itself without end* (my italics [cm]); b) the condemnation of

pure unifying, law-creating intellectualism, which is to say, the death sentence for philosophy.

Further on, Papini writes, "Thus, the post-Romantic problem, in its duality, has only one solution: the strengthening of force. Philosophy is disappearing; rationalism is perishing on its own in automatic formalism, while on the other hand, previously hidden and despised forces—new, mute forces lying dormant in the *subliminal self*—are appearing."[3]

In light of these truly instructive quotations, is it not obvious that there is a deep bond between the disposition of a youth who has been raised on fascism—who, like Mussolini, was an enthusiast of dropping bombs on Abyssinian villages— and the work of philosophers and writers who make the *subliminal self* the source of ideas and inspirations? Is it not the case that the sword that found its way into the hands of madmen was forged by the works of those modern Romantics who destroyed faith in the gravity of thought, which is never the ultimate source of judgment for them—the ultimate source of judgment is X, so fluid, so unknown; it is life itself. Do not be ashamed; be naked. Discard the corset of conventional morality imposed upon you by the propriety of rules. If I experience joy from watching peasants' huts collapse from bomb blasts, why shouldn't I say so out loud? If I feel contempt for the scientist who devotes his entire life to proving the primacy of feeling, instinct, and action, but submits to thought, while I am all feeling, all instinct, all action, why shouldn't I spit in his face and burn his books in the square? Nakedness, a yearning for nakedness, is the obsession of all reformers of human nature—to appeal to man in his naked state, alone, liberated from both divine and conventional ethical intervention. The daydream of all theoreticians of "natural goodness," from Rousseau to Gide, is to see man *beyond civilization*, man himself, with the result that, fighting against "Platonism," they introduce it through a side door, since "free man" is their Platonic ideal. It is indeed strange that such unbreakable ties exist between this tendency and Protestantism. Writing about Nietzsche, Gide is well aware of this. He insists that Nietzsche is the inescapable consequence of Protestantism, that Protestantism *had* to lead to Nietzsche: "Without placing any limits on free evaluation, [Protestants] created a religion without boundaries, thus one that is impossible to define, which—on the day when free evaluation introduces atheism into it—will know if atheism is a part of itself or not; a religion predestined to disintegrate in the unbounded circle of philosophizing, to which it opened the gate."[4] It is just this quality that Gide recognizes as the most attractive aspect of Protestantism—its ability to evolve into new forms, its not keeping man back at any stage.

What, then, is the ultimate goal? One cannot speak of a goal, just as one cannot speak of the goal of a plant; growing is itself the goal. Anti-intellectual currents eagerly employ the legendary concepts of "strength" and "growth." In truth, they are not concerned with the transformation of reality, with man's mastery over matter, since all types of transformation always aim in a certain definite direction. Rather, we are dealing here with purely psychological approval of the *experience* of strength, the *experience* of vitality. A more sated, more settled version of vitalism which is cultivated in wealthy capitalist countries gives pride of place particularly vividly to *delighting* in the seething, the very churning of life. What the result may be is irrelevant; it is the act itself, like a moment of powerful, penetrating feeling, that fulfills one. Arousing joy, the physical joy of the muscles, sinews, and nerves, it spurs one on toward the next, ever more daring activity. Gide, a worthy son (or at least not a prodigal one) of Western democracy, the literary mirror of contemporary currents of his time, exhibits to perfection this more passive, connoisseurlike aspect of Dionysian enthusiasms for movement, upheaval, activity. His characters live and act disinterestedly; they are continually sundering anew the chains of necessity, not in the name of some definite convictions, but in tune with something deep inside their organism, in search of its most flamboyant, its grandest rhythm, which might guarantee a blissful state. They rebel against the commandments of existing morality, against the family, against warm domestic feelings, solely because by destroying the things that have grown up around them, as Papini says, they affirm for themselves their "I." This is childish destruction, an urge to bite, eternal childhood, full of curiosity and contempt. It is rebellion for the sake of rebellion, action for the sake of action, will for the sake of will—in complete isolation from consequences, from any evaluation of those consequences. The world is dying before their eyes; the gashes their deeds carve out are unworthy of their notice—go forward, never look back, imprison life in a moment of illumination. Everything that provides that moment of illumination, that intensifies vitality, is the truth. Gide's chief theme is *the rapture of self-liberation*, the rapture of destroying everything that exists now. Rapture. This word should be emphasized, since self-liberation and destruction take place not in the name of the superiority of a new truth, but as a program of inner experience, as ecstasy without end. His "prodigal son" returns to his parents' home in rags without having achieved anything. He returns beaten up, but when his younger brother runs away, he does not restrain him; he is proud of him, even though he knows that in his wanderings the boy will find only disillusionment. The beauty of existence is in fighting, regardless of what the fight is about and how it will end. "Our life is waging war," but the goal is just the product of warfare; resilience and youth create goals that are somehow tacked on and insignificant in relation to the blind, joyous will in search of pretexts. Unlimited output of emotional life, that is what is concealed in the question posed by Nietzsche and by Gide: "What is man capable of?" Because here capability is really capaciousness. That question, transformed to reflect its authors' intent, would go like this: "What can man experience?" Greatness and splendor of deeds are not measured by the changes they introduce into human relations, nor by an internal, statistical injunction such as the codex or the catechism. They are measured by the gift of internal simplification, the feeling of strength they bring to the actors. Whoever desires but does not act, destroys; whoever does not act will ultimately stop desiring. This principle is the principle of exercising for the sake of exercising; it incorporates, whenever it serves as the foundation for social consideration, the conviction that all intensive human activity is good in and of itself.

The intersections and kinship of these antirational directions are highly complicated. Nevertheless, the future, always erasing differences and bringing similarities into the light, will undoubtedly reduce them to some common label. Then, too, there will certainly come a time for demonstrating their role in the creation of fascistic movements. Now when I speak of André Gide, a bizarre thought comes to mind: that the ignorance and divine nonchalance of artists are no less capable of wreaking destruction and ruin than the cold calculations of strategists. The delicate hands of intellectuals are stained with blood from the moment a death-bearing word emerges from them, even if they saw that word as a word of life. Perhaps their books are not read by the masses, but the journalist who writes articles for the daily press reads them. These articles are read by the tribune of the people, the teacher, the man in the street. And so the coin of ideas, of thoughts, starts rolling; along the way its more subtle letters are rubbed out until, smooth and simplified, it reaches the masses in the form of a single motto, a cheap slogan. Then the time comes when a demagogue picks it up from the pavement. What are the speeches of dictators made of—dictators accompanied by the applause of millions? Mottos harvested from popular pamphlets, transparent enough to be understood by everyone. They have to be preceded by the work of scholars and artists; then the popularizer takes them over. Thanks to this process, they are lively and complex enough so that the ordinary man, deafened by their roar, cannot distinguish their falseness. The fascist programs were amazingly modest with regard to objectives that could be subjected to rational evaluation. They appealed to emotion, to imagination. The masses were made drunk on action as action, heroism as heroism, might as might—the rapture of self-liberation and destruction. Self-liberation to what end? To crime and slavery. Farther down the road, that is what awaits all these people possessed by a Dionysian frenzy. "The most important intensification of Romanticism," to use Papini's language, in reality made man appear naked, caused intellectualism to become a dangerous transgression, while the new powers concealed in the *subliminal self* found their voice. The search for "spiritual adventure" changed into a much too real adventure for the entire globe.

Those same social transformations that gave the world the antirationalism of James, Nietzsche, and Gide engendered historical materialism. It, too, deriving from the same sources, treats every idea as a human creation, as an instrument for action. It, too, denies eternal life, immutable truth that is separate from the world and possesses a life of its own. Yet historical materialism is the mortal enemy of currents that appeal to blind energy. Stanisław Brzozowski has already commented on this. "It is undeniable," he wrote, "that today's progressive, urgent question in philosophy is the struggle between pragmatism and historical materialism. Other struggles are archaeology."[5]

For historical materialism, the foundation on which ideas

arise is not the X of human nature, the depths and abysses of our psychophysical makeup, but the labor of the human collective. For Marx, it is insufficient to be propelled into action by thought: "He recognizes that thought has to be something other than a rum ration distributed to soldiers before a battle . . . so that thought is not alone in moving him to act, but in order that by action he is able to bring thought to fruition."[6] Action creates thought, but thought, in turn, since it now exists, must be a lawgiver. Energy and action claim a different proof. Among pragmatists of all types, the proof was the joyful emotion itself of the one who acts; here, an objective goal, the transformation of reality into a means defined by thought, becomes a kind of proof. The meaning of action, looked at from the perspective of its consequences, is the opposite of great pleasure. This argument is truly the most important argument in contemporary history, and while it was taking place on paper, the forces that were about to transform it into a pitched battle for life or death were already taking shape. It seems that an appropriately reconstructed pragmatism is the sole ideology of totalitarian regimes. Thought served up in doses measured by propaganda bureaus fulfills a function no different from rum before a battle. "The truth is what intensifies our energy to perform deeds prescribed by the system of the conditions in which we live."[7] That is how Brzozowski summed up the fundamental conviction of the pragmatists. Those leaders whose lips did not hesitate to state the most obvious lies—just so long as they could extract the maximum of vitality and energy from their peoples—would have subscribed to this conviction. And what about Gide? Will he find a successor who will want to sing a hymn in honor of the "fruits of the earth"? And will Europe recognize the wave of irrational intoxication that swept across her after the war of 1914–18? Probably not. Probably, a slow, laborious construction will be Europe's lot. It is perhaps wrong to saddle a writer with responsibility, to accuse him of crimes he did not commit. It would make no sense, just as accusing Nietzsche would make no sense. And yet, readers who designate a place for them in the stacks of their libraries, valuing them as creative writers, have the right to reject them as moralists—to reject them and to condemn them in the name of things that are greater than literature. This would require them to condemn some part of themselves, some corner of the heart. When these works fade into the distance, when they disappear within the colors of their time and none of their pages can awaken internal dialogues, they will return as evidence . . . but will they return as beauty?

Beyond Truth and Falsehood

This happened around the time of my high school graduation. I was experiencing doubts then that could have been called religious doubts had they not extended much further than the sphere of religious dogmas. I asked about the right to bear within oneself certain vague convictions, certain fantasies that elude rational explanation—those imaginings and convictions that become the raw material for the creative work and thought of one's entire later life. I sensed their weight and significance only vaguely, but they did not fit within the framework of any system; they were living contradictions, a jumble of wishes that the world might be one way and not another. It was then that William James's *The Varieties of Religious Experience* fell into my hands. What peace, what joy, what unexpected support! This book taught that I was free to give myself over, without any scruples at all, to my timid visions and beliefs without worrying about their truth. It taught me that it sufficed that my beliefs gave me strength and certitude, that they guided my steps through chance and experience. It taught that there is no other truth than the truth of human desires and aspirations, and that what contributes to internal clarity and goodness requires no other test. I am not sure that I understood the mechanism of pragmatism correctly, but after reading this book, I suddenly felt happy. The truth was revealed as if by listening in to the work of a young organism. It flowed with the blood; it rang out with the hammer of the heart. The harmony of the world was just such a truth as one's joy on a June morning when a bright stripe falls on the table through the parted drapes and the aroma of fresh baking and the voices of a market day float in from the street. I understood that not everything can be expressed in rationally motivated assertions and that this unclear, unknown part is more important than arguments and disputations. Beyond the ranks of words, there existed something alive and powerful, and every faith existed beyond the boundaries in which "yes" and "no" are in force.

I speak of this not to demonstrate the influence of James or other pragmatists on a certain generation. "Influences" are too complex a sphere and one that permits too many liberties. I would like to consider the experience of reading James as a phenomenon in and of itself, a phenomenon sufficiently frequent and disturbing that it is permissible to devote a moment's thought to it.

Let us assume that, just as in this instance, a young man grows up in a traditional atmosphere where religious and ethical values are joined together. Slowly, new ideas and convictions that are contrary and foreign to the religious spirit creep into his world. He attends classes in apologetics or Church history and hears about dogmas, the Holy Trinity, redemption; he learns about Thomas Aquinas and Saint Augustine. The whole system possesses an internal cohesion and harmony; it is sustained by medieval thinkers. But then, in his nature and history classes, an entirely different understanding of life and of man penetrates him, totally foreign to the medieval hierarchy of values. Descriptions of persecutions, revolutions, the collapse of centuries-old cultures and belief systems do not fit within the static, medieval image of the world, established seven or eight hundred years earlier, with a power that is eternally binding until Judgment Day. Nature's workshop—where he places slides that he has prepared himself under the gleaming new microscope, where he looks at living beings similar to himself and developing according to the same laws—leads to other thoughts that were neglected by the doctors of the Church. "So what!" someone might exclaim. "For a hundred years millions of students have existed in this strange, bifurcated dimension; the catechists continue to draw popular arguments against evolution from their brochures or mock naturalists in the name of the new discoveries of physics." True. But this does not alter the fact that every time this affair begins from the beginning, the incompatibility of two habits, two methods, begins anew. It has been called a conflict between faith and reason. This is no more precise than if we were to speak of the conflict between faith and faith, or reason and reason. For the Christian system is far removed from pure emotionalism, just as what we usually call scientific thinking is far removed from pure reason. Rather, it is a conflict between two equal spheres, equally powerfully armed both emotionally and intellectually—two spheres, each of which has its weak points and its superiority. Reading natural science or history emphasizes their obviousness and builds upon those thousands of concepts and judgments that appear in black and white in newspaper columns, that shout out from the traffic on the streets and race along the telegraph wires. But when it comes to placing values into a certain order, history and nature begin timidly, clumsily, hesitating between their complete negation and attempts at biological or social grounding. Here, readings in religion, by stimulating an intuitively understood assessment of good and evil, nobility and baseness, are without a doubt the winner. A seventeen- or eighteen-year-old boy is incapable, however, of uniting these two separate spheres into an intellectual whole. The sums never add up. Ten "buts" lie in wait for every "yes." In this continual balancing, in his lack of equilibrium, he joyfully welcomes a book that relieves him of the effort of choosing between two extremes, that allows him to preserve both spheres as being equally (he feels this) important and precious. True, he pays a rather high price for this: it demands, by way of transferring the entire problem to the domain of practical applications, an almost total relinquishing of pure understanding. "Perhaps," the young reader says, "certain of my beliefs are in conflict with each other, but God does not reveal himself, and even though people were taught this in the Middle Ages, I have no rational data to lead me to believe that he exists. Perhaps, in this world of struggle for existence and the persecution of the weak, the good is only a slightly useful fiction. But *let* God exist, *let* the good be valued; that's what I want. If I can divide my food and drink into what is good for me and what is bad, I am also free to do the same with my beliefs and views. Let us follow the demands of the heart."

This intellectual experience would probably not deserve to be studied were it characteristic of only the years of adolescence and religious anxieties. Instead, it appears to be at the source of a great many important and powerful cultural currents, and it is one of the permanent points of a certain period, like the notion of dissolving into Nature in the works of the Romantics, or the vision of the primitive among Rousseau's contemporaries. What is the essence of this intellectual experience? Several totalities, several value systems coexist in the mind even though they cannot be mutually reconciled. The search for a higher level of judgment that could reconcile them follows upon this. If these systems are incompatible in their intellectual elements, they may, perhaps, accord perfectly in their background or in their other components. Two geometrical figures traced on a blackboard may very well not be similar, but they are drawn on the same board and with the same chalk, and that brings them closer.

Wronging the weak is recognized as deserving of condemnation, but at the same time wronging the weak presents itself as a universal law of both nature and human society. This is clear contradiction, from which, perhaps, one can extricate oneself only by rejecting one of those assertions; it is a contradiction that was the driving force of Byron's creative work. But perhaps it is a mistake to present this contradiction in all its intensity and nakedness. Perhaps both the one and the other assertion can be transferred into an arena where they will lose their sharp contours, where they will dissolve in a broader and greater whole. Yes, definitely—but only under the condition that human thought be assigned a much more modest place, and instinct, habits, and reflexes be heard. Instincts, habits, reflexes, or whatever we call them, require no proof. They exist, and that is sufficient. They can be experienced; they cannot be completely enclosed within the parameters of a syllogism. They can be classified into the experientially healthy and unhealthy by observing the life of individuals and of entire societies. Whoever seeks equilibrium among several mutually antagonistic value systems must rely on experience, on the vital activities that regulate the clash of intellectual complexities. Such an operation does not take place, however, without leaving its mark. The philosopher multiplies suppositions and hypotheses without reaching any definite conclusions, but it suffices to keep on rowing, to work the earth, to live in a community, in order that life may flow independently of any hypotheses and that many doubts may be resolved automatically. Whoever has even once performed this operation would be inclined to agree with this. The ideal of an active life slowly begins to eclipse the ideal of knowledge for the sake of knowledge, wisdom, and inquiry. The student in romantic novellas who still pores over the pages of a book by candlelight in a garret, whom astonished birds visit at dawn, begins to change, is transformed, and finally emerges as a participant in demonstrations, a ringleader in political brawls and scandals. He demands of philosophers and sages prescriptions for saving the world by fast-acting, immediate, and, one might say, technical means. Inquiry that does not aim at a clear, already established goal is becoming less and less popular.

Is this the inevitable consequence of the collision of several value systems appearing in a simplified form between the hour of history and the hour of religion? I think not. But certain inclinations, certain intellectual constructs, attaching themselves to the phenomena of collective life that are difficult to comprehend, tend toward oversimplification. One might say that only these oversimplifications count; only these oversimplifications have social consequences. Thought bears fruit, and man is not, alas—or, perhaps, thank God—a thinking machine.

Considering the illnesses of the present, Professor Johan Huizinga (famous as the author of *Homo ludens*) considers one of the most dangerous symptoms to be advanced irrationality, the renunciation of cognition in favor of life, and, as a consequence, the weakening of the ability to make judgments. Did any previous civilization contradict the ideal of cognition, the intellectual foundation itself? he asks. His answer is in the negative. "Systematic anti-intellectualism, both philosophical and practical, which we are witnessing today, appears to be an absolute novelty in the history of human civilization . . . If spiritual currents ever rebelled against the logical instrument that reason is," he says, "they always did so in the name of a super-rational element. Culture, which today aims at adopting a certain tone, opposes not only reason, but consciousness in general, and it does so in the name of the subrational element, in the name of passions and instincts. People are taking the side of free will, but not in the sense of Duns Scotus, who steered it toward faith."[1]

In support of this, one can cite, obviously, a great many names, a great many directions from the spheres of philosophy, art, politics. Perhaps most important is the general atmosphere that conspires to make the high school student, following a clearly marked path, repeat on his own the experience of the great warriers who undermine the importance of reason. One measure of the reach of these phenomena about which Huizinga speaks is their universality, their penetration into the very style of life. Reconciling "yes" and "no" on some higher level of judgment, man learns how to transfer the center of gravity from those "nos" and "yeses" to whatever it is that tests them, to that higher level of judgment, and going even farther, he loses the ability to ask disinterested questions about the world. He begins, instead, by asking about the goal, about what it is that those questions are meant to serve. From contradictions rooted deep in our system of knowledge, a conviction has arisen about the fundamental unknowability of the world, along with an understanding of truth with limited responsibility, truth for human use, with no pretensions whatsoever to being eternally binding. One arrives at that truth not through an effort directed at some indisputable axioms, but by reaching for its underpinnings, for biological or social determinants. Both conventionalism and Vaihinger's philosophy of fiction, both pragmatism and Bergson's anti-intellectual stance, all create the impression of being the germs of a process whose coarse, palpable results are expressed in political doctrines and in complete systems of fictionally based, freely constructed historiosophy. A young man raised in an anti-intellectual atmosphere, fed on popularized Freudianism (whose destructive results have yet to be comprehended), may very well be unaware of the general coloration of his aspirations. All our connections with the era in which we live are unclear and are visible only to our descendants. Nonetheless, even in the battling currents of our era, there exists a certain common background that creates their historical bond. Perhaps Huizinga is not thinking, then, when he observes melancholically, "When one looks around one can see that among educated people, most frequently among the young, a certain indifference to the degree of truth possessed by the world of their ideas has become common. Rarely is a distinction made now between the categories of fiction and history, taken in their simple, commonly accepted meaning. One no longer cares to know if in the spiritual realm the degree of truth is provable. The fashion of accepting *myth* is a striking example of this."[2]

We know this word only too well. It was in the air before 1939; there was hardly a field of human creativity in which it was not spoken. Who is without sin, and who can pride himself on his lips never having uttered it, his pen never having written it? "Myth" is a highly respected word; the glow of ancient Greece is reflected from it, the glory of demigods and heroes. Lately, however, it has taken on a new meaning. It appears to designate every truth, every system of meaning, which is accepted not because of its logical necessity, but through an act of will. People believe in myth not because they simply believe but because they yearn to believe in it, because they have faith in its positive effects. Neither a broadly expanded justification of this state of things nor elaborate proofs based on observation of collective life can change the fact itself.

For the vast majority of programmatic Catholics, Catholicism is a salvational myth; they are conscious of being Catholics in a way that is similar to Brzozowski's approach. For them, the question of the truth or falsehood of dogmas in general is nonexistent; it does not possess the severe, clear contours that it had for people in the Middle Ages. Catholicism for them is a wondrous discipline of human nature; they see in it an outlet for the most beautiful aspirations and instincts of the human soul, and at the same time as a guarantee of some sort of moral order in people's relations with one another. It is a kind of symbolic image of the perfect proportion of spiritual elements, and the dogmas are an expression of a farsighted wisdom that, in establishing them, was concerned with the harmonious construction of the whole. They are almost prepared to justify fasts on the basis of hygienic needs. Questions about the persons of the Holy Trinity, and about Adam's original sin that weighs upon the entire human species, are usually obscured in a fog of allusions and transferred to the sphere of blind faith. It may be that only militant atheists treat Catholicism as seriously as Catholicism has wished to be treated throughout its many centuries of existence. In this context, one might mention Professor Baudouin de Courtenay, who thought that imagining a kind God who permits the suffering of beings created by Him entailed a purely intellectual harshness and absurdity; he conceived of original sin not as a myth but as a matter that should be submitted to the judgment of reason, just as it was for Saint Augustine, Saint Anselm, and Saint Thomas Aquinas.

The revival or, rather, the creation of myths enjoyed its true triumphs in the field of political thought. The popular slogan "Let us seek an idea" already contains within itself the conviction of a great force inherent in the so-called idea, a force capable of moving crowds in the desired direction. That direction is more a subject for deliberations than the "idea" itself, which is more appropriate as an instrument than as an ultimate goal. One need not even speak of the myth of race, which is entirely elusive from the intellectual point of view; it is enough to recall the myth of labor or the myth of the dictatorship of the proletariat, propagated by the various branches of Marxism. It should be noted here that orthodox Marxism wages a fierce struggle against a pragmatic understanding of truth, which acknowledges as its foundation the acquisition of

an objective knowledge of reality, although this does not pre-
vent Marxism from denying the possibility of "pure" knowledge separated from economic conditions, nor, in practice,
from subjugating knowledge to the tactical and strategic demands of the Party.

Thus the young man whom we were discussing carries the
burden of great events. His experience of reading James is the
first droplet breaking down his soft sandstone. It could as easily
have been a good experience with a different book born of the
spirit of the age, if that book taught him that certain problems
should not be stated *in crudo*, that the delicate mist of sentimentality, habits, and instincts is more important than the
intellect's casuistry.

Is there a way back from this path? Is it possible to return to
absolute truth, achieved through purely intellectual effort, to
truth unruffled by anger, emotion, the yearnings of the heart,
or considerations of the needs of thousands and millions of
hearts? To a disinterested, eternal truth, even if it were limited
to a few elementary principles, with all the rest given over to
the ruminations of constant and systematic doubt? That does
not seem likely. Writing these words, I am subject to the
changes of the era in which it has been my fate to live, and
no different from those who seek medicine for the illnesses
of civilization (judging the tree by its bitter, oh so bitter, fruit),
I ponder the possibility of reviving intellectualism. No different from Professor Huizinga when he observes that "philosophy, which lays the foundation of truth from a defined
form of life that it serves, is dispensable for the representatives
of that form of life and without value for the rest of mankind."[3]

No doubt, the cult of disinterested knowledge, independent
of social consequences, will never return, at least not in the
near future. Who knows, though, if the circle is not closing
now, if anti-intellectual tendencies, brought to their maximum

tension, are not becoming reconciled with each other, and that by knowing more about instincts, reflexes, the mechanisms of social life, we are not acknowledging the proper place of dim human semiconsciousness, precisely in the name of the demands of collective usefulness and developmental prospects.

The Experience of War

We actually know very little about how people are experiencing this war internally, this war that is being waged over an idea about man and the world and that therefore resembles religious wars. Just about the only source of such knowledge is to reflect on one's own experiences, but even this is not such an easy thing; the absence of a language applicable to these new experiences is an obstacle, and we know how convention can transform even the most sincere response. The numerous attempts at forging the experience of wars into literary form while they are still "hot" are good examples; for the most part, these attempts have been unsuccessful. We will know about Europe's experience of wars only when it becomes a social fact, that is, when it erupts into new philosophical and artistic currents, when it is recorded in a struggle with creative material—in words, clay, paint, sound. Obviously I am not thinking about recording the theme of war, which is a secondary matter, but rather about the general atmosphere, the change in internal proportions, on which this great collective experience cannot but have an influence.

In the meantime, we are condemned to self-examination. Since the personal tone is completely justified in this instance, let me say that I see a certain internal logic and internal development in my own attitude toward wartime reality, which is perhaps not solely, and not exclusively, my personal experience. I have been trying to discern, to trace the contours of this tangle of painful matters, and even a partial success in this effort leads me to the conclusion that there is something that can be called a specific experience of war, that it is a mechanism of some sort that one can discuss, just as one discusses the experience of love or the mechanism of cruelty.

It is not possible at present, however, to name all the components of this complicated mechanism. Therefore it is necessary to seek the help of writers who have attempted to define if not identical, at least similar feelings. I am thinking of Tolstoy's *War and Peace*. Seeking analogies (even though exact analogies are impossible), we often stop to consider the Napoleonic Wars. Despite their relative innocence in comparison with the march of the National Socialist doctrine, they must have been just as strong a shock for people in those days, particularly in their most implacable and bloody manifestations in Spain and in Russia. The two most imposing documents of war in European culture, Goya's drawings and *War and Peace*, were bequeathed to us by Spain and Russia. If this is just an accident, it is an eloquent one. *War and Peace* came into being several decades after the events that are its theme, and it is already a polemic vis-à-vis the Napoleonic legend. Tolstoy's great authorial intuition, however, allowed him to conquer the distance of time (perhaps that distance was indispensable for him) and to give a penetrating analysis of the phenomenon under discussion. Good books live a rather rich and complicated life, and each generation can find its own reality in them. Thus the Russian writer's novel contains passages that acquire a thoroughly new expression for participants in a demonic spectacle. It is worthwhile, then, to call them as witness and, using them as a pretext, to aim at advancing our self-awareness if only by a fraction.

Already in the war of 1812 aspects of total war were present, even if only still in mild form. Moscow in flames and a crush of carriages on panic-stricken roads are close to our present understanding. The observation of war from the perspective of a civilian participant is what brings several chapters of Tolstoy's epic closest to us; and what Pierre Bezukhov lived through during those critical days for Russia forms a study of the experience of war worthy of the most rigorous philosopher's pen.

Pierre is in a state of "excitement bordering on madness." He is overcome by a feeling of obscure but powerfully experienced obligation, the necessity to participate actively at any cost. Driven by this madness, he completely loses the ability to evaluate events realistically and exists in a world that resembles hallucination more than a waking state. His reasoning functions are completely blocked. Despite the instincts for self-preservation that should have demanded that he flee along with the rest of wealthy Moscow—to which Pierre, as an aristocrat, belongs—he swims against the tide and stays put. A vague imperative, incomprehensible even to him, crystallizes into a bizarre decision: Pierre decides to stab Napoleon, the author of all his fatherland's woes. He does not believe fully in the justice of this decision. As we would explain it today, everything takes place in his subconscious. The true motivations for his decision are unknown to him, but a sense of solidarity with the fate of his people resides somewhere deep within him, and that, along with a yearning for sacrifice (not devoid of emotional tenderness toward his own presumed death), requires an external support in the conscious part of his self. So he creates just such a support, like a bee building a larger cell for the queen under the pressure of a mysterious instinct.

His intention to murder Napoleon is fantastic and unreal, but it affords him a reason to remain in Moscow, at least at first, because later on his decision dissolves imperceptibly: "Do what you must and be gone." Such is the first stage of the experience of war, the emotional background—the destruction of equilibrium between the conscious and unconscious parts of the human being, along with submission, more often than normally, to instincts that a perceptive person will be incapable of naming, and if he does name them, he does so in a way that coarsely falsifies them. These instincts need not be, as is evident from this example, the lowest, purely biological instincts; they can have a beautiful moral sheen to them, but they exceed the individual's ability to understand them. They belong to the sphere of great collective raptures that are often expressed in inadequate words or in deeds that are entirely useless as judged by common sense. Anyone who recalls the autumn of 1939 and the frenzied movements of human atoms, some of whom struck out for the east and others for the west—while for still others, remaining in the place from which other people were fleeing was a goal achieved by dint of the greatest sacrifices—will agree that some powerful forces must have been directing people, forces arising from the intersection of their personal habits and their inclinations, with a solidarity experienced one way or another, to be together: with one's family, one's native city, the army, one's party, one's own milieu. The solutions kept multiplying, and depending on which of them won out, individuals elected to go in this or that direction. Without a doubt, these atoms had some reasons of their own and communicated those reasons in words to other atoms similar to themselves. But for the most part, those were only their ostensible reasons, and justifying their actions by saying "It's better to act thus and so because . . . ," people placed after "because" a reason that was minuscule in comparison with the enormity of the elemental force that flowed through them.

Thus, perhaps the first response is more dependent than it is in peacetime on a hidden current that runs through the body of society, thanks to which even the most benighted man becomes an active participant in processes that greatly exceed his understanding. The intelligentsia is not of much use here: "excitement bordering on madness" is a condition of intellectual disarmament, born from a feeling of intellectual defenselessness in relation to an inner compulsion (to go, to act, to fulfill commands, to be in a crowd, etc.). Later, new elements emerge—awareness of human cruelty and one's personal destitution, destitution in the biblical sense, the death of loved ones, hunger, humiliation.

Pierre Bezukhov, captured by French soldiers, put on trial, and conducted to the place of executions, watches as his comrades, plucked at random from the Moscow crowd, are shot "as an example." All the details of the executions unfold before him with great clarity: the comatose gaze of the condemned who, to the very last moment, do not believe that it will happen; the nervousness and anxiety of the soldiers who are doing the shooting; the hasty burial of the still moving, shuddering bodies. "All these men clearly knew that they had committed a crime and that they must eradicate its traces as quickly as possible." Under the influence of this sight, a sudden break takes place in Pierre, not in his consciousness, but in those deepest strata that had been shaken by the war—a sudden departure from the circles in which we normally exist when we are living within traditions accumulated over the course of centuries. "From the moment Pierre saw that terrible slaughter committed by men who did not wish to do this, it was as if a spring had broken in his soul—a spring that allowed everything to cohere and to live, so that now everything collapsed and became a heap of meaningless rubbish. Though he did not acknowledge it to himself, his faith in the purposeful design of the world, in humanity, in his own soul, and in God, had suddenly died."

The second layer of the experience of war: we can call this the loss of faith in civilization. Living according to values accumulated by the labor of generations—values composed of the efforts of saints, thinkers, artists—man exists within certain frameworks; his thoughts and feelings develop according to a particular ritual. From the words of the prayer that his mother teaches him, through his readings and studies in school, to his experience of social life, he draws from the storehouse of humanistic hierarchies. Without being aware of it, he assimilates values; he understands his own existence and the existence of humanity as a struggle for ever more perfect goals. He senses that man is not only an animal, but something greater. His moral sense finds support in customs, in law, in religious commandments, in the current language of slogans and appeals to his fellow citizens. It is a critical moment for him when this fragile surface is sundered and he sees the depths of human nature. Everything collapses; everything seems artificial and ephemeral in comparison with these elementary facts: the cruelty of human beings that is identical in its results with the cruelty of nature; the ease with which in one second a sentient, thinking creature turns into a dead object; the treatment of individuals (each one of whom, he had believed, is a unique being) as toys to be destroyed, thrown from place to place, mutilated. At such a moment all possible perspectives for contemplating man disappear; there remains but one—the biological perspective. The rest appears to be an unessential superstructure.

This breaking point must be much clearer in this great war of the twentieth century. Whatever else they were, the Napoleonic Wars were a battle of powers within the framework of civilization; no side was proposing a program of toppling man from his pedestal and placing in doubt his centuries-old dignity. Where the individual experiencing that breaking point has to bear not only the sight of man turning into an animal but also the influence of a doctrine that justifies and glorifies naked bestiality, the possibilities of breakdown are much greater. Onto a soul bowed down by a sight like that which Pierre Bezukhov witnessed, words of propaganda based on the worship of absolute power and (despite the gains of Western culture until now) worship of "natural" man— shaped not by the Gospels, the sacraments, or the customs of benevolent coexistence in accordance with *jus gentium*— descend like a blow. These words can act powerfully and leave lasting traces in the unconscious (but important for behavior) sphere from which the instincts of thought and action are born.

What can be the results of this sudden loss of faith? Are they not expressed in a change of the collective spirit; do they not imprint themselves upon the behavior of society? Pierre Bezukhov falls into a stupor, a completely vegetative state, and that is one of the possible consequences—a kind of dreamlike condition, indifference to surrounding events, internal paralysis. This is actually the condition his persecutors aim to create; it suits them. Another possible response, in individuals who are more active and crafty, will be to stop at the point of internal revulsion and to make an outward display of completely cynical activity. These individuals derive justification for the most vile acts from the annihilation of values; since nothing enduring exists, since life is nothing but a meaningless swarming of vermin that devour one another, everything is permitted—in which case, let us help ourselves. In this respect they follow the path of those concealed or blatant criminals produced by every society; but in exceptional periods more of them are born than usual, since the internal brakes have failed.

Nevertheless, the types of consequences mentioned here do not appear to be sufficiently common for us to fear their pouring out as a great wave that will swallow peaceful forms of social existence. More dangerous are effects that comport with the strivings of human nature and therefore occur much more frequently. The innate yearning for moral harmony, the drive to establish some form of hierarchy simply in order to have one in place, can push people to get comfortable in the ruins of the ethical world, in the ruins of faith, and this getting comfortable is called the deformation of values. Doubting the heritage that preachers and prophets left them as they issued their summons to fight for God's kingdom on earth, people must discharge their fervor, their fondness for noble and sacrificial deeds, and feverishly seek something suitable to worship and adorn, just like architects who adopt ruins as a model, affirming them as the most beautiful creation of architecture, unaware that somewhere there are truly beautiful, undamaged monuments of art. National Socialism understood that need superbly; arising in an epoch when the experience of war had scorched the souls of millions of people, and exploiting the strong current of doubt in civilization that engulfed the Germans, they established a new divinity, their own tribe, in the place of the overthrown gods, lending it the traits of divinity and equipping it with all the virtues of truth, beauty, and goodness. To be sure, there is no truth, no beauty, no goodness—but there is German truth, German beauty, and German goodness; and thus the void was filled, and within the confines of the new canon there was room for heroism, dedication, friendship, and so forth.

How, then, does a representative of defeated Europe behave if it is his lot to recognize this spiritual defeat? Having lost his faith in the mission (a faith by which the nineteenth century lived, quite perversely, to be sure), his horizon blocked in all directions by a landscape of ruins, it may well be that he will fail to summon the energy necessary to emerge from that accursed circle and will acquiesce in running his home in a way that is appropriate for ruins and ashes. Then, nursing his hatred for the enemy and in search of something with which to oppose him, he follows in his enemy's footsteps and sets against him an opposite ideal, but on the same scale: he will set up his own tribe against the enemy tribe and worship it, recognizing its industriousness and strength as the highest criterion for action. Man, humankind—these concepts evoke in him only a reluctant reflex and become linked once and for all with bitter memories, such as the impotence of the League of Nations, or the pharisaism of democracy. Such an attitude, making one's fatherland into an altar on which the individual is immolated, permits him to unload all his reserves of nobility and heroism, the more so since, as long as the oppression lasts, this altar is simultaneously an altar of suffering mankind. Victory must bring a rupture, however, and will bring to light the question of the primacy of goals. If such an atmosphere became universal, the continent would soon be threatened by a new danger arising from the exaltation of one's own country, to which nations that have suffered greatly are inclined.

I have derived the above ruminations from our experience of war, but it would be an error to claim that it alone is the driving force of these changes, which have far more complex causes. Nevertheless, the experience of war contains the history of the last few decades in condensed form, as it were. It is enriched by accumulated material, it reshapes man more powerfully than other experience, and it touches even the least impressionable of men. Let us proceed. Does the loss of faith exhaust the entire extent of this phenomenon? No. Tolstoy makes his hero lose his faith and then rebuild it. Pierre Bezukhov descends into the vale of misery in the prisoner-of-war camp, and it is precisely there—among absolutely primitive conditions, ill-treatment, and death that sweeps away his fellow prisoners one after the other—that he experiences his great transformation, emerging reconciled to the world and internally free. This occurs through his encounter with man's fate in all its simplicity, with transience and pain. One might say that he is healed by the presence of the neighbor who shares his pallet, the simple peasant Platon Karataev—his even breathing during the night, his calm resignation, his complete acceptance of everything that the next day may bring, are for Pierre a new experience, difficult to name. Perhaps it is simply called love of one's neighbor. Pierre, walking barefoot over the soil of frozen Russian high roads, his feet bleeding, discovers that man is not only evil but also truly good; that the earth and life are good, and evil should not conceal from us the great and wise harmony of existence. Even weakness and human insignificance do not disturb this harmony; they enter like a necessary factor into an ultimate accounting. Tolstoy does not hesitate to describe Pierre's behavior during the execution of Karataev, who is too weak to keep up with the convoy. "Karataev looked at Pierre with his kindly eyes, clouded with tears; he was inviting him to approach, evidently wishing to tell him something. But Pierre couldn't trust himself. He pretended that he did not notice that look and walked away . . . Behind him, more or less from where Karataev had been sitting, a shot rang out. Pierre heard the shot distinctly, but at that moment he remembered that he had not yet finished counting up how many stages separated him from Smolensk . . . And he began to count."

Is the solution given by Tolstoy the only solution? Doubting in man, can one regain one's faith only by renouncing everything that well being, social distinctions, and the exploitation of material comforts bestows upon us? Can one accept civilization only when it is subjected to the fiery test of severity and simplicity, forcing men to bind up among them those knots that develop "in suffering, in the innocence of suffering"? Such a solution is very Russian, and it has recurred in Russia in various permutations for years. It is a paradox that Europe, defending itself from accepting this solution, was compelled by force to descend into the purgatory of primitivism and poverty. Europe's traditions, however, do not rest upon evangelical Christianity. "Elders" who have abandoned their families and property do not wander across Europe in order to "save them-selves" in the primeval forests beside the Ob' or Pechora rivers. Europe's monasteries were active, dynamic, engaged in eco-nomic, political, and educational enterprises. Perhaps that is why Europe is so reluctant to surrender, and why she prefers to treat her humiliation as a temporary phase without imagining (to herself) a future based on a harsh, stringent model. Many of her citizens are undoubtedly fated to experience what Pierre Bezukhov experienced. A touch of a hand, the word of a prison cellmate, will break down difference and enmity and will again raise man aloft, and "the world that collapsed in the soul will arise again, more beautiful than ever."

Tradition, which speaks with redoubled power during a period of convalescence, imposes its own formulas, its own lan-guage. The demonic elements of human nature were widely acknowledged in Western Christianity. From the moment the individual broke free of the Church's guardianship and trusted to his own powers, anything could be expected of him, and the most extreme bestiality was, in the eyes of a Catholic, the ex-pected consequence of innate corruption. That is why man, continuing the tradition of Western Christianity, is better pre-pared to emerge from the lack of faith to which baseness drives him. His crisis is less severe, the action of the antitoxin swifter and more effective. Despite the depths that are often revealed, he persists in having hope and constantly anticipates the brotherhood of men by dint of the very subjugation of those depths and his entanglement in the reins of biological drives.

The conclusions that flow from consideration of the experi-ence of war are quite disturbing. Believing firmly in the de-struction of the doctrine of a racial superman, one may ask if such a powerful load of evil can be buried and forgotten, as people sought to do after World War I, clinging to delusions of "prosperity." Everything depends on how man copes with doubt in his own conscience. If he becomes comfortable with it, if he accepts the struggle for "living space" as a natural condition, realistic politicians will appear on the scene who will see in the balance of powers and the mutual checkmating of states the sole foundation of international relations, which, as we know, no longer leads to "little wars" between two states, but must end with a party for the entire globe. If man overcomes doubt and reverts to the old path of daydreams about one state of united humanity, it is still unclear what formula he will adopt. Will he, acknowledging that civilization in its present form is fundamentally evil, wish to destroy it, to turn over its soil and build a new one, educating the masses in the brotherhood of poverty and the loss of individuality? Or will he, adhering consciously or unconsciously to the tradition of Western Christianity, wish to renew civilization, to enrich and improve it, changing its obsolete institutions and subjecting them to new demands? We do not know.

In addition, there still are the eternal conflicts of interest and egoisms of nations. Their significance varies, however, in relation to the spirit of the age and the names that each generation learns to attach to them. They are like certain illnesses: as soon as a sick man knows that he is suffering from a particular ailment, his symptoms will manifest themselves a lot more painfully. Egoisms are difficult to eradicate, but a great deal depends on what remedies are recognized as acceptable. Even the difference in degree between the application of a protective tariff and the extermination of a nation that stands in the way of the march to power means a great deal.

I said that I know little about my own and others' experience of war and that I was only pondering Tolstoy's understanding of it. I have tried to deduce its inner structure from several features and to extract those allusions that the Russian novelist seems to have enclosed in his simple sentences. Perhaps the experiences of people during war in the twentieth century are more varied and profound; perhaps they develop according to different laws. And perhaps applying Tolstoy to them is as inappropriate as, for example, applying descriptions from pacifist novels about the war of 1914–18. For the time being, however, we do not have a great deal to choose from.

Zdziechowski's Religiosity

During the two decades of the interwar period, in the low-ceilinged auditoriums of a university in Wilno, Marian Zdziechowski, a little old man with an ascetic face, delivered his lectures. He held the position of rector, and his name was surrounded by a halo of righteousness and wisdom, but for the majority of young people engaged in heated arguments between the extreme right and the left, he was only a respectable relic of the past. In our opinion (mine and that of my peers, who were engaged in discovering our own Americas during the years 1930–34) the old man had no idea about the so-called problems of the day, and his warnings about the danger threatening the world from the sides of communism and nationalism were tinged with a pitifully maniacal coloration. His eschatological vision of the impending arrival of something inescapable and horrific coincided with the vague feelings of his listeners and readers and agreed with the atmosphere of the time. But only his vision. His entire way of understanding, his conclusions, his warnings—all passed right by the aspirations of the young, who saw salvation precisely in those currents perceived by their professor as the work of Satan. What for him was night, they perceived as "the radiant face of the dawning day." Only later, after the passage of years, did many of them, by way of bitter experiences, return to certain truths proclaimed by Zdziechowski and acknowledge that these same foundations might be useful for something, even though the "historical sky" had changed.

This example illustrates quite nicely the mutual relationship of two separate generations. We were taught that there exists a constant law under which "children" must always rebel against "fathers" and treat their ideas and work contemptuously, and only when they themselves become "fathers" and are repaid by their heirs with the same measure of alienation and incomprehension would they give the past its due. Such a law is probably a fantasy that, like many other fantasies, derives from accepting as an unchanging principle of human nature phenomena that are common for one or two centuries. There is no such law; there is, instead, a mutual enmity of the generations, but it exists only in a few periods, and there is no reason to assume that it has to exist always and everywhere. What is the source of that enmity? The average person imagined, until recently, that what was truth for his grandfather could no longer be truth for him, that he was wiser than his grandfather—wiser not thanks to his own efforts, but his personal partaking of the changes in civilization. Grandfather did not fly in an airplane, he did not read Lenin, he did not watch films; therefore Grandfather, even in his best and most creative moments, had to be less clever, "did not take account of the achievements of science," and therefore his works, if he left any, might add to the number of volumes in the library, but nothing more. In truth, this is a very important matter; it touches on the continuity of tradition and the weight of authority. Generations that are vying with time are convinced that the Ten Commandments change every few years; they identify progress in means and form with progress in truth, and they expose themselves to the risk that no longer every few years but every single year and even every couple of months a new solution to the puzzles of the world will be found. So "schools" and "trends" multiply, and recording their short-lived history demands at the very least the same effort as recording the history of ancient kingdoms. Man is no longer valued, then, on the basis of the aspirations and works of his entire life, but according to how he has acted most recently, or the last thing he said in print, because the continuity of his development is divided into small segments, each of which is evaluated not in proportion to the whole, but in proportion to the surrounding intellectual fashions. Can one imagine a different order, in which the enmity of generations would yield to deliberate continuity? It is possible, but it can happen only if and when the myth of automatic evolution dies out. Progress would then be the fulfillment of one human truth in continually new conditions and shapes. It would not be the pursuit of constantly changing revelation. Evolutionary thinking, however, is so ingrained in the thinking of the masses that it will outlast even the collapse of faith in "progress" and will slowly disappear only if the generations join together in accepting some universally binding principles.

The example of Zdziechowski inclines one to thoughts of this sort, but they would have to form a separate chapter. Here I would only like to give Zdziechowski his due, to settle the debt that the "children"—let us be frank, the "terrible children"—owe him.

Against the background of the interwar decades, his figure is distinguished by a rare characteristic—a complete lack of flirtatiousness in his relations with the younger generation. In writers who wish to catch up and not lose their significance, flirtatiousness often becomes their main working rule. One can distinguish several degrees of authorial flirtatiousness. The most blatant consists of submitting to collective opinions, catering to the *mentalité* of the elite or the crowd. This means adapting the coloration of one's thoughts to one's surroundings. After 1918, our optimistic faith in a lasting peace under the wings of the League of Nations, in the splendor of the slogan of self-determination, in social reforms, in Pan-Europe, in technocracy, in democracy, was just such a general coloration. In those days, when young writers of the Skamander school were echoing the cry of triumphant vitalism, Zdziechowski openly condemned self-determination as one source of the unbridled egoism of small ethnic groups. In 1922 he was capable of writing, "We are a small part of Europe, we are linked with her fate, we are infected with the same diseases of communism and nationalism as she is, and together with her, biting at each other in a mad rage, we are rushing headlong into the abyss."[1] This means that he did not succumb to what was then the first and most dubious point of the catechism of the "right-thinking citizen," that he did not have to wait for the despair that engulfed Europe in the 1940s; it was present in him many years earlier.

Another variety of flirtatiousness is the flirtatiousness of vocabulary, images, and definitions. It was common to say about many older writers that they possessed the secret of eternal youth. How often, though, is this not true youth (which is manifested by a capacity for internal changes, by fervor), how often is this only a skillful grasp of current language and current themes? Clever old men know their own minds, but they write about the nonsense that interests their milieu. They pretend to be naive, because they understand that certain words and definitions are taboo for contemporary people and might bring down upon their heads the phrase that is deadly for fame: "He's finished." It is not good to be too serious, to gaze from too great a distance at momentary tastes and fashions. Someone for whom the new novel he has just read or Piłsudski's trip to Geneva are events heralding a new era in the history of literature or politics will respond reluctantly to people who are too thoughtful, who casually dismiss these temporary phenomena, people who are intent on observing the current of history. The third variety of flirtatiousness, which is a characteristic of the technocrats, ought to deserve our praise. Since prophets are never viewed kindly, especially in their own country, they therefore often don the garments of ordinary people and speak in a style that is least offensive to the reader, which does not hinder them from believing firmly in things that are usually well concealed beneath a volley of ironic or scientific sentences. Zdziechowski, however, did not possess any of these varieties of flirtatiousness, and that may explain his lack of popularity. He spoke like Cassandra, and his every sorrowful prophecy is "pitifully maniacal." The well-fed citizen who enjoys the pleasures of this world turns away with disgust from the voice of Cassandra. Thus, Zdziechowski was a voice calling in the wilderness, striving in vain in his speeches as rector to guide the souls of youth.

Wisdom often earns the epithet "divine." People say "a divine sage." I think that the most divine characteristic is incommensurability with the flow of time experienced physically and emotionally by millions of human beings. I picture Zdziechowski as he walks the streets of Wilno, divining from the clouds—baroque as always in that city—the tragedy of crazed and doomed mankind, and right beside him a band at a student dance is still playing the tango "Like a Panther in a Gilded Cage," and young human beings experience their first initiation into worries, fears, touches, odors, the dramas of the heart. I do not know what remains of the lilac gowns, the secretly exchanged kisses, the meeting of trembling hands. Perhaps, in some ultimate reckoning, it is no less than what remains of the most powerful efforts of an industrious mind. But those kisses, that whirling to the music's beat, the rosiness of dawn on the windowpanes, and the emotional dramas—

they no longer exist. There is no way to recover their traces; they are ephemeral, like the human beings who experienced them; and this fact settles the argument, and not in their favor—but a thinker moves onward, beyond the bounds of death.

Two phenomena are interwoven in Zdziechowski: religious pessimism and historiosophical catastrophism. I would like to take up the first of these for a moment.

To define someone as a Catholic writer is not to define him at all, because Catholicism, while preserving the identity of dogmas, is constantly acquiring new forms, is continually realized anew, and by the very necessity of struggle in a changing historical environment, it profits from new ways of understanding the world. Not only every century has a different Catholicism. Among Catholics who are close to one another in time, there exist immense differences in religious style, depending on which element acts on them more powerfully and what in particular they emphasize. Chesterton was a Catholic by virtue of his enchantment with the mysterious complexity of life, its mythical character; Zdziechowski, by virtue of his sensing the enormity and menace of evil. This is sufficient to show how baseless are questions about whether Catholicism is pessimistic or optimistic, if such extreme and contradictory positions are encompassed by it. Pessimism and optimism are inseparably intertwined in it; each of its pessimistic statements about man is accompanied by an optimistic correction, and vice versa. Nevertheless, there are individuals who find that such correctives allow them to intensify more effectively the truth contained in their assertions, because it unties their hands, designating the limits to which they can go as the blackest of pessimists or the rosiest of optimists. Obviously, this opposition is only one of the many possible oppositions in religious style that I have mentioned, and reflecting on Zdziechowski's pessimism, one must try to discern its nuances, its internal structure.

In the history of Catholicism, the date 1885 is very important. That year, approximately, is the pinnacle of the development of positivism in France and the beginning of a turn away from positivist positions. Until that time, "even among the faithful themselves, in the bosom of orthodox Catholicism, the conviction that religion cannot be reconciled with modern ideas, that one must choose between it and science, was deeply ingrained."[2] Only around that date does the Church's separation from the state of science begin to sway and weaken. Following Parodi, we can enumerate the chief manifestations of this turning point that sparked the great changes in mentality, changes that we live by to the present day. The religious movement began from purely aesthetic sympathies for religious sensibility, from the equal treatment of all feelings (even religious feelings), assisted by the refinement of artistic forms.[3] Under the slogan "to feel everything is to understand everything," people began valuing the naïveté of faith, longing for the primitive, and having sentimental feelings for the enchantment of religious rituals. Numerous conversions took place among poets, painters, musicians. Negation came to seem too coarse and too limited in its approach to the complexity of culture. At the same time, the bourgeoisie and the clergy saw in religion the best antidote to socialism, anarchism, and the specter of revolution; therefore, through the lips of their writers, they exhorted people, if not to a sincere and true faith, at least to preserving a religious gesture, to following the forms. But a gesture changes the actor playing a role; thus, "people moved, like Brunetière, from gesture to sentiment, and from sentiment to belief."[4] Science itself was helpful here, especially in its two youngest and famously developing disciplines—psychology and sociology. In psychology, religious experiences were encountered as facts that could not be denied. William James exerted a powerful influence by defining the normal nature of religious experiences (according to him, normality is recognized by practical efficacy, by the fruitfulness of efforts), which the religious element in man fulfills perfectly, creating harmony that is unattainable in its absence. Durkheim recognized religion as a sociological fact and admitted its great significance in the development of societies. Philosophy, meanwhile, contributed to the disappearance of beliefs about the world as a mechanism. Subjecting our scientific thinking to analysis, it discovered a certain distancing of our scientific hypotheses from the world of phenomena, which Bergson would later push to an extreme. This was not all. Renouvier, studying logical judgments, distinguished in each judgment an act of concentration, hence of choice, and an effort of the will. Since not everything can be found out, the first and most general principles are recognized because we want them that way. Even the trust that we have in reason assumes a voluntary accession, a postulating of its appropriateness as an instrument. "Since then, in addition to knowledge and even at the roots of knowledge, a place was found for faith."[5] That is also the source of the natural striving for support in intuition, for listening to "the voices of the heart."

This great debate in defense of irrationality took place during the years of Zdziechowski's youth and could not have passed him by. But as one reads his writings attentively, one is inclined to presume that it was the following, later wave—that the true foundation of his religiosity was the positivist division between faith and reason, the style of thinking before the turning point of 1885. Zdziechowski did not underestimate reason; he did not explore its suspicious labyrinths. Feeling and faith on the one hand, and intellect on the other, were for him two separate and conflicting wholes. The opposition was the more apparent because, for a Catholic of that period, the Scholastic slogan that God is recognized through intellect gave no support at all; on the contrary, that was precisely the source of his irritation. Reason in the nineteenth century was something quite different from the Scholastics' reason, so that considering these two entirely different concepts as identical had to result in an insoluble puzzle. This is what Zdziechowski admits to:

> As I grew older, and the more I knew of life and the world, the more clearly and painfully did I become aware that the world, when one understands it through thought, as a unity, is an absence of harmony and an absence of reason—not, as we are taught, a work of reason; it did not proceed from the hand of God. 'There is no God,' Nature and History cry out in a great voice . . . but that voice is lost in the harmony of psalms and hymns, in that great, eternal confession emerging from the most profound depths of the soul, that like 'the earth without water' is the soul of man without God. God exists. Only the fact of God's existence—this is something that exceeds the bounds of thought preoccupied with the external word; this is a miracle. *Le monde est irrationnel . . . Dieu est un miracle.*[6]

And elsewhere: "Thoughts about the problem of religion have always guided me, and today they still affirm me in my conclusion that faith is violence done to reason; what takes place on earth testifies too loudly, cries out against God."[7]

Now let us permit ourselves a comparison. Let us reach for a book by Zdziechowski's contemporary, the well-known atheist Professor Baudouin de Courtenay.[8] His public confession is a shocking document. An intense, frank personality that knows no compromise is revealed in it. "I see only evil in the world," he writes; "so much injustice, so many cruelties, that I cannot burden not only a just, but also a kindly and merciful Father with the responsibility for this. Blaming the sins committed by the human beast on the creator and on providence is very convenient, indeed, but it is also senseless and immoral."[9] "The worthless human brute ascribes his criminal and sadistic impulses to a God created in his own image and likeness, calling that God of his not only just, but also merciful. A man who permitted himself such acts would be considered a criminal, but God is honored precisely because he is the God of vengeance."[10]

Is not the tone of Zdziechowski's confession similar to that of de Courtenay? It is similar because its background is the same conviction about the irrationality of faith and, even more, the impossibility of reconciling faith with an ethical sense. "After all, God is love, so whence come suffering and evil?" Zdziechowski asks. "This is explained to us as the sin of our forebears. But is not such an answer a slap in the face of our moral thought?"[11]

Where de Courtenay saw endless night, however, Zdziechowski perceived a glimmer of hope. God is a miracle, and the existence of this miracle is testified to not by a merciless and blind Nature, nor by history, but by the inner voice, the demands of the heart. And here we arrive at the kinship between Zdziechowski and Modernism. He felt this kinship powerfully himself and often defended the Modernists against excessively severe, uncompromising condemnation. Modernism, after all, was what followed that turning point; it was the first and too garish flowering of that turning point, and therefore it could not be alien for a philosopher who was painfully experiencing the nineteenth century's splitting in two. Perhaps not in those fragments of the Modernists' doctrines where they strove to soften revelation, to make it less threatening, lighter, more accessible for a man of that time, where they thereby drew close to Protestantism, but certainly where they proclaimed the irrationality of achieving knowledge, Zdziechowski was at one with them. And he was with them when they strove to replace a superterrestrial God with an immanent God. He appeared to agree with Tyrrell that "the idea of a God who dwells in the heart of man, let us rather say in the hearts of saints, continually eradicates the superterrestrial God installed on a heavenly throne: that is the source of the inclination to broaden and reimagine the idea of the Church; the Church is neither this nor that community, but the entire human race which is directed by the Divine spirit."[12] And what pointed words he used when he spoke of rationalistic Christianity: "In and of itself our temporal world is a lack of harmony, a lack of meaning, it is irrational; we have to close our eyes in order not to see or hear this. At the same time, sages and poets in Christendom as in Greece, by closing their eyes and blocking their ears, all of them, with very few exceptions, were preoccupied with one thing only: convincing themselves and others that everything that is, is rational."[13]

In 1909, Albert Leclère's book *Pragmatisme, modernisme, protestantisme*, containing an uncompromising critique of Modernism, was published in Paris. The author condemns those Catholic thinkers who, under the influence of James, forget that faith is an act of reason and, protecting themselves from the temptations of positivism, fall into the mysticism of the religion of the heart. "After all, those thinkers are sentimental when they propose as the deepest foundation for religion that which is darkest in the soul, least known, existing somewhere deep down, under a layer of consciousness; they are sentimental when they elevate in religion the element of personal experience."[14] Today we recognize the correctness of such a severe critique, for we have recently seen the ramifica-

tions of irrationalism. But for Zdziechowski, as for many en-
lightened Catholics at that time, the matter did not seem quite
so straightforward. Zdziechowski does not agree with Leclère,
and if he did not go beyond the Church's teaching, he at least
praised the services of the Modernists in deepening religious
life, and he made the leading Modernists, Loisy and Tyrrell,
appear much more attractive.

This entire set of issues, however, is developed in Zdziechowski's writing as an attempt at fitting an uncompromising,
despairing pessimism (which he himself ascribes to the philosophy of the East and indirectly to Schopenhauer) into the
framework of Catholic faith. Not only the sight of cruel and
indifferent Nature evokes in him revulsion and a feeling of the
impermanence, the vanity of all things. Whoever looks into
himself must notice there elements that link him to Nature;
must admit that as a biological being, he is nothing but a chaos
of drives and desires, and that located within the order of Nature, he commits the most base acts all the time, prettifying
them before himself. The East, and Schopenhauer following
the East, recommends purification by annihilating in oneself
the will to live. Zdziechowski did not go that far, but the voice
of yearning for a Divinity, which he heard in himself, was for
him the voice of hope against hope, a yearning for a miracle. If
we move a step beyond this, we may ask how Catholics who
opposed the Modernists did this, and what entitles us to trust
that voice. If "the world lies in evil" and we ourselves are
flawed to our very depths, lying ceaselessly, do we have the
right to believe that the voices we hear inside ourselves, along
with our entire inner experience, are not also stamped with
falsehood? Is it not too risky a proposition to rescue religion by
reference to feelings emerging from the darkness that is every
human soul? Is not a harmony imposed by reason more worthy
of recommendation than echoes of the subconscious? Zdzie-

chowski did not take that step. Had he done so, he could not have defended the irrationalist position, because he would have had to admit that the errant, unstable intellect is the lesser of two evils, that it leads us astray less often than a constant—but lying—heart. Perhaps such a step would have been for him a step into an utter, absolute abyss. Or perhaps there was one more factor here: the influence of Russian religiosity.

I think that in Polish culture, people who have experienced the East in themselves best understand the danger of the East—people for whom the words "the Russian soul" are not only an empty sound but a laughable simplification. To gain an intuition of "Russianness," one must pay a price; one must, at least in part, succumb to its temptations. Zdziechowski had that intuition to a great degree, and therefore we may assume that he often yielded to the seductiveness of Eastern Christianity's thought, as his books confirm. It is not for nothing that he was formed in Russia, not for nothing that he frankly idolized the Russian philosopher-mystics, Trubetskoi and Solovyov. Perhaps it is not even a question of their influences, but of that confluence of thoughts that arises on the grounds of internal kinship. The split between the evil world and a good God never reached a more extreme position than in Eastern Christianity. As Bogumił Jasinowski demonstrated, the spirit of gnosis is still alive in the religious thought of Russians to this day, and one can find it not only in prerevolutionary sectarianism, but also in Berdyayev and Solovyov.[15] The abyss between God and the world, "which did not issue from the hand of God," dates back to the teachings about the hierarchical construction of the Divinity proclaimed by the Gnostics. The world is evil because it is the work of a lower demiurge. According to Solovyov, it arose when the Soul of the World fell away from God's goodness and wisdom, so that the Soul of the World would be a lower element of the Divinity, yearning to merge with oneness. Although "we can, we have the right, we even ought to believe that from the position of the universal, pre-eternal order, from an idea that is inaccessible to us but leads him higher, everything that acts upon this atom has a deeper meaning,"[16] we will never be capable of discerning that meaning; God is absolutely incommensurable with the world, and even reason illuminated by grace is incapable of approaching understanding of God's attributes. At the same time, suffering acquires cosmic dimensions; it ceases to be only a human means of experiencing the world—human, because only man is able to assign values and to suffer because of the suffering he sees around him. The act of accusation directed against being in general embraces equally the suffering of the ant crushed by someone's heel and human suffering, both the agony of mi-crobes and social injustice. This must give birth to despair, for we are unable to make a single movement, perform a single action, without causing pain to other beings; perfect altruism would be, perhaps, suicide, although who knows what the cells of our organism would say about that? Naturally, Zdziechowski did not argue for suicide or a return to nirvana. Nor did the Russian theologians argue for this. But for them, as, for exam-ple, for Solovyov, Christ was a cosmic principle—the redeemer not just of mankind, but of all creation, of flies and ants, too. Zdziechowski wanted to add the influences of pessimistic phi-losophy to Catholicism, and he defended its positive results in an audience with Pope Pius X, arguing that thanks to this philosophy, "we learn to feel more actively the essence of the Christian view of the world, which we express in our daily prayer in which we refer to the earth as a vale of tears."[17]

In the great debate that developed around Modernism, the Church, in the encyclical "Pascendi," condemned those among the faithful who were attempting to construct a Catholic phi-losophy on a heritage derived from Kant. It firmly proclaimed that Kantian and post-Kantian immanentism, subjectivism, and agnosticism cannot be reconciled with doctrine. It recom-

mended Scholastic philosophy as the sole foundation for Catholic metaphysicians. By doing so, it drew a clear boundary
around the growing efforts to reconcile faith with philosophy.
But until that moment, the field of observations had been
open, both for those who drew from the new achievements of
the theory of knowledge arguments against the Scholastics,
and for those who, like Zdziechowski, were approaching Kant
through Schopenhauer and Eastern philosophy.

   In comparison with the intellectual structure of the years
1918–39, Zdziechowski is decidedly anachronistic. Most anachronistic is his meditation on "the pain of existence," expressed
in sentences that mean nothing for the younger generations, so vague are they and so alien to all caution in attacking
the ultimate, greatest matters.[18] We are separated from him
by the same things that separate us from Jan Kasprowicz's
Hymns, Wacław Berent's *Dry Rot*, or the works of Tadeusz
Miciński—something that does not lend itself to brief definition. Although more readable than these authors of Young
Poland, Zdziechowski has the same insatiable hunger as they,
and he seems to hold the same conviction that there are always
experiences that conform to the words we use, or at least that
"problems" lead a separate life. The poetry of Young Poland
is so bad because a poet saying "Spirit" or "God" felt he was
using expressions as concrete as "table" or "willow," and when
saying "table" or "willow," he assumed they were just as concrete as "red table" or "blossoming willow." Transferring these
stylistic features into the sphere of thought, one can explain to
oneself why several generations responded with great seriousness to such concepts as the Absolute, the Will to Live, the
Naked Soul. Similarly, Zdziechowski never tested the material-
ity of the terms he used; he sailed over the sea of "great concepts," collected and evaluated the thoughts of philosophers as
if they were creations independent of place and time. When

he stood before an audience of youth after World War I, this was precisely the chief reason for their clash of views. Those young people valued an entirely different species of concepts, which in their opinion were much more alive and subject to proof. They were preparing themselves for nationalism and communism, since nationalism derived its slogans from the so-called immutable laws of biological struggle, and communism reduced the entire question of truth to changes in the economic base. Zdziechowski did not go beyond the dialectics of ideas themselves, and he did not gather these ideas into new generalizations, recognized by the young as something very important and actual. Had he done that, he might have achieved at little cost the popularity of Berdyayev, for example. He treated changes in history as deviations from a definite pattern. He attempted to discover that pattern by relying on his Christian conscience, and not only did he disagree with the opinion that such a pattern does not exist at all, but he also did not want to recognize that the same pattern could be observed in constantly changing shapes under a covering of conspicuously different lifestyles.

The neo-Thomist Catholicism professed in the interwar period by certain literary-political circles went hand in hand with a universally felt revulsion against murky meditations about the essence of existence, with a turn away from metaphysics. It responded to the need to grasp earthliness. Even the religious question stemmed from questions touching upon the organization of earthly life, the relation of the individual to the collective, and so forth. Particularly in Poland, where religiosity rarely emerges from inner life and often stems from political yearnings, this process achieved great intensity. The majority of Catholics who promoted Saint Thomas grounded their Catholicism with the help of sociopolitical inferences, with the help of a vision of a new Middle Ages that could be incarnated only by relying on a Catholic worldview. What followed was a total inversion of the entire problem of religion; outcomes were supposed to justify and create an internal faith which no one was courageous enough to cultivate. It is not at all surprising that those Catholics linked Saint Thomas with ideas taken from fascism, because at bottom, without realizing it, they accepted Catholicism as one more fiction, useful for the goals of the political structure. Thus the specter of freedom and practicality in the acceptance of truth, which had already visited the Modernists, returned from a different direction and in a much more vulgar form. One cannot make that complaint against the French Thomists. Yet even in their writings there was very little of the metaphysical current that, whatever one might say, constitutes the true life of religion. The closed form of sentences borrowed from the *Summa theologica* entered like a substitute article, saved the Thomists from floundering into open engagement with mystery. The infinite number of subtle distinctions rose up like a useful wall between man and naked (if I may call it that) existence.

The skillful Scholastics played off their contemporaries' affection for precise terminology and turned their attention, first of all, to that requirement. In addition, they were in excellent control of knowledge about historical impermanence; they adopted historicism, using it for their own purposes. In this variant, Catholicism, drained and intellectualized, preoccupied with the human world and not with the world in general, was ripe for the taking by minds that were far removed from concerns about the Soul of the World, the Absolute, Ormuzd and Ahriman.

But wasn't the price that had to be paid for the turn away from the spirit of Modernism way too high? What drove people toward it—that hunger, that anxiety—is worth something, if religion in general is worth something. If someone disagrees with Zdziechowski that only the internal voice, despite everything we know about the world, opens the gates of heaven, it does not mean that that inner voice can be replaced with syllogisms demonstrating the necessity of the existence of God. Be that as it may, the Modernists and their sympathizers, like Zdziechowski, were the last religious thinkers—not Catholic philosophers (because there were many of those who came after them), but truly thinkers who probed the meaning of religion. Standing beneath a starry sky or experiencing empathy for the sufferings of a fly is a phenomenon that lies at the birth of faith and rituals, whereas Saint Thomas's judgments are only one of the ways to codify metaphysical dread. When one turns to Zdziechowski through so many biases and layers piled up by time, one must notice one thing: intensification of mystical terror is rarely met with. Naturally, one may ask immediately, What is this, and might it not stem accidentally from the conditions of the era in which Zdziechowski lived, from its concepts and the language used in it? I dare insist, however, that this is not the case, and that if one were to discard all the accretions of historical style, what would remain is a despairing man, alone in the presence of a God who rises above a world "which did not issue from" his hand. And not just man as a document of his epoch, but rather as a document of certain eternal matters that are eclipsed today by the restraint and inhibition of our means of expression.

I have compared two formations of Catholicism: the Modernist one, in which there was space for the doubts that beset Zdziechowski, and the neo-Thomist, which eliminates similar anxieties by observing precise terminology and is more interested in man than in being in general. It is possible to discover in this a lack of consequential reasoning: if I ascribe Zdziechowski's particular religiosity to his tendency to use vague and inflated words, and to the *bogoiskatel'stvo*—the Russian

God-seeking of the past—then why do I say that this type of religiosity is something eternal, noble, higher even than the worries of Thomists satisfied with their intelligence?

Certain constant elements of human nature are one thing, and the means of their expression, imposed by an epoch, are another. Historical time introduces and changes many elements; but not everything, I believe, is time's creation. For example, "seeking the absolute" is a description of an old need, constantly renewed by people, but it is a description within the framework of a particular style. If one should reject that style and consider it one of those matters that have already been surpassed, this does not necessarily lead to rejecting the need itself, which has assumed and can still assume the most various forms, yielding to transformations, thanks to that modality, but not to the extent of ceasing to be a need. One may cast doubt on Zdziechowski's assertion that the inner voice speaks to us unquestionably about the existence of God, especially since that same inner voice is at the root of religions without a Divinity, such as Buddhism, and of religious atheism, such as that of Professor Baudouin de Courtenay. After all, the metaphysical yearning that speaks so forcefully from Zdziechowski's books is something real and enduring, not just the pure modality of history. All the difficulty rests in the fact that by naming this yearning, we give it a name borrowed from the language of a given era, from the philosophical concepts peculiar to a given period. What Zdziechowski spoke of as the ideal part of the human soul, yearning for God, bore the name "The Metaphysical Sense of the Wonder of Being" in Stanisław Ignacy Witkiewicz, who belonged to the following generation, and it found its expression not in religion, but in art and ontological investigations.

I mentioned the possibility of the generations moving closer to each other on the ground of mutually accepted principles. That is why I am trying to reach beyond what was temporary in Zdziechowski, what was the accretion of German idealism, of the Romantics, or of Russian mystics. Zdziechowski is the nakedness of religious feeling (as we call it), and also an uncompromising ethical stance, in which evil cannot be justified even if we summon the loftiest slogans to our aid. It is an eye on the absolute boundary that divides good from evil, something very rare in a time of advanced relativism.

Perhaps Catholics of the newer formation also considered the existence of evil, or, reading the first volume of the *Summa*, they considered whether "God is the same as His essence, or nature." Maybe so. It happens, however, that part of a doctrine is taken to be the necessary completion of the whole, even though sensitivity to what that part represents has vanished. A suspicion arises that something similar happened with the metaphysical part of Catholic doctrine and that while Catholicism was expending most of its forces on turning to systems harnessed by worldliness, the faithful lost their desire to venture into territories that always carry the threat of heresy. The last to do so were the generation of the Modernists. Jacques Maritain may be a splendid philosopher, but his efforts at bringing Saint Thomas closer to us have yielded good results only in the realm of aesthetics, ethics, and social affairs, but not where even the best intellectual apparatus must toil in vain if, as in contemporary man, there is a lack of real experiences that stir the imagination.

In Poland during the course of the interwar decades, not a single religious book written by an orthodox Catholic was published, it seems. Obviously I use "religious" in the sense that we mean when we speak of Pascal or Cardinal Newman. In order to find a living "metaphysical current," we must turn to authors who stand either outside the circle of Catholicism or, in general, outside the circle of any religion. Zdziechowski, who arrived in the interwar period with his faith lived according to his own accounts, belongs among the exceptions, and remains as an example of the inner acuity possessed by passionate atheists or despairing believers.

1943

The Boundaries of Art

(Stanisław Ignacy Witkiewicz from the

Perspective of Wartime Changes)

I

Stanisław Ignacy Witkiewicz predicted that "ethics will devour metaphysics" and that future humanity will be happy but will not know three things: philosophy, art, and religion, which are already living through their period of decline today. It is not my intention to seek to clarify the sources of such a conviction in Witkiewicz; that is, I am not going to cite authors who might have influenced him or concern myself with the sources of Pan-European catastrophism. It will have to suffice for us that there was in Poland a gentleman on a grand scale who, despite his many eccentricities and artistic failures, stood immeasurably higher than the majority of his contemporaries. Arguments and polemics in Poland during the interwar decades seem quite shallow in comparison with what concerned Witkiewicz. Furthermore, the atmosphere of the interwar period was described much more successfully in his two fantastic novels than in many a supposedly realistic book by esteemed novelists.

In order to understand this, it was necessary to live through the year 1939; the endings of Witkiewicz's novels *Farewell to Autumn* and *Insatiability* are, after all, exactly the same as the end of Piłsudski's Poland. The subject of these novels can be summarized in a few words: the disintegration of a certain civilization in which the majority of people not only do not realize that it is happening but even succumb to the pleasant illusion that this disintegration is proof of health and strength. Only a few individuals feel that these are the last days, but that is precisely because they are degenerate persons who are still dragging along in that phase of civilization, and who, at the most, are still permitted to exist. In the next phase, if they should live to see it, only madness awaits them, or what Witkiewicz himself chose—a large dose of Veronal and slitting his own veins. I shall have more to say about this later. For the moment, there is still praise for the language Witkiewicz used; it is an absolutely polite masculine language, straightforward despite external appearances—minus all ornamentation, metaphors meant to be charming, cadences of phrasing, and similar devices.

This language possesses great flaws, but it does not possess the one greatest flaw that has recently become widespread: the *préciosité* and suspect melodiousness that so stubbornly characterizes Polish prose, which is difficult to break free of when writing in Polish. Witkiewicz attempted to load language to the maximum with meaning, and if several fragments of his novels give the impression of verbosity, it is not because he was intoxicated with the music of style, but simply because the meaning he wished to express often loses its gravity for a later reader. These characteristics of his language appear in his novels and essays and in other forms of expository prose—that is, in writings that he did not recognize as artistic creation. I shall not attempt to speak about his numerous plays or his painting.

The most irritating of his flaws is his tendency to hyperbolize certain psychological processes, a tendency evidenced in the overuse of powerful epithets. This suggests that he emerged from the school of Young Poland and was far removed from moderation. The "monstrification" of his novels makes it difficult to consider them as literature that has a chance of lasting, other than as documentation, as content, as intellectual load. It is this load that we must concern ourselves with now, constructing, with the aim of being informative, something like a condensed version of the writer's views.

One should not believe, Witkiewicz asserts, that such phenomena as philosophy, religion, and art are eternal. They appear at a certain stage of development, after which they may well disappear. Subordination to the collective, which is constantly at work, leads us to that conclusion.

Imminent wars, slaughters, and revolutions do not engender primitive anarchy as their final outcome. On the contrary, their result will be the victory of social justice and the transfer of power into the hands of the working masses of the world. The process of democratization is irreversible, and there is no chance that we could return to a condition in which a few splendid individuals develop at the expense of the abasement of millions.

The individuality of the average citizen first found its voice in Greece, where everyone was guaranteed great freedom of thought. When, however, individual thought born in Greece achieved great results, these results were assimilated by society, which, in its own interest, began to suppress individuality. The necessity to simplify the demands of technology—and the satisfaction, with its assistance, of the ethical postulates derived from Christianity—must inevitably lead to complete automatization; that is, citizens will be granted no freedom of inquiry, and the freedom to choose one way of life or another will be very limited. Obviously, the most essential feature of automatization is the absolute happiness of the citizens, who believe that the slogans of propaganda are their own thoughts, and who are completely satisfied with their place in the social machine.

Witkiewicz considered himself to be a philosopher above all, a philosopher from an already vanishing breed, because he

was concerned with the essence of being, and considered ontological investigation as the sole inquiry worthy of philosophy.
One of the fundamental concepts in his system was the concept of Individual Actual Identity. He derived that name from
the feeling of being identical with oneself that each particular
human being has—and not human beings alone, but theoretically each Individual Being. This feeling is hard to describe;
it is given to us through experience, and we must think of certain moments we have experienced in the dawn hours, immediately after waking, such as the reader may have known. It is
a sort of astonishment that one is oneself, that at one time one
did not exist and that one is heading toward death, and yet one
is—and one constitutes an inconceivable unique being within
the multiplicity of one's situations and the surrounding world.
One of the English "metaphysical poets" (Thomas Traherne),
writing a song of a newborn child, places words of astonishment in his mouth about possessing hands, feet, eyes, and a
mouth: "But that they mine should be, who nothing was, /
That strangest is of all, yet brought to pass." It is precisely that
astonishment that Witkiewicz was thinking of.

Questions: "Why am I precisely this, and no other, being?
In this place in infinite space and this moment in infinite
time? In this group of beings, on this particular planet? Why,
in general, do I exist, since I could have not existed at all? Why,
in general, does this or that exist?" and so forth, are a form of
wrestling with the mystery with which humanity has been
wrestling from the beginning, and the principle of this mystery is the principle of Individual Actual Identity. The metaphysical feeling of the strangeness of existence flows precisely
from my being identical with myself and constituting a
unique being in duration and extent. This anxiety is what led
to the rise of religion, philosophy, and art.

Humanity first sought answers to these disturbing ques-

tions in religion. Religion, however, lost its influence on leading minds at the moment when philosophy took upon itself an
inquiry into the truth of existence. Religion then began to
grow ossified, limiting itself to mechanically accepted rites and
dogmas; it ceased to assuage the metaphysical anxieties of believers who from then on sought to relieve their anxiety in
other fields. This happened in Greece, and it happened in
Europe at the end of the Middle Ages.

For many centuries, philosophy created systems that had as
their goal the discovery of Absolute Truth. Witkiewicz writes,
"Our forebears, aiming at unachievable absolute truth, attempted to emerge from under the curse of the principle of
Individual Actual Identity, to construct an edifice of thought
that time could not destroy, a system of ideas extracted from
the accidental nature of a given system, that would be obliga-
tory on all existence." Independently of the relative inaccuracy
of these systems, it must be stated that "only belief in objective truth created truly valuable ideas and systems of
thoughts." Gradually, however, philosophy reached a point
where it noticed that there is a limit to our concepts and that
by using the concepts available to us, we exhausted, in coarse
outline, all the combinations leading toward a solution of the
mystery. The invalidation of philosophy took place during our
time. Philosophers behaved like the fox in the fable, however;
since the grapes turned out to be too high, they proclaimed
that they were green and not worth the effort to gather them.
A narrow interdependence with social changes that blunt the
sharpness of the experience of mystery led to the feverish activity of denying the mystery—on paper. Insoluble problems
were declared to be illusory in an attempt to demonstrate that
they depend on a misunderstanding. Witkiewicz feels limitless
contempt for the pragmatists and for Bergson because their
writings express most clearly a lack of interest in struggling

for a stark, unambiguous truth. Every theory, Witkiewicz says, is, from a certain perspective, self-delusion in order not to experience directly the monstrousness of existence. But it is one thing to lose courage and head for the tavern, stupefying oneself consciously; it is quite another to confront difficulties head-on.

The pragmatists raised all sorts of irrational nonsense to the level of truth if that nonsense seemed positive for the development of societies. "Ideas that people strived for in former times were independent of direct utility and were true or false not because they helped or harmed a given social group. Perhaps they had value for one class or another, but that value was not a criterion for their creators. Pragmatism always existed, but it was not programmatic. The characteristic attribute of our times is the programmatic nature of certain ideas." The human spirit tried to break out of the false circle of relative truths and "with truly superhuman effort aimed at absolute value in horrific struggle with the Mystery." "Throughout this entire struggle over truth with the Mystery, new veils kept falling from the Mystery and a time came when we saw the naked, hard body from which nothing more could be removed, impenetrable and invincible in its dead statue's indifference." Pragmatists attempt to shatter the statue; they simply deny that it exists. Bergson now recommends some sort of new "intuitive" understanding, beyond comprehension in accordance with the laws of logic. Is that, asks Witkiewicz, why we have sharpened our minds over so many centuries—to relinquish everything that has already been won for a pitiful phantom of the truth, for intuitive hallucination? But we deserve this. "Every epoch has the philosophy it deserves. In our present phase we deserve nothing but the worst kind of narcotic, with the goal of deadening in us any antisocial metaphysical anxiety that would interfere with automatization."

Thus, philosophy ends its life by gradual suicide, pretending to the world that it is still alive. What philosophers are doing now, having killed off metaphysics, is nothing but performing an autopsy on the corpse and filling out its death certificate. They write entire volumes in order to prove the impossibility of philosophy, to demonstrate that its value is purely a matter of convenience and practicality, that it is only the foam on biological surfaces or social processes.

There remains art. Religion and philosophy have tried to intellectualize metaphysical anxiety. In contrast to them, art is the externalization of the direct experience of anxiety.

The metaphysical feeling that is the source of creativity and the embryo of every work of art is polarized in a layer of ordinary life sensations and imaginings, in a layer of the intellect, and a layer of Pure Form, or simple intellectual qualities. It is like a flame that cuts through these layers and unites them into an inseparable whole.

Unity in multiplicity—that is the definition of a work of art. A human personality, being also a unity of multiplicity, preserves its oneness in symbols because they are united in a necessary fashion. A work of art, providing the artist who created it the highest sense of his own ego, in turn—through its own inner correctness and necessity—awakens metaphysical anxiety in the recipient. The feature that distinguishes a work of art from other beautiful objects is that unity is its exclusive goal. Therefore, for example, it is entirely unimportant in a painting whether it represents one person or another, or if it renders a particular landscape faithfully. Only the directional tensions (a term introduced by Witkiewicz) evoked by the brush are important, and it does not matter if, to create them, the painter used human faces, trees, chimneys, or only lines and planes that represent nothing from a worldly point of view.

What is more, liberation from inessential elements that only interfere with achieving unity would be the ideal. Painting "from nature," the desire to represent faithfully the natural colors and shapes of objects, their solidity, perspective, etc., binds one to the service of matters that are entirely alien to art. Pure Form in painting has nothing in common with noting down our surrounding reality, just as Pure Form in music has nothing in common with the expression of the so-called vital feelings—of sadness, joy, yearning, and so on. Obviously, seeking content and form in a work of art leads only to misunderstanding what art depends on, for there is no artistic "content" that can be separated from form.

Throughout the course of history, man and his metaphysical strivings have undergone great changes. In ancient times, when man found relief for them in religion, he preserved a certain type of inner equilibrium, and the art forms he created then had the dignity of peaceful beauty. When, however, religion lost its power to convince people, and philosophy died out, eliminating itself, man, who was metaphysically unsated, grasped convulsively at art and began to transfer his dread and sickliness to it. The old peaceful form discovered by people who knew other outlets for their anxiety no longer satisfied him. He now demanded too much of art; it had to substitute for former dogmas, rituals, and inquiries into the essence of being. He had to unite elements that were more and more contradictory and distant from one another in order to achieve thereby a moment of short-lived gratification.

The more these rebellious elements, rushing toward independence, have the artist under their control, the more acutely does he experience the condition about which we are speaking; and this condition is stronger if it is achieved at a greater cost. This phenomenon, which Witkiewicz calls insatiability by form, leads to increasingly greater complexity of the means he uses. For contemporary art, harmony and symmetry no longer suffice; art is intoxicated now with dissonances, disharmony, the anxiety of asymmetrical, disordered planes. This leads to perversion, to using as material loathsome, bizarre elements, shocking colors, eerie sounds. A perverse simplicity appears, a seeming simplicity that conceals within itself weights of gigantic complexity and hidden monstrosity. Art stands on the brink of madness because the people who are creating it today are the degenerate heirs of ancient masters who were on honorable terms, once upon a time, with Mystery and who shaped their works in a world made harmonious by religion. Yet the insane works of a van Gogh or a Picasso are the only form of beauty accessible to us. In order to feel what Giotto felt when he painted his saints, and what an ancient seer felt, we have to increase the dose and move toward the ultimate impossibility, toward absolute insatiability by form, when all the limited combinations of intellectual qualities that we still have at our disposal are exhausted. Then art will finally die, although for a long time people will continue to imitate it, and individuals capable of experiencing metaphysical anxiety, but no longer capable of any realization—potential artists, in other words— will be locked up in institutions for the mentally ill. Already today, individuals gifted with a sense of Mystery are the exceptions; the rest are rapidly maturing into automatization, recognizing as art only what touches upon their political interests (patriotism, social renewal).

This is one of the sources of today's dissonance between artists and society; excellent contemporary works do not stand a chance of connecting with rural dwellers. What some people tell us about a radiant future era is a fairy tale; according to them, great talents, languishing until now, will emerge from the human mass, which will be raised up to the highest level by a system that guarantees a just division of goods. A system that hopes to manage the unbelievable complexity of the economic life of our times must destroy what results from liberating the masses, and the peasant who now may be raising cows will be freed to participate in culture, but he will never know the luxury that is intellectual self-sufficiency. The ant heap's haste will harness him to its routines; he will never know the loneliness from which metaphysical amazement is born. He will be happy. But what will remain for us if not ethical values? "Beauty has gone mad, truth lies at our feet, torn apart by contemporary philosophers, and from the trio of ideals only goodness remains for us, that is, the happiness of those who did not have the power to create beauty, nor sufficient courage to look Mystery in the eyes." "Ethics will devour metaphysics and one must accept this as a natural phenomenon, without shedding tears, just as we accept the fact that people die and ripe apples fall to the ground. It may be bitter for the degenerate heirs of ancient civilization." "From cattle we came and to cattle we shall return," says one of Witkiewicz's heroes. Nevertheless, it will be painful only for the few, and only the few will realize that this chapter has come to an end.

The victory of ethics signifies the victory of relative values over absolute values. All attempts at a metaphysical justification of ethics, or imputing to ethics a meaning of universal rules, permanent and unchanging, would be absolutely hopeless. Ethical prescriptions always present a particular pragmatic point of view; they are an expression of the interests of one or another social group and have a temporary, instructive meaning. Religion, philosophy, and art are purely individual creations; they express the relationship of the individual to Existence, whereas ethics presents the individual's ties with society—ties that are subject to constant change.

I have summarized Witkiewicz's views to the best of my ability, because decency requires this. Witkiewicz considered intellect to be the only precious thing in man; he wanted to be treated as a philosopher and not an artist; he himself confessed to the bankruptcy of his artistic efforts. Now I can allow myself some observations.

Ideas that depend upon defining cycles of humanity's development, particularly if they aim at illuminating, one way or another, a particular brief moment, the so-called "our times," arouse suspicion. The mythological depiction of the ancient Germans by German scholars is an almost too glaring example of this. Doubt always arises as to whether what is at stake is not the mythologizing of contemporary life for various reasons, while contemporary understandings are imputed to people of past epochs who had no conception of, nor ever experienced, phenomena such as we have; and these ancient people, appropriately presented as specimens, are supposed to serve as proof of the correctness of some thesis or other. When Witkiewicz writes about ancient artists ("muscles like ropes of steel"), or about ancient rulers experiencing the wondrousness of existence on a gigantic scale thanks to the limitless freedom of individuality, it often occurs to us to interject perversely that ancient rulers were not as healthy, after all, as Witkiewicz wants them to be, nor did they exist in a sphere of sensations of such high quality, and that the cruelties perpetrated by them derived less frequently from their lordly caprice and more often from the rules of the struggle for power.

Prettification of the past is, in general, a very interesting phenomenon and a real obsession among some people. Rousseau prettified primitive man; in the Renaissance, people prettified Greece; Stendhal prettified people of the Renaissance; between 1918 and 1939 the Middle Ages were prettified; and furthermore, nostalgia for the so-called ancient splendor is usually linked with a revulsion against the present day. Witkiewicz is clearly obsessed with decline. This horror does not fit perfectly into an intellectual framework; it is a presentiment that visited the most impressionable people, especially in

Poland, separated as that country was by a narrow border from the new world in the East. Who knows, perhaps various Polish pessimisms from that period were simply "the quaking of the little man before the big," and everything else was only secondary, additions, decorations. At any rate, in both of Witkiewicz's novels the new civilization of automatons comes from the East—the first time as a revolution of levelers, the second time as an invasion of Europe by Chinese-Mongol armies. In both novels the finale is death against the background of a beautiful Polish autumn. In *Insatiability*, the Polish dictator Kocmołuchowicz is cut down by the Chinese; in *Farewell to Autumn*, Bazakbal is executed by the levelers. Witkiewicz committed suicide when the Red Army entered the eastern territories of Poland, and this took place against a background of exactly that same nature.

In his novels, Poland (a fantastic Poland, seemingly transported into the future but really interwar Poland) is represented as a temporary creation, hanging on in part with the support of the Western democracies, in part through the strength of powerlessness. An optimistic drowziness reigns there, and a craving for pleasure, and, suspended over everything, the boulder of inevitable catastrophe dangles on a slender thread. It makes no difference whether this image is realistic or not; what is important is that the ambiguity of Polish weakness exerted a powerful influence on the direction of Witkiewicz's thought, lending it a totally hopeless coloration. Faith in the irreversibility of the historical process and, at the same time, a passive fixation on this process, as if one were hypnotized—that was a very widespread phenomenon during the interwar years. Witkiewicz understood the weight of the changes taking place in Russia; their dynamic force, compared with the carefree atmosphere of Polish life, reminded him constantly of the fragility of the peripheries of capitalism. Historical fatalism, which paved the way for great mass movements and thereby for war, reaches exceptional tension in him. That he attempted to swim against the current and did what he had to do, knowing beforehand that it would end in defeat, connects his works to perhaps the one serious current of the interwar decades, a struggle without anticipation of any reward. Convinced of the demise of metaphysics, he writes an essay in which he explains his metaphysical system. Convinced that automatization and the enslavement of the intellect are inevitable, he defends the rights of intellect at every opportunity. (To be sure, while calling for engagement with philosophy, he considered nineteenth-century German philosophy the only philosophy worthy of that name.) At times he even wants to believe in the possibility of a planned utilization of automatization to resurrect philosophy and art, but at the same time he knows that it would be fruitless. His hero Bazakbal, who plans to commit suicide on the border with Slovakia, is haunted by the thought that after all, the historical process can be reversed by the force of human will. So he hastens to return to Poland in order to proclaim his idea there, and the first border guard he encounters liquidates him along with his plans.

What has been happening in Europe since 1939 exceeds Witkiewicz's descriptions. Many of his predictions have been confirmed, but from a kind of distant perspective; both his predictions and their fulfillment have been forged into a single temporary mass, and all his opinions may turn out to have been formed under the excessively suggestive power of the predicted moment. One can say of him that he was tragic; one can take him as an example of a stormy petrel, a bird that senses an approaching storm. One can also accuse him of various weaknesses, above all of decadence, which it is always so easy to persuade oneself and others to adopt. Furthermore, convincing oneself beforehand of one's own decadence paralyzes an individual's or a class of people's ability to resist, if that is how they view themselves. One can also compare

Witkiewicz with the Russian intelligentsia of the years preceding 1917 and look for differences or similarities—the same generation, but a different sort of impending defeats. I will not attempt to make that comparison. I only insist that he is a very serious figure and that those who feel distaste for him after reading a couple of excessively brutal erotic scenes in his books are wrong. He may well not be an "exceptional writer," but exceptional writers occur so rarely that if one were to restrict the history of culture to them, it would be a very skimpy history indeed. Since so much has been written about Stanisław Brzozowski, because it is easy to squeeze various slogans out of him that are dear to the hearts of fascists, why should one not speak about Witkiewicz? Neither is a great writer, but if one wants to identify at least a couple of people in Poland who thought about something, one must encounter Brzozowski, who is repugnant, and Witkiewicz, who is not pleasant, although at least he had no intention of being the nation's instructor. Ultimately, the movement of collective life does not always have at its service personalities who are well balanced and classic; perhaps the lack of them is the price that is paid for bravery and desperation. Nothing will remain, in any event, of the enormous number of "masters" of the novel, verse, or short story, but something enduring will remain from the work of Witkiewicz, who was by no means a master—and this is important not only in Warsaw or Kraków, but in Sydney and Pennsylvania, too.

II

What will endure in Witkiewicz is the form he provides for the intellectual events that characterized the first half of the twentieth century. Let us take that period's history of art. One can learn a great deal from the opinions expressed by the average educated man around the year 1930—for example, about painting and sculpture. Were one to construct a questionnaire and ask him to answer three questions, let us say, the results would be more or less as follows:

QUESTION: What periods in the history of art do you value most highly?

ANSWER: I probably don't need to say that the art of primitive people can serve us as a model of creative conciseness and creative deformation. Among the epochs we know from history, Egyptian art is great and so is early Greek art, as long as it preserves Egyptian influences and only slowly frees itself from them. Later, spoiled by aspirations to realistic faithfulness, it degenerates. Sculptures from the classical period testify to a decline. I do not understand why our ancestors liked the *Venus de Milo* so much, or the *Discus Thrower*, but dismissed with disdain the works of ancient Greece or Etruria. Medieval Italian painting before the fourteenth century is great art; then the Renaissance began, falsifying the goals of painting and paving the road for almost photographic naturalism. I think that a conscious return to the true goals of art can be sought only in contemporary art.

QUESTION: When you look at a picture or a sculpture, do you yield to the suggestions of the subject represented in them?

ANSWER: Never. I only seek perfection of the artistic resolution. It makes absolutely no difference to me if the subject of a picture is a landscape, a still life, a human group, or an abstract composition.

QUESTION: Whom do you think of as the patrons of contemporary painting?

ANSWER: The Impressionists. They freed us from the

tyranny of the subject and allowed us to focus all our attention on purely painterly values. Since then, arguments about the preservation of this or that human issue on canvas have lost all significance. Every subject is good if it becomes a pretext for an artistically fine composition.

That the average educated person would have given exactly those answers can easily be confirmed by reading articles about art and criticism in the periodical press. They would, of course, be the most simplified, universally accessible findings. Witkiewicz's beliefs were identical in their general outlines. When he published them in 1918 (in his *New Forms in Painting*), he was considered a revolutionary on Polish soil, just as his father, Stanisław Witkiewicz, was long before him. In 1918, the middle-class milieu that took an interest in art had not yet moved beyond the boundaries drawn by Witkiewicz *père*; they agreed, that is, that the subject of a picture is of no particular interest, but they demanded from the painter precise observation and faithfulness to nature. It did not occur to them to set up African sculpture or Italian primitives as a model, and a landscape with cows earned recognition if it was "just like"; furthermore, the cow could even be green, because such light can occur. So, light is all right (it's an element in nature), but this is still far from programmatic deformation and treating a picture as only a collection of colors and planes. In a short time, however, under the influence of innovations from the West, there were many changes in Poland, too.

What can be deduced from this change in taste and the parallel change taking place in the themes pursued in evaluation? A nineteenth-century man would have been offended by African sculptures with protruding tongues and erect phalluses. He would have seen only a lack of talent in folk carvings of holy images; and in Italian painting, he would have preferred Raphael to Cimabue and Giotto. Even the early Impressionists made him anxious, not only because they freely assigned colors to objects, but also because of their freedom in choosing their subjects. Manet's *Le déjeuner sur l'herbe*, with a naked woman sitting surrounded by men wearing clothing, was a first-rate scandal, not lessened by the recollection that Giorgione had already painted similar groups. If, then, a citizen of the first half of the twentieth century evaluated paintings entirely differently, he evidently had reasons that were previously unknown.

The change from being interested in what a picture or a sculpture represents to being interested in the work itself, independent of its original model in nature, gives us pause. Anyone who would ask if the colors or shapes used by the artist were faithfully observed, or if the neck of the person in the portrait was too long, would have given proof of his boorishness and bad taste. I shall not say yet whether such questions are justified or not; I only state the fact of a new attitude toward art, which is significant enough.

Once upon a time, Courbet had to fight for the right to paint everyday things: people in frock coats, a peasant funeral procession, artisans, labor. Then the Impressionists managed to arouse rapture by bringing to light the wonders that the human eye sees in grass illuminated by sunlight, in flowers, in the bowers of a suburban café's garden. There was still a hierarchy of subjects, though, which was dictated by ties with society's general aspirations; that is, there was something extra-artistic at the heart of painting, which it would be hard to attribute to visual impressionability alone. In the opinion of our interlocutor from 1930, it makes absolutely no difference what is painted. But in the Middle Ages, in an atmosphere of religious exaltation, figures of saints were painted not because the saints were a better pretext for achieving "formal tensions"; on the contrary, technical skill clearly served a superior intention. The Renaissance discovered the naked human body in paintings not because its beauty was suddenly recognized, as is frequently said, but because the disrobing of the body signified for the artist a return to legendary Greece, an attempt at rediscovering the continuity of civilization. The interiors of Dutch homes expressed the intention of Holland's wealthy, cultured burghers "to see oneself in one's own nature." Poussin's mythological scenes are embedded in the world of classical literature. Similarly, in the Impressionists, in their observations of street life, cafés, the theater, in their noting of fashion, their sensitive observation of the French landscape, there is the joy of possession so characteristic of the nineteenth century, an affirmation of progress and its various possibilities.

Nevertheless, there must be some truth in the opinion that the Impressionists "freed us from the tyranny of the subject." Their aim was the painterly exploitation of what surrounds us; that is the source of their freshness of impressions, stemming from the resistance that untouched and unformed humanistic subjects present—for example, Degas' ballet dancers, who had not been painted previously, or the crowd enjoying itself in a *bal musette*. A purely intellectual approach to reality usually conceals within itself, however, possibilities for exhausting and replacing the power of stimuli with the power of impressions, and so that same grass and the women with parasols, for example, who originally possessed the charm of something captured for the first time in history, later become a pretext for ever more inventive means. When the positivist faith in progress broke down, the successors to the Impressionists painted landscapes and still lifes as if they did not care at all about the uncontrolled, new connections among things that had arisen all around them. In this way they signaled, consciously or unconsciously, their disdain for expanding the circle of familiarity by including phenomena of this world—which can be reflected only through an idea that brings order to these intellectual occurrences; a super-painterly and even super-artistic idea, as for

example the ideas of the Renaissance; or the progressive realism of the nineteenth century. A still life repeated in countless
variations sufficed for them because they were reconciled to
what is given and has been elaborated on. Following in their
footsteps came new theories of art proving that the meaning of
painting lies in the construction of self-sufficient form, free
from any kind of imitation. Medieval art was valued so highly
because it was strange, eerie, just as African religious works
were strange and eerie; people forgot that what was taken to be
pure form in them had arisen as a consequence of belief in a
particular, magical understanding of nature by the people of
that time.

Poetry followed a similar path. I am thinking of John Sparrow's book *Sense and Poetry* (1934). Seeking continuity in contemporary poetry from Baudelaire to the present, Sparrow
elaborates his thesis that poetry has been characterized by a
process of increasing irrationality or the disappearance of logi-
cally deducible meaning. In Baudelaire, the language of poetry
began to express certain contents connected with the sphere
of human relations that were external to the work itself, although there were also elements in it which, if separated from
the whole, would convey no meaning. In other words, verse
becomes a planetary system in and of itself, as it were, independent of people's ordinary means of communication. In
Mallarmé, thinking is already replaced completely by arrange-
ments of words designed to create a mood. Valéry introduces
the architectonics of a poem, isolated and absolute, as the foundation of poetry. This was all accomplished by substituting
rules of association for rules of thought; images are always
connected in a strictly private manner, and the key to them is
lost. Someone once loved a girl in a blue dress, so he associates
love with the color blue; for someone else, chestnut trees and
nasturtiums symbolize the family home. But the reader has
different associations, and though he may submit to the au-

thor's suggestions, he will not perceive the logic of consequences, he will perceive only poetic necessity. What has taken
place is that "the movements and transitions in the work . . .
form a psychological, not a logical, unity."[1] Sparrow does not
intend to impose on poetry the duty to instruct, inform, or exert an educational influence. He merely remarks that poetry is
impoverished when thought is abandoned. In many instances
"the effort to discover what it is that he is meant to understand
prevents the reader from enjoying the images and ideas as they
are presented, just as the random method that governs their
choice precludes him from understanding their connection."[2]

These convergences may be described concisely as follows:
just as the transfer of attention from subject to technique, for
which the subject is only a pretext, occurred in painting, so in
poetry poets have locked themselves into rules of the game
that are binding only and exclusively inside a closed chalk
circle. This does not mean that just any work of art can be
conceived of apart from the rules of the game. Every picture
or poem constitutes a world in itself, but its links with the
broader world that surrounds us may be very strong or weak, or
totally broken. Degas' ballerina exists among other living ballerinas; she is a unique instance of them, but she is based on
the reality that ballerinas do exist. A Cubist portrait does not
derive its justification from the person whose portrait is being
painted, but from cylinders and cones that are not the most direct, but rather the most roundabout, path to its goal. The poet
of associations and metaphors enjoys the journey, the process
of the poem developing in time, and as it approaches the end,
it turns out that all the while he was circling around an insignificant thread.

Among the many theories that have developed in this atmosphere, perhaps first place belongs to the praise of "pure
poetry," such as has been elaborated by Father Bremond, the
author of *The History of Religious Feeling in France*.[3] It is no

accident that a historian of mysticism achieved such success when speaking about poetry. Art required justification for its new form, and as it moved toward external phenomena, it could find that justification only in the artist's own emotions or in the emotions of his readers. I want to make myself clear: external justifications, those that can have importance beyond the work—for example, Dante's description of hell or the motif of Beatrice—are a way of giving form to Christian ideas; Whitman's hymns find their sequel in the idea of progress and in the life of the developing American democracy; in the Romantics, what is external to their verse are the human emotions that may be more or less universal and have therefore buttered the bread of generations of professors.

In a lecture delivered beneath the vaulted ceiling of the Académie Française in 1925, Bremond began by allying himself with the representatives of pure poetry, from Edgar Allan Poe and Baudelaire to Mallarmé and Paul Valéry. In accordance with his yearning for purity (pure painterliness, pure theatricality, pure musicality), in order to arrive at poetry's essence, he attempted to exclude from poetry everything that is of secondary importance and subservient. Long ago, during periods when poets modeled themselves after ancient authors, the features that a work was supposed to possess in order to be beautiful were enumerated, although it was often admitted that poetry has certain wondrous features that cannot be explained. Today, Bremond argued, we no longer say that in a particular poem there are living pictures, noble thoughts and feelings, a little of this and that, and in addition something that cannot be expressed (something ineffable.) We say instead that first and foremost there is something *ineffable*, which is inextricably bound up with this and that. That mysterious element alone constitutes the true life of poetry, and poetry is liberated from its burdensome and alien obligations by recognizing that it has a right to play that role. The most ingenious analysis cannot explain why a particular line of verse awakens a vibration in us and a condition that is similar to prayer, while the same line, with just one word changed, leaves us cold. This is an internal current that cannot be understood intellectually; it is pre-visual, preconceptual thinking. Elsewhere, Bremond cites Bergson. This internal current, then, has nothing in common with an image, a thought, the author's feeling, or even with the beauty of a sound, although it is closest, perhaps, to music. What, then, remains? According to Bremond,

> everything in a poem that directly occupies or can occupy our superficial activities (*nos activités de surface*), our reason, imagination, sensibility, everything that the poet appeared to want to express and actually did express; everything that, as we say, suggests something to us; everything that a grammarian's or philosopher's analysis can extract from a poem; everything that a translation is capable of preserving, is not-pure. As is easy to surmise, the subject or list of objects in a poem, but also the meaning of each sentence, the logical flow of ideas, the progress of the narrative, the details of descriptions and even the emotions that are directly awakened in us—all are not-pure. Prose would serve perfectly well to instruct, relate, paint, produce a shiver or extract a tear; that is its natural task. In short, eloquence, by which I mean not the art of speaking a great deal so as to say nothing, but the art of speaking in order to say something—is not-pure.

It would be difficult to go further than this. But Bremond knows that pure poetry rarely appears. It is a flash of lightning shimmering across one or two lines of verse and suddenly dying out. Words, as the material for externalizing the mysterious current, are at the same time an obstacle. Excellent poetry strives for silence; it exists beyond the boundaries of speech. It is a mystical state (imperfect, to be sure), a communion, a presence; its sources are the same as the sources of prayer, which Bremond later demonstrated in his book *Prière et poésie.*[4]

Bremond was a very French phenomenon. His attacks on "rationalistic poetics" are understandable in a country that produced the poetics of Boileau and in a language more inclined than others to eloquence and tirades adorned with stylistic figures. Nevertheless, he expresses the tendency of his time perfectly. Let us attempt some substitutions. Bremond's *ineffable* is nothing other than Witkiewicz's Pure Form, after all. Not-pure elements that appeal to reason, the imagination, sensibility—these are Witkiewicz's "vital emotions" or his imitation of nature. The mystical state of visitation that draws poetry close to prayer is the metaphysical insatiability arising from a feeling of Individual Actual Identity. The silence toward which the excellent, maximally tense weight of poetry aims is the ultimate insatiability by form that marks the boundary of art.

When we dispense with differences in terminology, we see that Witkiewicz and Bremond stand at the edge of mystery, and that association with mystery, with the same meaning or lack of meaning of being (pre-visual and preconceptual thinking) that becomes visible through colors, words, sounds, is for them the only value of a poem, an image, a sculpture, or a musical work. Because both their theories were formed under the influence of general artistic changes and were professed with only minor deviations by the majority of educated people, in particular by artists, we are free to draw some conclusions from this. We may risk asserting that the entire process of the so-called liberation of art from the subject is intimately connected with the dying out of religion, at least with certain aspects of it, in particular with the metaphysical-dogmatic aspects. The need for a substitute arises; perhaps it can be explained in part by the religious upbringing of children who, once they are grown up, drift away from religion. Such people transfer the array of unfulfilled desires to the high human activity that is art, creating a kind of sect of the initiated. They perceive in it a metaphysical source that churns up various beauties of form; in addition, they are more sensitive to its internal rhythm than to any other of its properties. Proust, who is otherwise utterly distant from religious interests, represents an almost religious attitude toward art. Bremond was right to seek support for his conclusions in Proust's descriptions of Vinteuil's sonata. It is also sufficient to recall the death of old Bergotte at the picture exhibition, and the yellow spot that strikes him as something perfect, something he had aimed for his entire life, in vain. In Polish literature, in Iwaszkiewicz's short story "The Mill on the Utrata," someone recites a poem in English to a dying man, and this is like a substitute for the last rites. These tendencies of artists met with a rather sour reception among Christians. Maritain, who is so perceptive, warns that "art is not angelic bread" and that it would be vain to expect "super-substantial nourishment" from it. Indeed, art understood in that way becomes a religion of the laity, appearing as a rival of ossifying religions.

Theories of art such as those proposed by Bremond and Witkiewicz are the final stage of a long process; they have a tradition behind them. Various strands are interwoven in this tradition, and there is no reason to ignore their variety and attempt to sketch "great theses," which would certainly be false. This is a boundless field through which one can wander peacefully, selecting from the entire history of culture examples of the particular honor that people have accorded poetry, for example, because they detected in it the reflection of things that are inaccessible to rational understanding. Because, however, lovers of pure poetry place special emphasis on the purging of programmatic aspects that began in the nineteenth century, they are free to join Bremond in citing Poe and Baudelaire. Poe, in his essay "The Poetic Principle," explicitly excludes

truth and passion from the domain of poetry: "the manifestation of the Principle is always found in an *elevating excitement
of the Soul*—quite independent of that passion which is the
intoxication of the Heart—or of that Truth which is the satisfaction of the Reason."[5] Poetry, according to him, has only an
accidental contiguity with truth and duty. It is "the desire of
the moth for the star," "the prescience of the glories beyond
the grave," "those divine and rapturous joys."[6] Under the influence of beauty we are moved to tears, and they are tears of
angry, impatient sorrow rather than satisfaction: thus does the
feeling affect us that here on earth we can come to know true,
otherworldly exaltation only for a moment, only fleetingly.
According to Baudelaire, we return to heaven through beauty;
we recapture for a moment the fervor that was the normal
condition of people before original sin. And owing to that
"insatiability," to use Witkiewicz's term, that yearning for unattainable lasting happiness, the characteristic feature of the
highest manifestations of art is sadness. "Melancholy is thus
the most legitimate of all the poetic tones," says Poe.[7]

Now a question: How should one respond to aesthetic theories of this type? How can one appreciate them without renouncing simplicity and the unique meaning of words? These
are phenomena that are too close to us for us to be able to treat
them as only a chapter in the history of culture. For them to
become the past, they will have to be overcome by mental effort and a new formulation in practice. In this new formulation it is not, by any means, a question of negating and erasing
all metaphysical understanding of beauty. Too many valuable
works have arisen from this belief, and this motif returns too
stubbornly in the history of art. One can only say metaphorically that if someone wishes to return to heaven through art,
he should remember that an angel with a fiery sword stands at
the gates of heaven. Putting it more precisely: absolute purity
destroys human activity, because fewer and fewer human mat-

ters interest us, until at last we come to focus on a nail in the wall or on plaid trousers, as Witkiewicz's heroes do after taking a large dose of cocaine. Then art ends; all that remains is silent contemplation, for that is the price of entering forbidden territory. There is something embarrassing, even indecent (Witkiewicz would say "degenerate") in deliberately contrived products of pure art. They grate on us, even if they are beautiful, because their beauty is not accidental, arising tangentially as the outcome of pursuing a more general aim, but rather, established from the beginning as the one and only aim. In a way, this resembles what happens when someone tells a joke and laughs at it himself, preempting his audience's reaction. We like Degas' painting because it aspires to the ballerina, to analysis of her movement. Dante aspires to Paradise through Hell and Purgatory, a medieval painter to his ascetic vision, Mickiewicz to the idyllic Lithuanian countryside. If one of our contemporaries, unable to follow Dante in his faith, were to detect in the poet's descriptions of his journey a beauty separate from the ideas of his time, if he were to insist that those beliefs served Dante as only a pretext, he would be making a grave mistake. He would also be mistaken if, having lost acquisitiveness in relation to matter, which was so characteristic of the nineteenth century, he saw in Degas only harmonious colors and a sketch, and in Rimbaud's trembling agitation only a dazzling flood of words. The bet that artists place is always larger than later generations think it was, because as time passes, so-called formal achievements obscure their struggle. The consequence of a formal relationship to the past is an increased capacity for delectation. Works from the past, severed from their ties to civilization and held up against a single measure, constitute an immense gallery in which everything has its place. One can then successfully construct a history of artistic technique, placing side by side a folk carving of a holy figure and a sculpture by Maillol, but this reflects negatively on new artistic creation, which always lives by struggle and not by delectation.

If I seem to stand in opposition to the element that Bremond called the *ineffable*, that is only illusory. Actually, I criticize Pure Form out of love, because although one is pining for paradise, one may refuse oneself permission to return, if that return would only result in corruption. There is danger in a programmatic recognition of Pure Form as the root of art. It is odd that Witkiewicz—who said that "pragmatism always existed, but it was never programmatic," and that the curse of our times is in the programmatic nature of certain ideas—did not arrive at the straightforward assertion that, in just the same way, Pure Form has always existed but was not programmatic, and that when one takes programmatic aim at Pure Form, one inflicts on it an incurable wound. There are mechanisms in culture so delicate that when one points one's finger at them, they immediately change into something else because of the excessively strained attention focused on them.

III

Now I shall attempt to show that Witkiewicz appeared as a witness for one of the sides in an ancient and extremely pettifogging lawsuit. The sides in it are (*are*, because the lawsuit has not yet been settled) *ethics* and *poetry*, and the latter acts as the legally empowered representative of art in general. Perhaps the sides are wrong to have taken this to court. As if understanding this, they often withdraw their suit and reach an agreement. The experts insist, however, that the agreement is illusory and that even when they collaborate, each side tries to harm the other.

The first of these sides calls itself truth and virtue. It chooses reason as the foundation for its actions. The other side has difficulty defining its position, and when arguments are demanded of it, it dances, laughs, weeps, or utters unintelligible words. More than one judge is inclined to rule against it, because of its obvious dementia or the underdevelopment of its intellectual powers. Plato proclaimed that it is three steps removed from truth and dwells amid fantasies and phantoms. Where reason is capable of grasping the idea of things, poetry sees only mistaken illusions.

For reason, a chair, a table, a bed, or a pitcher can be reduced to dimensions and weight; how we arrange them is irrelevant. A painter, that unreasoning person, sees something new in the same object every time, depending on the angle from which he views the object. A poet, a person no less lacking in reason, delights in descriptions of passions and emotions, over which reason must pass as if over the lowest part of human nature. Furthermore, what is untrue is also immoral; the poet is immoral, because he shamelessly wallows in terrors, nostalgias, melancholias, placing in the mouths of his heroes complaints that a rational citizen would be ashamed to utter in public. In this way he infects viewers and listeners with tolerance for the animal part of people, for what is fleeting and transient. There should be no place for poetry in a perfect state. With one exception—if it legitimates itself in relation to truth and virtue with something useful, singing, as it ought to, of gods and heroes.

Since Plato's time, more than one defense of poetry and more than one condemnation of it has been written. In the nineteenth century, the largest-scale attack was launched by Tolstoy. Because we are concerned with the fate of contemporary art, it is worth pausing for a moment over a certain polemic that took place in France in 1937. The young author Roger Caillois attacked poetry according to all the best models. True, this time not as a believer in virtue, but as a believer in speculative thought. He accused poetry of a "lack of necessity" and the falsification of physical truth, acquired through difficult effort, slowly, but permanently.

The best explanation of his intentions would be to cite an old schizophrenic who uttered this biting assessment of beauty: "Look at these roses; my wife would call them beautiful, but for me they are only a collection of leaves, petals, thorns, and stems." Benjamin Fondane* responded with his essay "La conscience malheureuse." In this argument between ethics and poetry, Fondane accused ethical thought of acting in bad faith. He detected the old Platonic attempt in his antagonist Caillois's concern for the purely intellectual apprehension of the world. Ethical thought and speculative thought are the same in relation to poetry, just as they were in Plato. In actuality, this is a unified ambition to transform reality as it is recognized by us into a purified, ideal schema. Only what contributes to a rational understanding of the world should count in poetry. The rest—just like the changing shape of a chair that is continually moved into a different position—is fantasy; it is the most complete irreality. For Caillois, poetry exists in servitude to the senses, servitude to physiology. The old schizophrenic probably said the same thing about his wife: seeing a beautiful rose instead of a collection of petals, thorns, and stems, she did not know the truth about the rose and was enslaved to her senses. Whoever accuses poetry of having an "animal nature" acts in a similar fashion; the "animal nature" of desire, despair, regret, intoxication, or the physicality of impressions is always the inessential, external stratum of a world that possesses an internal structure, the goal of our intellect.

On what is the bad faith of speculative-ethical thought

---

*Benjamin Fondane, a French poet, was of Romanian Jewish descent. A student and friend of Lev Shestov, he died in 1944 in Birkenau. [Author's note added for 1996 edition] based? That it acts, presumably, in defense of poetry, while poetry, not endowed with the gift of logical expression or the capacity for making clear distinctions, listens with open mouth and assents—to its own destruction. It assents when speculative-ethical thought broadly justifies the role that poetry ought to play in the service of truth or virtue. It applauds Hegel when he frees poetry from the bonds of everything that is "finite and particular," that draws boundaries for the spirit. But poetry lives precisely by what is finite, particular, real, animal, fleeting, and transitory. Brightness and knowledge destroy it. Ignorance, darkness, fables, and mystery nourish it.

Having listened to the speeches of her opponent, who draped herself in the toga of a barrister, poetry forgets who she is and what she should thank for her existence. Ultimately she is no longer able to dance, laugh, and weep in answer to arguments. While she was able to do so, she was strong and could issue a challenge. Tamed into politeness, she is ashamed of herself, and it is precisely then that the "bashful conscience of the poet" emerges. The poet does not trust himself. The poet needs a *reason* to act, and that reason is supplied by obliging, diabolically perverse, speculative-ethical thought. On the last rung of development—before 1939 it was the school of surrealists—poetry programmatically turns to the subconscious, to dreams, instincts, irrationality. But this is nothing other than the *rational exploitation* of irrationality, instinct, dream, the subconscious, with Freud (and Marx) in hand. It is a closed circle: rational miracle; rational fairy tale; rational, programmatic physiologism and animality. This is the trap into which the naive and infantile muse was drawn by her resourceful rival.

It appears that Fondane hit the nail on the head and identified the main thread in the drama. We remember how many schools or groups of poets there were before the war. The most important part of the equipment of each poet was the doctrine justifying his right to practice poetry, that poetry does have a function in the social organism (obviously, only the poetry represented by that poet's school).

Speculative-ethical thought dealt so courageously with poetry because it had experienced a great triumph in all areas. This appears to be paradoxical. After all, it is precisely those currents that are hostile to reason that form the foundation of mass delusions, and it is precisely contempt for the truth of reason that insured their triumph, aiming successfully at the masses—and yet, this both is and is not the case. There is in these mass delusions the glorification of blood, instinct, strength—ultimately, the glorification of stupidity—but justified philosophically, no need even to mention how and on what sophisms it depends. Just as the old schizophrenic looked at the rose, scientifically and soberly; just as the surrealists scientifically and soberly attempted to awaken hallucinations, dreams, and "the unleashing of the five freed senses" in themselves; just as scientifically and soberly, working from the standpoint of biology, did they look at the life of the human animal, agitating for a planned animality (no longer the involuntary, accidental animality of poetry). The right to murder the weak, to establish state slavery, to conduct breeding experiments with people, *had been proved.*

The theory of pure art is like the bashful self-defense of poetry, burdened with complexes, against an increasingly more powerful opponent. This took place through poetry's slow withdrawal from positions to which the other side made claims, just so long as she could retain something for herself in her modest circle, something that might remain untouchable. "They accuse me of immorality? I have nothing to say; this is not my business; I have nothing in common with virtue," poetry responded reprovingly. Others arrive with a desire for truth (today they rage against poetry because it "does not express the truth of our era"). Poetry then advises them to rely on reason, because truth is beyond her competence. Poe and his faithful pupil Baudelaire state this explicitly, black on white. According to them, poetry possessed only accidental ties with the realms of the will (virtue) and reason (truth). They also bracket out the passions—or the "vital emotions" of Witkiewicz. We saw how few of the permitted components remain in Bremond. At the same time, however, poetry, the very same one who once mocked before Plato "the crowd of wise men who want to rise above Jupiter," now obediently attempts to explain her virtues in the language of wise men. She borrows their terminology and attempts with their help to erect a rampart around her minimal possessions. She succeeds only if she permits herself religious or metaphysical emotions, as did Poe, Baudelaire, Bremond, and Witkiewicz. She does not succeed if those metaphysical emotions are to be rejected: then the last scrap of ground slips away from under poetry's feet, and she wakes up completely in the power of ethical-speculative ideas. She will have to obey the party, the state, or the interests of the revolution. Even preserving some piece of the territory of "pure art," she languishes, because she has too little space, she is suffocating, she senses a lack of reality. Having given up a range of intentions, she must endure being called contemptuously a toy for connoisseurs, a childish thing—and her shame deepens. Poetry wants to be serious. She wants at least to be seen as a grown-up, even if she is not treated with the respect she deserves in consideration of her gray hair. This explains the wholesale rejection of pure poetry by poets; they are moving under the solicitous wings of ethics, because then they will finally be serious. A mediocre poem about a great leader, about the sufferings of the fatherland, about the new social order— now that is finally something that counts. A perfect verse that is only poetry is pretty, sweet, pleasant, but no more than that.

So there is something utterly wrong in the tactic that poetry adopted in this difficult argument. She allowed herself to be drawn into discussions in which she will always come out badly. That's one point. The other point is that she has been surrendering for so long that she has lost almost everything, and she is getting rid of what remains out of incurable shame.

It would be completely useless to point out the paths to salvation. Either they are the same as the paths to salvation of a civilization based on freedom, or they do not exist at all. One could create ten more theories and poetic schools, and it would be to no avail. The fate of poetry is too closely tied to the fate of every free creative work of the spirit for it to be worth the effort to prescribe some separate medicines for her.

Let us see what might have happened had the poet not agreed that the schizophrenic was fundamentally right. First of all, he would have recognized him not as a serious person and his wife as not a serious person; he would only have asserted that they experience the same phenomenon differently. That would have liberated him from shame. Undoubtedly, when the schizophrenic stamps his foot and yells, "You idiot, why do you say that a rose is beautiful? Don't you see that it is only petals, leaves, and a stem?" the wife can say nothing in her defense, and she need not. An unabashed poet would not have relinquished truth and virtue so hastily to the ethical-speculative schizophrenics, retaining only beauty for himself. In other words, he would not have withdrawn into the circle of pure poetry, where "melancholy is the most legitimate of all the poetic tones." On the contrary, he would have insisted that it represents reality and only reality; that the charm of a rose, a lament on the death of a loved one, desire, and fear are not mere phantoms, unworthy of a purely rational, transparent construction of the world.

IV

Reading Tolstoy's *What Is Art?* one arrives at the most astonishing associations. What came to my mind was a dance hall in the little town of Baranowicze, which I saw before 1939, one of those establishments for the spread of cultural trash that always provide grist for social workers' arguments. In truth, Tolstoy's reaction to "unhealthy" art did not differ greatly from the internal spasm I experienced in that bar.

Tolstoy pretended to be a simple man and used what was obvious as blackmail. One feature of such outlooks on life as the desire to always think exclusively about ideals that will ensure the happiness of societies is their ostensible (but only ostensible) validity and irrefutability. That was the case with both Tolstoy and Plato.

It should be obvious from this sketch that art exists between two extremes. On one side it is threatened by a freedom purchased at the cost of renouncing its influence on human relations, as can be seen in the proponents of "pure poetry," "pure form," and "art for art's sake." On the other side, it is threatened by enslavement to social ideas. We are so saturated with thinking in collective categories that it is difficult for us to imagine, for example, that it might not be permissible to condemn the imitators of Nietzsche or the propagandists of racism. The world has entered a phase in which every sort of poets' delirium, though seemingly divorced from reality, immediately has some kind of serious consequences. The controls of sobriety and ethics can no longer be avoided. And that is precisely why it is so important to seek the boundaries that we, like the mass of simple people who worry about social justice, must guarantee our poets.

Perhaps it all comes down only to a choice of ethical-social visions. Some of these visions are hostile to free development along the lines of constant motion and changeability. They frighten and blackmail us with the so-called decisiveness of a single point in history. The others, at least, do not proclaim that the world is either ending or beginning at precisely this moment, that we have been living in falsehood for hundreds of years and only now have the scales fallen from our eyes. These are the natural allies of culture.

Ideas that want to realize the happiness of mankind *hic et nunc*, speculative-ethical hubris assuring us that it knows what man needs and what prescription to use in order to guarantee him a state of bliss once and for all—these are matters that the poet and the defender of poetry ought not to trust. If they cry out that it is now or never, that we are living through a turning point such as mankind has not known since the beginning of existence, and that one may not be concerned with anything but that turning point, the defender of art and science would do well to suppress, in himself and in others, that cry of topicality. What follows from such a posture of restraint is not that one should take the side of those who say that everything has already happened, that injustice and violence are eternal, and that one should mind one's own poetic or scientific garden without expecting any changes. On the contrary, one can say with perhaps greater legitimacy that everything is always new, if not in the elements themselves, then in the proportion of elements. Even at the very bottom of our decline, reason convinces us that hunger, murders, the misery of the masses, and wars, are not inevitable, though they exist now. The civilizing form that emerges from a line of verse, from the subject and the presentation of that subject in works of art, awakens hope, averts doubt. It is greater than the praise of this or that political system. Because whatever is realized in practice is always more or less dead for art and science worthy of their name. Practical discoveries are the gift that science, aspiring to its own super-practical aims, brings to people. We fly in airplanes, but at the same time a scientist is laboring over a discovery whose practical consequences are unclear to him; he is incapable of foreseeing them. Art is loaded with future forms and future systems, even though it still has no clear conception of them, because if it had, it would be only an obedient craft.

What I thought while reading Tolstoy played out against the background of that remembered tavern in Baranowicze. If we could show it to people of diverse characters and inclinations, we would obtain a test of those contradictory positions I have tried to represent. Tolstoy would say that this spectacle arouses disgust, and if that is all a civilization is capable of producing, it does not deserve a good fate. We should eradicate it and begin building on different principles. A politician who frightens us with the fulfillment of history would say the same: "Look, that is what the corruption in which you are living has come to. Does any of you dare to defend it? Aren't you and your entire junkyard of subtle beliefs and convictions condemned by the fact that instead of providing the inhabitants of this town with books, works of art, good and hygienically run restaurants and clubs, you have given them semiliteracy and a pitiful imitation of Western cabarets?" The timorous artist would agree with him, blushing: "Yes, yes, so what shall I do to destroy this worthless civilization? I shall devote myself body and soul to the service of the new, even if I myself should have to suffer. I will break with everything that I believed in heretofore. I do repent." Some other artist, someone like Witkiewicz, would insist that it doesn't concern him in the least. He knows, however, that Tolstoy and the politician and the timorous artist are not mistaken, that the future is opening out before them. He will not go along with them and asks only that he may die in peace.

But there is one more response. The dance hall in Baranowicze, Gothic cathedrals, Dante, and Shakespeare are products of the same civilization. Terrifying wars, exploitation, and degradation, and also the idea of a united humanity, workers' unions, insurance, and universal education are all products of this same civilization. Is it necessary to strike at the foundations of this civilization in order to uproot everything that encumbers it? Should what has grown up in it organically and out of respect for man be replaced by a new Plato's Republic? No.

Warsaw, 1943

LETTER ESSAYS OF

JERZY ANDRZEJEWSKI AND

CZESLAW MILOSZ

|

Czeslaw Milosz to Jerzy Andrzejewski

Dear Jerzy,

In the course of this third year of war I have often thought
of writing a new "confessions of a child of the age," such as
Musset wrote over a century ago—a confession that would exceed, in its violence and scream of pain, that Romantic era's
settling of accounts of the conscience. I assume that I would
not lack for reasons to complain and hurl curses against the
world. This is what I would like my future reader to see and
comprehend: my first memories of childhood, those long rows
of refugees' wagons on the crowded roads, the bellowing of
cattle being prodded along, the red glow of the fires of 1914,
revolutionary October in Russia and again the year 1920 on the
battlefields, and then growing up in the blind, unconscious *lu-
cidum intervallum* between the wars, the university in which
blind, unconscious people lectured about some by-products of
knowledge acquired in the junkyard of the nineteenth century.
I regret the silence that conceals the lofty and so foolish first
youth of my friends' and my Wilno, our dreams of revolution,
ended for many of us by years of imprisonment. I regret that
no voice will be heard explaining what a terrifying desert is
a society without a sense of the tragic, how in this desert a
couple of people, like Marian Zdziechowski, spoke up and
were completely misunderstood by the youth with whom they

might have been united by their common understanding of
the threat of coming events, but from whom they were separated by the impoverished education that these youth received,
with no sense of tradition. In truth, here, "where every deed is
born too soon, and every book too late," it would be worthwhile to speak of our own and others' sins, that blush of shame
when during our takeover of Cieszyn from Czechoslovakia I
was ordered to prepare radio communiqués and I did not simply spit on the orders, did not say "No"—through that same
lack of civic courage that has brought millions of Europeans to
the very depths of disgrace. It would be worth telling what
paths led my friends, after the Soviet troops invaded the Wilno
region, to commit treason against their own fatherland, against
honor, and about how an old Jewish woman on the Romanian
border handed me a slice of bread and asked me why we were
carrying on a hopeless struggle, and I could not find an answer,
and I was right not to, other than that worn-out shibboleth
"honor"—and how she grimaced with a bitter smile and said,
"So, honor, honor, and thousands of murdered women and
children, that's honor!" Perhaps I'll write about that someday.
But I doubt it. There would be too much pathos, too many cries
in it, too much rage, which we can wring from ourselves with
impunity only when we have destroyed something hateful that
oppresses us, when we raise our voice to protest against the
placid peace of an era grown fat with prosperity. But when one
exists on the ruins of Europe, tangible ruins more in the spiritual than the physical sense, what is there to destroy, and for
what? The evil that I might have been able to rebel against revealed itself in all its grandeur; it surpassed expectation and
analysis. There is no need to hunt it down and point out its disguises for people's eyes. It is tangible, near, and words have no
priority here. Therefore, all my effort turns, instead, to constructing, if not the new edifices of an unknown tomorrow,
then at least the foundations leading to a new systematic

doubting that might be capable of unearthing the few values worthy of rescue and development. And then a new note steals into my lamentation, my fury, my anger and pain—a note of calm deliberation, perhaps the same as that which caused an imprisoned Chinese poet around the seventh century A.D. to write this line: "In the midst of the storm that knocked me down, weeping, I write gentle poems." Faced with the simple and elementary things in people's lives, faced with physical suffering and death, it makes no sense to play hide-and-seek with oneself. The spiritual ruin that has befallen Europe has not passed us by, either; rather, it played out in us first (understand that as you wish, in either a narrower or wider sense), and the rest arrived as an inevitable consequence. Happy is he who cannot say this about himself—but I confess that I will suspect that such a man is lacking in candor, or I will doubt his self-awareness. Yes, "Know thyself" is harder today, perhaps, than ever before. If a man has stopped believing in something, he likes to believe that he still believes; if he has not yet begun to believe in something, he behaves as if he already believes. How difficult it is to look clearly at oneself and at others, to not tell lies, not create myths. For some time now I have been concentrating my efforts on this, but sometimes I am overwhelmed with doubt as to whether it is possible to achieve such clear vision. The times are no good, no good. Perhaps no worse than other times, but in any event, we have to take this time as it is, with goodwill, with affirmation, we have to say "yes" to the suffering it brings, to accept that this is exactly how I have been fated to live, and there is no recourse. A time (perhaps future memoirs will understand it this way) in which people prayed although heaven was empty, without God the Father on his throne, without bands of angels, without thunder ready to strike the unjust. A time in which philosophy was still pursued even though it had become a game played by the initiated, the escape of the rabbis of logistics, and had ceased to be the divine entertainment of wise men. A time in which art was still being created, when one paid with one's life for banal and quickly forgotten compositions of a few colors, a few expressions, when people tried in vain to track down greatness, thousands of miles removed from that rudimentary process known as contemporary art, that child of despairing irrationalisms. Am I really to name this time, to define it? That's not my business. Let historians of culture evaluate those dull rumblings of history preceding the great spectacle in which the assembled riches of optimistic theories, hypotheses, ideas, so vital in the last century, appeared to people's astonished eyes as a pile of rotten wood and straw—the proverbial miser's treasure suddenly brought out into the light of day.

So here we were, fated to live somehow in this time of feverish and vain trying on of all the old costumes with which we tried to cover our pitiful nakedness. Socialism had turned wormy and fallen apart; the idea of democracy had perished; Catholicism had been transformed into a desiccated mummy, its exterior varnished and lacquered, and once again was fashionable among the elite; philosophy was drowning in conventionalism and fictionalism, while Marxism "of the general line" jeered mercilessly at the "rotting" of western Europe— the bastard son, marked with the same stain of disease and degeneracy as its mother, who had rocked him in the arms of Hegels and Marxes. In the midst of this upheaval we heard the pleas of those in search of a so-called great idea ("We're in desperate need of a great idea"), the incantations of high-placed charlatans who understood "idea" as a device for influencing the mob, a device with which they could electrify those mobs and lead them blindly toward a more down-to-earth aim than that idea. Whatever in the world of ideas had no direct practical value, whatever did not serve immediate action, was rejected, unnecessary, laughable in its suspension and detachment. They came noisily to people like you and me, who were formed and prepared for work in the fields of thought and artistry, and not of the great deed, hurling insults at us for our separateness, our isolation, our lack of contact with the masses. "Oh, you intellectuals," they said contemptuously, "why don't you speak out in support of one side or another now, when struggle divides the world and it is necessary to stand on this or that barricade, why don't you subordinate your life to the idea that will transform the world, why are you not standard-bearers and drummers for the new movements? Twittering on the sidelines is unnecessary today; the only worthwhile man is one who has joined the ranks. You, you, suspended in a vacuum, torn from your roots, repeating out of habit a number of old phrases about humanitarianism, about the rights of man— phrases that entered the grave along with the cadets defending the Winter Palace in what used to be Petersburg, what kind of delusions are you treasuring, you who are as comical as old man Verkhovensky in Dostoevsky's *Demons*, who found it unbearable that a pair of boots is more useful than Raphael's *Madonna*. You, young men, but still clinging convulsively to what is dying, perishing in front of your eyes, carrying on snobbishly about Flaubert and Baudelaire, about lonely artists who create in opposition to the opinions of their contemporaries; why did you take them as models? Perhaps you know now what kind of fate awaits such aristocrats of the spirit today. When the enemy comes, one bullet or an executioner's club will destroy your subtle brain, your unborn works. What cries out in today's man is not the yearning born in a pampered intellect; it's a cry: to live, to live at any price, and those who desire to live must be as one, devoting their all.

What can one respond to such intellectual blackmail, to being pushed against the wall, when there is only a choice of "yes" or "no"? Should one enter into competition and hurl even more brutal, more obvious and simplified slogans? That would be useless. The dialectics of great totalistic currents, made into a devilishly efficient implement applied to the simplest minds, cannot be defeated by any form of argument. And yet, as you know, I have spent time in Russia, and when a Communist unfolds his iron dialectic in front of me, I shrug my shoulders because I believe my own eyes more than his reasoning. And yet, I have been living now for a couple of years under the rule of a "national revolution," and when someone begins to admire totalitarianism, I look at him as if he's a madman. So perhaps there dwells inside man some kind of intercessor that those currents do not consider, an intercessor that proclaims its veto against so-called unassailable arguments. And although so many undertakings and beliefs lie in ruins today, perhaps not everything has turned to dust, perhaps there is some foundation on which one can stand. To find it and to define it even in general terms—maybe that is the task for people of goodwill, who are not fated to mourn that which has passed, nor to grieve over what is, but to think about the future, even if it is not their own. I am bold enough to declare that I am not an adherent of any so-called idea, at least not of any that are currently in vogue. I don't think an antidote to the narcotics of the most varied myths can be a new narcotic, stronger than the previous ones. Perhaps because of this I am deserving of condemnation and contempt. But I have seen too many destructive results of great communal "dynamic" slogans, too much blood with which they mark their path, to be able to trust them. The so-called monolithic worldviews are monolithic only in that they fill the more difficult and complicated places with blindness, simplification, and mania. I have no intention of piecing together a catechism or confession of faith for myself, or of putting my signature beneath one that already exists. "Aha," they'll say in response to that, "an anarchistic individual." Not in the least. Those names, those labels are losing their meaning today, just like the whole repertoire of the past century. I desire only one thing: to be a man. That is both very much and very little; I suspect, however, that it is more than being a Communist or a racist or a liberal democrat. I have mentioned that intercessor which opposes the cacophony of doctrines, even if they are smooth, glib, incontrovertible, and wise with the evil wisdom of the unhappy—*excusez le mot*—sons of the earth. That intercessor—a grain of wisdom and ethical sense—is certainly not mine alone. I find it in an old woman who has pity for a Jewish child. I find it in an executioner who hesitates for a moment before committing murder. No, this cannot be called a delusion. And it is not a bland and banal thing. If one were to measure the currents of thought and works of art by that measure—a measure that was forgotten and rejected before riches burned, before capitals collapsed, and man again, returned to his primal nakedness, understood that only in that way is he different from a beast— oh, that is work for generations of thinkers and artists.

The demon of our age, the demon of practical application and direct action, responds: "Aha, so it's humanitarianism you want, noble and elevated. We know it, we know it well." After the 1914–18 war people also cried out in chorus, "Don't kill!" and issued pacifist manifestos. And those choruses of noble people, disgusted by the flow of blood of the tenderhearted, are the very ones who prepared a new and even crueler war, who disarmed the West's democracies, placed a sword in the hands of madmen, and were unable to pry it loose. No, whoever yearns to allow people to live must arm himself in pitilessness and fury, and hatred for those who do not want to support life. He must forget more than one beautiful commandment in the name of a future time when a better and happier humanity will be able to adhere to those commandments. From this follows the necessity of ideas that are technically efficient, that are capable of bringing order to human societies and holding them in check for as long as the name of humanitarianism is weakness. The devil uses tried-and-true means. Observe how eagerly he applies labels, how eagerly, as part of his blackmail, he makes use of the device of assigning people to a particular rank, what contempt he has for imagination that succeeds at proposing forms of communal life other than what has heretofore existed. The kernel of wisdom and ethical sense is not easy to cultivate, that is certain. Those good-hearted people made a great mistake when they assumed that it would be possible to eradicate wrongs and suffering automatically with sermons, instructions, and warnings. They were pacifists; they applied a bandage of sentimentality and tenderness to Europe's suppurating wounds. They thought that war and only war deserves the highest condemnation, that it is a misunderstanding, at the conclusion of which it is appropriate to wipe away its traces and return to previous good habits, preserving reminders of it in museums and books as an eternal warning for future generations. It didn't occur to them that industrial and social currents can be carriers of the germ of crime. They were unprepared for a blow from this direction. Deaf to the tales told by Russian émigrés, they transferred their warm feelings for the old French Revolution to the Russian Revolution, and fascism did not provoke any anxiety in them. Their humanitarianism was not the first link in the chain of efforts controlling European thought, but an addition, a lovely branch planted on top of the nineteenth-century edifice; it was intended to conceal the bitter, great crack produced by that war. They were certainly too optimistic and, whatever else one might say, they revered the conviction, instilled in them by their teachers, that progress could be harmonious and continuous—they were the last believers in the word "progress," which has been expunged from today's dictionaries. You surely remember Thomas Mann's "Warning for Europe," which is typical in this regard.

The development of this pinch of common sense, the appeal to moral law in man, demands a penetrating mind and a close connection with experience. But the experience of the last thirty years is not the type that leaves no traces. I repeat: this is foundational work, new work founded on principles, a complete revision of ideas, and not only of their applications. The prolonged labor of even the best preachers will amount to nothing if the evil spirits of the collective, a Nietzsche, a Sorel, or an André Gide, freely develop and enlarge upon their views alongside them, while Bergson or Freud turn the seriousness of human thought into dust, if liberal indifference permits the flowering of hateful doctrines that conflict with the most elementary demands of conscience. In the final analysis, the work I am speaking of does not—and should not—lead to universal disarmament, to that dangerous fiction that knocks weapons out of the hands of the guardians of law and places them in the hands of criminals, nor does it lead to capitalist democracy, or Cubist art, or to a philosophy that falls flat on its face before "the laws of life and blood." It can be called humanism, humanitarianism, whatever one wants, but the label will change nothing related to the value of that one life ring, the one way out that history has flung at us.

The devil says, "That's weakness." I confess that I don't know what is weakness, what is strength. I know that I am seeking a philosopher's stone, that I would like to begin to build something lasting, but can one build something lasting if the goal is not truth, but power? The few, most penetrating minds of that time understood that what constitutes the sickness of contemporary culture is the repudiation of truth for the sake of action—the opposition would appear to be absurd, monstrous—but nonetheless it has been transformed today into flesh. Like Pilate, that culture asked, "What is truth?" and washed its hands. Weakness! Is it not worth waiting for the final judgment to pronounce on this? Does strength not sometimes appear as weakness? Does not the same yearning that I feel in myself resonate in millions of human beings? But when that comes to pass . . . !

Weakness. I have no intention of ducking, of running away from the problem of weakness. On the contrary, today it is growing into a problem of the first magnitude. All of "good" Europe, the Europe of humanistic traditions, whose history is filled with cruelty and crimes but never openly praised as such—this Europe turned out to be laughable, powerless, impotent. "Evil" Europe, the Europe of openly worshipped lawlessness, transferred its affections to flamboyant effects, violent means, simplified ideas monopolized by the organs of propaganda. People listen with pleasure, but also with disbelief, to whoever still speaks the language of the good Europe. It sounds like a fairy tale about the happy isles in an age of bombers and tanks; it sounds like the words of the Gospel that priests perhaps read to soldiers on the battlefields of Russia. Let us agree that it sounds feeble, insubstantial, that it seems unmanly and stamped with hypocrisy. But in this battle of evil with the moral law in man, no words have yet been found to condemn doing harm to one's fellow man, no words that would resound like the trumpets of battle—at least, they have not been found since the angry, vengeful Jehovah of the Jews fell silent and was succeeded by a weak, mild Christ. If the remains of the good Europe are marked by hypocrisy and an excess of humanitarian phrases, that is not why they deserve to be condemned, since a thief who is ashamed of his deeds is worth more than a thief who praises himself with laughter.

My dear friend, don't interpret my words as a manifesto and don't lend them too programmatic a color. In the midst of destruction, I wish only to see something that opposes destruction, and it seems to me that not everything is lost yet. This era has brought all principles, all currents, to their ultimate consequence. And in that, perhaps, lies hope. Before fruits in the garden of thought ripened, patient gardeners allowed all species of trees to grow. But when the fruit on some of the trees turns out to be poisonous, is it not time to distinguish among species? Even if insane gardeners were to insist that the poisonous fruits are the tastiest, the healthiest, and sing out in a chorus, "Who will prove to us that they are poisonous, how will they do it, since they serve us admirably?" would that provide a sufficient reason to doubt a normal man's intuition?

August 22, 1942

II

Jerzy Andrzejewski to Czeslaw Milosz

Dear Czeslaw,

You have raised so many different questions, considering some of them at length and with precision, while barely touching upon others, that to tell you the truth, now that it is my turn to respond, I am in a tizzy over which reflections, generalizations, feelings, and doubts to engage with from among this tangle, and what to pass over in silence. Speaking frankly, I would like to deal with all these threads and not pass over any of them, because while some of them appeal to me with their common sense and orientation to the future, others awaken doubts of various intensity, up to and including unequivocal opposition. It seems that it would be hard to have a different initial reaction, a colder one, shall we say, one that carries with it from the very first the capacity to make choices and establish hierarchies. The times in which we are living, along with our experiences during the past few years, both prewar and wartime, have made us particularly sensitive to human voices, including those that resonate piercingly and find listeners throughout the world, along with those which, like yours, resound in isolation or, at the moment, in dialogue. The boundlessness of human suffering and the equal boundlessness of the most despicable human instincts lead us ever deeper into the spectacle that is playing out before us, and imagina-

tion, often against our will, inclines us to pay distressed attention even to those human voices whose whisper or scream re-
sounds far away from us on battlefields, in prisons, in the
camps, and under the roofs of existences that are unknown to
us. As for me, I find in myself so much ignorance and doubt,
and at the same time such a need and yearning to achieve at
least a scrap of knowledge that would solidify the ground under my feet and give solace to my gaze, so that I might know
how, be able, or want—choose which of these verbs to accord
primacy to—to depend on myself alone in the hope that there
and only there will I find the strength that I need, the intercessor who will illuminate what seems dark to me, unravel what I
judge to be indecipherable. Until very recently I still thought
that isolation that is unlikely to be breached is the sole and ultimate lot of human fate from the moment of the first glim-
mers of independent thought up until the final hour. Conrad's
pathos-filled comment about living and dying in isolation
struck me as a truth that both my own inner experience and
my observations of other people's lives confirmed. Today I am
not so certain. Rather, I am inclined to think that despite what
hatred, contempt, and cruelty reveal to our eyes, despite evil
and devastation, people are united by a solidarity that is deeper
than one might think, a deeper fraternity, much deeper than
the three triumphant slogans of the French Revolution. I
think that one must look for help from people and that one can
find it there. I would also argue that the burden of isolation
that has so tragically crushed man in recent years was assumed
voluntarily by man; even more, he began to consider this hopeless stain as a noble sign of his distinction and tragic pride.
Because man has always and everywhere been capable of heroism, the delusional cursed circle of isolation has closed off
many an act of heroism, sometimes in works of art, sometimes
simply in life.

But wait, my friend, I see that I am beginning to flee from

your letter with excessive haste; it is not good to float along in this problem as in a kayak on a swift mountain river. True, interesting landscapes might be revealed; such a route has so many charms and temptations that it would be best to go on foot now, and not to move along too quickly. It will be more peaceful this way; no one is chasing us, after all, aside from our own impatience, and you know what an unreliable friend that can be. In order to rid myself of temptations, taking up the thread I uncovered at the beginning, I must state that nothing other than the need and effort to open myself to the world outside complicates my engagement with your letter. Recalling the nice little tale about the donkey who was torn between two different feeds, it is possible to find the other side of the coin in a reaction like mine. Too bad. Because aside from my interest in its widely varying contents, your letter arouses my curiosity as a particular fragmentary manifestation of human individuality that, as you will figure out, is you in this particular instance. It contains two contradictory visions of the world: the one condemnatory, steeped in dark eschatological vapors, and the other its polar opposite, like a perfect form of wisdom and harmony carved from a block of marble; you admit that it is an entirely interesting object for psychological investigations, even more, for investigations that with luck might serve as a springboard for contemplating the type of self-contradictions in contemporary man, or, to be more precise, of the contemporary intellectual. I can already see the apprehension on your face. But don't be afraid, I shall not treat you as a guinea pig, even though a vague foreboding has whispered to me that I might reach certain conclusions by following that path. My unfortunate tact keeps me from performing that experiment. Also, not without a touch of envy, I have to recall that Witold Gombrowicz, if he hadn't changed under "the deep blue sky of Argentina," would have placed you on the laboratory bench without a moment's hesitation. As for me, reserving this opportunity for my strictly private use, not to be preserved even on paper, I shall take up only the problems you pose. In brief, warnings and doubts.

It wouldn't have worried me had you never written this new confession of a child of our age. It is very dangerous to publish a testimony for a generation while maintaining a lyrical posture toward events rather than an epic approach, which alone can resurrect people and affairs in their objective dimensions, in a way approaching the truth. I prefer Stendhal's writing about Napoleon to Musset's; *Confession of a Child of the Age* bores me terribly, but *The Red and the Black* and *The Charterhouse of Parma* are among my best-loved books. Years from now, perhaps, you will be able to bring to life the years of your childhood and youth, Wilno and your friends, those times of so many misunderstandings, tragic complexities—yes, years from now, but looking at those times, at those people, and at yourself from a temporal distance and never in the style you employ to write about those matters now. Our times are difficult, complicated, they are white-hot, painful. For years now there have been many open, maliciously festering wounds, many new wounds. To enter into that gloomy abyss, to walk on the coals and ashes, to observe the fires blazing everywhere, to hear the roar of embittered nations and so many voices of despair and suffering, perhaps to descend even deeper to where only silence arouses terror, and then what? To be inside this and write about it? No, I think one has to get past one's time in order to write about it. In a certain sense, one has to achieve insensitivity. Understand me. I am not thinking about coldheartedness, about some indifferent, practically inhuman gaze. No. I am talking about insensitivity to one's own time. About tearing away the most painful layer of sensitivity and impressionability. About closing one's ears to the cries of a mother whose only son was tortured in prison. Not to hear, not to see the millions of present-day sufferings. To pass by, with an indifferent gaze, the man who is suffering now and, being thus hardened against the world, to enter into communion in oneself with people, with people in general, not communion with a particular person, but communion with men, I repeat, in general. To sympathize, hate, share guilt, cleanse, condemn—yes! But beyond a man who exists in reality and in reality demands sympathy or the sharing of guilt, or who arouses real hatred. I am absolutely certain that to create a man in a work of art, and to live with a man, man to man, are, alas, very different things.

But these are only marginal notes, intended to explain, if only in coarsest outline, why I think that you, who are the most profoundly lyrical psychological construct, would be incapable of applying "the highest justice . . . multiple and unique, concealed beneath all sorts of disguises," to the difficult years of your youth. Understand, too, as a marginal note, my reflex of bitter astonishment when I read your recollection of the conversation you had with the old Jewish woman on the Romanian border in that famous September. Like you, I think that the word "honor," like many other "good" words, has been worn threadbare, but its dignity can be restored by the person who uses it. I hope that in this letter or in succeeding ones I will have occasion to elaborate on this and to stress more fully how it is that people whom you refer to as "of goodwill" feel a panicky fear of "good" words and "good" emotions, how easily they have allowed themselves to be blackmailed by the cacophony of criminals screaming at the top of their lungs, "Liberty, honor, justice, virtue, heroism!" how from excessive sensitivity they resigned their positions and handed over their most valuable weapon to the clutches of despicable men. Further: I am not convinced that "Catholicism has been transformed into a desiccated mummy," and that the faith we do not have (I will have a lot to say about this), but that is certainly held by many people, has "its exterior varnished and lacquered." I would be afraid of coming up with a formulation like this, if it is supposed to express something other than the definition of a subjective state. Your assertion that the idea of democracy is dying aroused the same hesitation in me. Who knows whether in the maelstrom of tragic entanglements we are not simplifying our task, murdering with the pattern of Shakespearean tragedies not people but ideas, one after another. I draw your attention to the fact that among many perverse inclinations of contemporary thought, one of them, which appears characteristically in people who for some reason or other yearn for renewal, is the yearning to find oneself in a cemetery. Like the majority of perverse inclinations, this yearning is usually carefully concealed, but one can discover material for a Tamerlane in the heart of more than one or two intellectuals.

Finally, let me put an end to these details, although I am expressing myself poorly, because each of these details opens up onto expansive, copious perspectives. If you will allow me not to be definitive, I shall express one more doubt. Speaking correctly about the inadequate resonance and echo nowadays of humanitarian phrases, as you put it, you write that "in this battle of evil with the moral law in man, no words have yet been found to condemn doing harm to one's fellow man, no words that would resound like the trumpets of battle—at least, they have not been found since the angry, vengeful Jehovah of the Jews fell silent and was succeeded by a weak, mild Christ." My dear friend, at the end of that sentence you should have hastily signed the names of Nietzsche and his disciples from various parishes, ending with Alfred Rosenberg, who used a similar definition of Christ in his *Myth of the Twentieth Century* as the Hitler regime's official judgment. I do not doubt that that confluence is far from what you intended. It struck me as either an overstatement in the heat of writing or, if it arose deliberately, then as, shall we say, excessive simplification. I would not feel comfortable in the skin of an exegete of the Gospels, so my one counterargument can be sending you back to the source itself. If you would go to the Epistles of Paul, or the Church Fathers, to Saint Thomas, even to the Spanish mystics, ending with Newman and the German and French Catholics of our day, that would suffice, I think, to liberate the figure of Christ himself and the teachings emanating from the Gospels from a global accusation of gentleness and weakness. If, however, you are concerned with the abstractness of words that fight against evil, I think that there have been a great many over the course of the centuries, and precisely ones that resounded like "trumpets of battle," because there is no other way to describe the voice of Bernard de Clairvaux, Francis of Assisi, Savonarola, or Teresa of Avila. No doubt there are similar voices resounding in our time, too, only perhaps we do not always hear them, and even if we do hear them, they seem too frail and anemic, incommensurable with the evil about which you have written. But many "people of goodwill" forget one thing: can the faint echo of the "trumpets of battle," their high-pitched call and the purity of their tone, be heard by the deaf or the hard of hearing? It's easy to detect danger in their passionate striving for a new word. The insatiability accompanying unremitting consciousness ("That's not it yet, not it!") can flow just as easily from the finest yearnings as from an inner acceptance of an eternal obstacle race in which the goal of the race is slowly forgotten and the race itself becomes its own goal. It is very easy to erase the image of objective truth and replace it with the form of one's own I, questing and insatiable. Do I have to tell you, my friend, what various consequences derive from those two similar positions that are not much different externally, but differ in essence! One more point, perhaps the most important of all. It seems to me that measured on the scale of human ordeals and experience, even the mightiest call of the "trumpets of battle" of good can never equal the intensity of the voices of evil. I am aware of

my inclination to favor well-stated but simplistic generalizations. But this is exactly where generalization strikes me as
most powerful, and perhaps I'm not far off the mark when I
say that in general evil does not require very much of us, while
good demands a great deal. With pity, anger, hatred, suffering,
we can finally, one way or another, respond to evil. But these
emotions need not transform us, and they do not make demands on us insistently for any effort on our part. Quite simply,
they either exist within a person or they do not. One person,
seeing a criminal, will weep, while another will cast a stone at
him. It's an entirely different matter when a distant echo of
the "trumpets of battle" of good reaches us; it really doesn't
matter, my friend, if it's a faint or loud sound. You yourself
write about the "ethical sense" that you discover in an old
woman taking pity on a Jewish child on the street. You admit
that this is a very quiet voice, and if one were to compare it
with the cacophony of monstrosities that the walled-in ghetto
presents (and, after all, that is only one portion of the crimes of
this world), it would sound fainter than the faintest of whispers. Nonetheless! So, perhaps we might agree that the intensity of a voice is not the most important thing, and that we *can*
perceive the lone voice of that woman as very, very resonant.
But what is hearing? Don't you agree that it is too little and
that as a matter of fact there ought to be something more? If
I am not mistaken, and I am relying here on my own experience, a step in the direction of that "something more" is quite
difficult, and further steps are still more difficult, and I think
that the farther one goes, the more difficult and risky it becomes. But it seems probable that the echoes of the "trumpets
of battle" are heard more clearly and more often with every
step.

    You are right to say that "the appeal to moral law in man
demands . . . a close connection with experience." It seems we
are approaching the center of a problem around which we

have been circling with a great deal of anxiety, and which you expressed in the very elastic generalization "to be a man." Ah, a man, a man! I imagine that with your distrust of "good" words and feelings, though you yourself placed a pathetic exclamation point over the idea of "man," you will soon hunt down the cliché in this. True, it can be a cliché. It is one of those assertions that are accompanied, like a shadow or an echo, by the question: "But what kind of a man?!" It seems that we have bidden farewell, for a long time, if not forever, to the principle of the equality of men, just as we have to the idea of continuous progress, or the doctrine of the innate goodness of the human being. The principle of the individualization of human beings is better suited to our vision of the world and our experience, as is our acceptance of the fact that there exist differences between us ranging from the tiniest and least important to the greatest disproportions. Yet you can imagine how easy it is, with such a viewpoint, to overstep the mark and, by asserting that each person is different, is unique and irreplaceable, erase all commonality between people. The fascisms of our time have presented us with a test case of what reality and the relations among people begin to look like when even the near universal fact that all human beings possess one head, two arms, and two legs has been questioned as evidence of a biological bond. I should add parenthetically that perhaps some deeper link exists between the individualistic urges of the Teutonic tribe and its current ideology. Who can say if the path from the medieval mystics, through Luther, Romanticism, and all the way to *Mein Kampf* and *The Myth of the Twentieth Century* isn't less circuitous than it might seem. We find ourselves in a bizarre and, I would argue, a drastic situation. On the one hand, we have been profoundly influenced by the conviction that human lives are unequal; on the other, fascisms and historical materialism, which are derived from different premises and on a different model, present us with dreadful spectacles of what the division between man and man can look like in practice. Taking this into consideration, when one looks at the Gestapo slaughtering Jews, or at the Communists liquidating the bourgeois intelligentsia, it is difficult to resist the bitter conclusion that the principle that measures their attitude to people is not, for us [?], such a foreign and distant concept. The paths of human thought are slippery, and sometimes a small step separates the intellectual at his desk from the hooligan acting upon his ideas. Man, in turn, despite what one might conclude from his improbable endurance, is a very delicate construct, and tiny touch-ups, seemingly innocent improvements, suffice for the whole to seem suddenly new, terrifyingly new.

If, then, we are faced with an urgent task, I think that task is the necessity of reconciling two contradictory principles, one of which individualizes people and the other of which binds them together by their commonality. Without a doubt, one can solve one's personal problems by the full sense of one's own separateness and by erasing one's solidarity with the human race. Religion opens the gate wide for such an individual. I shall refrain for the moment from judging such a stance, and shall only assert that within the confines of the life of the individual it is possible and, what is more, in exceptional cases it can bring quite significant achievements.

On the other hand, social approval, the law of collective life, must question such a position and will definitely do so, even though the sense and the hierarchy of the slogans shouted in defense of communal values are often quite dubious. A sentence that I recently stumbled across brought this home to me. It was spoken by the famous nineteenth-century preacher Father Lacordaire. Here is the sentence: "Don't worry so much about saving your own soul; worry about saving the world—and you will save your soul." I think that this advice makes sense even for someone who would prefer to separate the concept of salvation from its supernatural contents.

But let me return to that commonality. You write toward the end of your letter that "in the midst of destruction, I wish only to see something that opposes destruction." Before that, you made it clear in several places that you have been trying to find a similar value in man, sometimes calling that value reason, sometimes moral law or moral sanction. We are not going to quarrel about words! We know very well what this is about, and it seems to me that we are in complete agreement. But in this instance, to be in agreement is simultaneously both a great deal and very little!

I noted at the outset that I believe in people's ability to communicate with each other, and despite much experience, I believe in a deeper solidarity that unites people, and in a deeper fraternity among them. My life experiences (alongside that other one) and my inner necessity assert this.

But this conviction of mine does not in any way free me from the consciousness that all these ideas, taken individually and as a whole, weigh no more than a handful of sand. We know how often the words "fraternity" and "solidarity" fall from behind the barricades of those opposing fascisms. We know just as well that in the same way, and for the same words, people are dying who bring the world only destruction, the pride of the victors, and contempt for the defeated. So we say that we want to have nothing to do with this kind of fraternity and this kind of solidarity. "Then with what kind?" the question arises. And what moral law in man are we talking about? The law of a fascist, the law of a Marxist, perhaps the law of a Christian? Each of them brings a different world, different laws in the world, and a different man in the world and among people. A different man, that is, if it is a matter of the direction and goal of his aspirations. So it turns out that the concept of a moral law is still too little to unite "the sons of the earth" (to use your phrase) with a real, permanent bond. Here we have a new fracture, and once again what we hoped would support us opens up a chasm between people, commands them to trample and destroy each other.

I do not think that we ought to be in too much of a rush to abandon this position, however. On the contrary, I would be inclined to advise a thorough excavation and examination of the terrain. I can easily imagine what I would find in such an excavated trench: I would find myself, a man—more precisely, a man who is conscious of possessing a moral norm. It is still quiet, but we should not be fooled. We need only listen more intently to catch the murmurs approaching in the distance. Another moment, and massive detachments of armored moral laws will appear, some of them under the black spider of the swastika, others amid the flapping of red banners, and still others with crosses, portable shrines, and images of the saints. Ah, well!

I must confess to you that although I advise calm, I am somewhat anxious and nervous. Their ranks are drawing near. I am alone—a man with the moral law. I have to arm myself somehow. What can I do? Squatting in the trench that I dug for either my own destruction or my salvation, I ask, "This moral law, whose presence I sense in myself, sometimes as distinctly as the beating of my heart, sometimes as vaguely as nostalgia—is this law the subtle action of my brain or is it the reflection of a Truth that lies beyond me and, in general, beyond human experience?" Yearning for goodness, do I yearn as a man born in Warsaw in August 1909, the son of a merchant and an impoverished noblewoman, a Pole who has not completed his university education, a writer, or do I yearn as a participant in the world of creation, a tiny creature bearing within him from birth to death a grain of the highest Wisdom, one among millions who once lived, are living now, will yet live, and who are gifted with the very same grain, immutable through the ages?

Dear Czeslaw, I can already see the swastikas, banners, and portable shrines on the horizon. If you are sleeping, wake up; if you are eating, abandon your food, your work, and your house. Come to the rescue.

III

Czeslaw Milosz to Jerzy Andrzejewski

Dear Jerzy,

Doubt is a noble thing. I believe that if there were a recurrence of the biblical experience of Sodom, it would be necessary to seek the righteous among those who profess doubt rather than among believers. And yet, as you know, doubt is traditionally bathed in a glow and accorded dignity solely because it serves the seekers of truth as a weapon. Indeed, the most fervent people are doubters. Allow me, then, to take both sides, and do not think that when I speak as one who knows with a certainty, I do not also doubt; do not think, either, that when I doubt, I am not also sensing right beside me, close enough to touch them, definite, indisputable things. Just as human sight is capable of taking in only one side of an apple, human speech cannot encompass any phenomenon in its total roundness. The other side always remains in shadow. You summon me to assist in the struggle against armies of the most varied moral laws, armies equipped with swastikas, hammers and sickles, portable shrines, banners. Each of them insists that only its system of values is salutary, appropriate, useful. Each of them rushes around the world, exhorting people to join its ranks. Looking at this variety of mutually contradictory laws, you ask what is it that could convince you that your own intuition will not lead you astray; you ask about criteria, about guidelines. You ask, won't this stage be subject to constant change in response to particular social conditions, to a person's origins and upbringing, and if that is the case, can that constantly shifting line, that function of the most diverse factors, be the standard by which the currents and ideas creating contemporary history should be measured?

Yes, this is a vague, uncertain foundation, so vague and uncertain that it is easy to doubt its existence. All it takes is to raise one human generation in a new, changed way, instructing them in a different good and a different evil, and what a dozen years ago would have elicited universal indignation will elicit universal praise. The elasticity of human nature appears to have no limits; indeed, our own age is an age of monstrous experiences which prove this alleged truth clearly and persuasively. But still I must console you. Attempting to appeal to that nebulous element, the kernel of common sense in man, is nothing new, by any means; it is not like the discovery of a new continent. On the contrary, it is as old as the world, or, at any rate, as old as culture that can be traced back to ancient Greece. This element has been known by a great variety of names throughout history. Depending on the epoch, and on intellectual and linguistic development, it has been called reason, daimonion, common sense, the categorical imperative, the moral instinct. And although different faiths and different laws prevailed, enforced by the might of the sword, more than one Socrates drank poison in the name of that vague, wondrously indefinable voice, more than one humanist was burned at the stake. Only yesterday, Aldous Huxley, whose *Jesting Pilate* is such depressing, unpleasant reading (since it reveals the weakness of the West), that skeptical Huxley took a trip around the world in search of verities, and in this summary of the results of his journey he states that although almost all his convictions were demolished as a consequence of his contact with the immense variety of human beliefs, passions, and customs, still, he was able to preserve one conviction. That one conviction was his belief in the similarity of human nature, irrespective of race, religion, and language, his belief in the identical moral sense and similar definition of good and evil, be it in Europe or China or the Polynesian islands. Could it be that people like Huxley were the last, unworthy heirs of the European tradition? Could it be that their judgment was the last of the old world's delusions, a weak and deformed reflection of the final wave of humanism? And that in that case one ought to look at the extermination of people in camps, in prisons, with new eyes—look at it as a battle between red ants and black ants, without recognizing either the one or the other as in the right, but rather, granting that both species are right? Or perhaps we should instead admit that some human right, some fulfillment of moral law belongs to one side, and that their persecutors do not share that right. But if we take that position, we return to the vague kernel of ethical intuition; verily, this is not something that has long since been put to rest, that should have been consigned by now to oblivion.

At this point in my argument, I am overcome with shame. I bow my head in sorrow over my own tendencies, which prod me toward a greater zealousness than I desire. It is enough for me to loosen the reins a bit, and I begin to pontificate in the manner of a prophet or preacher . . . Knowing how easily I lapse into exaltation, I fear that I will soon mention the devil who summons people to mass by ringing his tail. I have very few qualifications to be a bard. So let us quickly extinguish exaltation with renewed doubt; let us return to bitter, scathing questions.

Over the last few years, observing the spectacle in which we all are also actors, I have been astonished—no less, I am sure, than you—by the plasticity of human nature. That man can endure relatively easily the loss of his property, of his family, his beloved profession, is not what I find most astonishing.

That he grows accustomed to hunger, to cold, to being beaten about the face and kicked, also fits within the boundaries of the understandable. But beyond that stretches a dark expanse of wonders, as yet unsuspected perspectives. Let us take the question of one's relationship to death. In so-called normal times (and perhaps ours actually are normal) death is surrounded by a ritual of magic gestures, incantations, and rites. The smell of death makes the neck hair of animals stand on end, but humankind drowns out the terror with the beating of tom-toms, the sound of organs, and the singing of mournful songs. Until recently, in Belorussia women mourners still keened over fresh graves. These rites give death the character of a singular event, the appearance of a phenomenon that disturbs the natural order; they make of death an event that is utterly specific, seemingly unrepeatable. As far as I can recall from my reading of the scholarly literature on this matter, the idea that death is inevitable is alien to primitive tribes—they ascribe death, if it is not the result of being eaten by wild beasts or being killed during warfare, to the influence of evil spells. Perhaps this, too, testifies to a ceremonious attitude toward death (if I may call it that). It is a different matter when, as today, new ideas are being born—for example, the idea of the mass extermination of people, akin to the extermination of bedbugs or flies. There is no longer any place for ceremoniousness. After a while these striking changes penetrate the psyche of the masses, who daily confront this phenomenon. A person lived, spoke, thought, felt. Then, the next day he's gone. (*"Jego voobshche nigde net"*—"In general, he's nowhere," as a certain Bolshevik told me when I asked him about the fate of Bruno Jasieński.) Death makes no more of an impression than the drowning of an ant makes on its comrades parading beside it on the tabletop. A certain insectivity of life and death, as I'd like to call it, is created. I suspect that we are beginning to look at man partly as a living piece of meat with tufts of hair on his head and his sexual organs, partly as an amusing toy that speaks, moves—but all one has to do is raise one's hand and squeeze the trigger and an ordinary object is lying in the same place, as inert as wood and stone. Who knows, perhaps this is the path to absolute indifference, including indifference to one's own death. It may happen that with good training and appropriate schooling, people will die easily, from a lack of desire; they will treat dying as almost an everyday activity, between two shots of vodka and a cigarette that they won't get to smoke.

In any event, this will certainly lead to indifference to the death of others and to a change in the classification of murder as an ugly deed. Causing someone's death is dissociated from the reek of demonism, pangs of conscience, and similar accessories of Shakespearean drama. Young men in perfectly clean uniforms can then shoot people while gnawing on a ham sandwich. Yet another novelty is connected with this: criminal law, paralleling the ethical feeling of civilized societies, has linked punishment to the fact of guilt. Because X is guilty, X must die or must be placed behind bars. Today, the issue of guilt is fading into the background, and how pernicious or dispensable a given individual may be in relation to society has emerged in the foreground. X dies, even though he did nothing bad; he dies because his hair color, the shape of his nose, or his parents' background are considered sufficient signs of his perniciousness. And it is difficult to cry out that this is happening outside the law, that these discoveries of a destructive war are the same as collective responsibility. On the contrary, the development of criminal law is clearly moving in this direction; the German and Russian criminal codes are symptomatic (see their definition of crime).

Down the road lie unequal rights and unequal obligations. For some one hundred years the democracies of the West have held to the conviction that all people are equal under the sun and should be judged according to the same principles—which in practice came down to a glaring inequality, depending on the amount of property people owned. The Middle Ages knew a strict caste system, which was gradually tempered by modern mores. The murder of a knight was not the same then as the murder of a merchant or a peasant, although genuine religiosity placed certain limitations on that disparity. In Sparta, as Taine reports, youths who trained for battle in camps would come out onto the roads at night in order to kill a couple of late-returning helots from time to time, for the experience and to prove that they had mastered the soldier's trade.

Today, the same differentiation is surfacing again, the same inequality of obligations and privileges. The claim that the democratic concept of equality is a definite model and ideal, and that what we see around us is a distortion and perversion, is therefore, at the very least, a doubtful proposition. To choose among the ebb and flow of the most varied aspirations of human mores, to take one period (and a rather short one, at that) as a model, and to condemn others—is that not a gross error, yet another error of untroubled evolutionism and faith in Progress?

Take the problem of freedom of thought. True, there have been periods when freedom of thought was placed very high, making it one of the hallmarks of man. But those years (from the start of the Renaissance, shall we say, until the end of the nineteenth century) are not particularly binding on us. Excellent educational results (and despite everything, we must include among them results that the Soviet Union can boast of) were achieved by the total elimination of independent thinking, and it turned out that people can get along quite well without freedom of thought. The question can also arise whether with the development of such technological means of communication as radio, film, and the daily press, freedom of thought is possible at all. Does this not mean constant infection with whatever ideas are in circulation, and even that when the masses are given ostensible freedom they may succumb to total unification?

Evidently, human plasticity is great and the search for constants, for an "eternal man" might turn out to be a risky undertaking. It does not seem to me, however, that this plasticity is limitless. It gives one pause that even the most incompatible moral-political systems appeal to the same elements in man and, independently of the various forms assumed by whatever ethical currents are in circulation, they make use of a similar ethical judgment. The call to heroism and sacrifice, whether in the name of the German people or the socialist fatherland of the working people, incorporates a scheme that is in no way different from the praise of patriotism and masculine courage in Plato's time. The propaganda of the various fascisms rolls out images of a "new order" in which, in contradistinction to the former democratic lack of order, people will be able to live happily, without fear of unemployment, wars, and economic pressure—that product of "Judaeo-plutocracy." The working people will be surrounded by care, mothers will have better conditions than in societies based on respect for money, and participation in the universal well-being and harmony will be shared among the people according to their deserts.

The falsehood of such assurances does not alter the fact that they appeal to the sense of rightness, to the thirst for justice in man. Propaganda devotes a great deal of effort to creating in soldiers faith in a "just cause," and the execution and torture of "worse" peoples has been given an equally broad justification.

These are not merely enemies—for enemies the chivalric code, so highly valued in Germany, demands a certain respect. These are enemies of the human race, subhumans, and as such they are released from the prescriptions of ethics. Photographs of Poles, Jews, or Soviet commissars, appropriately retouched,

are supposed to convince the viewer of the fundamental difference of these creatures, to inculcate faith in their inferiority.
The principles of honor and ethics remain in place, but as we
know, they always apply only to relations among people. Certain groups of people are bracketed out, and from then on it is
permissible to condemn them without breaking these noble
commandments in any way. The presentation of the Germans
as a people who have been wronged and hemmed in until
now—oh, those hastily unearthed strata of *ressentiment*—does
not differ from the depiction of the proletariat as an oppressed
class, which at long last is meting out justice. I dare say, too,
that the moral sense as a motor force is very much alive both in
fascism and in communism, and that when we observe the
monstrous things they do in practice, we should ascribe them
not so much to the disappearance of all ethical brakes as to a
change in motivation. This means that within those various
armies that carry around the swastika, the hammer and sickle,
portable shrines, and banners, there is one and the same ethical scheme, and that only its being filled with various contents
is what gives these varying results. One can compare this to
an algebraic model: depending on the values assigned to the
symbols in an equation, various combinations are possible.
National Socialism praises fraternity, collegiality, righteousness, nobility in relations between people, only "people" here
means Germans and, more exactly, good Germans who follow
their Führer's commands. The French newspapers, which have
lately been trumpeting the ideology of "national revolution"
with a significant dose of cynicism, have been competing with
each other in elaborating images of the nobility and beauty of
the "new order." Lies like that are extremely comforting. The
person who lies demonstrates that he recognizes a fictitious image as more alluring than reality. Indeed, propaganda is perhaps nothing but an appeal to man's instinctual sense of what
ought to be—a perverse appeal, to be sure, which falsifies in-

nate proportions. And although from time to time in the speeches of fascist men of state an open confession of crime can be heard that makes the blood run cold in our veins, the majority of their statements are lies, sentimental appeals to God to bestow his blessings, and the rending of garments over the other side's lack of morality. This demonstrates that Machiavelli's prescription is immortal and that a ruler would be acting badly if he appealed exclusively to man's basest urges. On the contrary, while doing evil, he must robe himself in the toga of a benefactor of humanity, a savior, one who exacts vengeance for injuries—a precept that today's pupils of Machiavelli are following quite faithfully on the whole. Yes, yes, this is all as old as the earth; this is all known, and undoubtedly only the absence of a necessary distance places in our mouths a sentence about man's total plasticity, the total novelty of what is being played out in front of our eyes.

Since we agree that even in the seemingly most predatory armies and programs an elementary ethical sense is surrounded with a certain degree of deference, we confront another problem. That same ethical scheme, that same sympathy for the good and disinclination toward evil lead to such varied deeds and are filled with such varied contents! The hierarchy of ethical values is easily overturned and its ranks reassembled. A German, a model son, husband, loving father of a family, will torment a subhuman, a Jew, or a Soviet soldier, because he is obsessed with his vision of duty and justice, which commands him to cleanse Europe of similar vermin. The fact that a characteristic dose of sadism is added to the mix still does not undermine my example. A purely bestial sadism, naked and plain, occurs much more rarely than motivated sadism, equipped with all the arguments needed to make it into a noble and positive inclination. Jews and Bolsheviks are responsible for the war, they are harmful, they murdered Germans, they are subhumans, they are filthy, they belong to the lowest race, which is incapable of culture—rationalizations like these come to the aid of sadism, the beast that slumbers in every man, when it feels like going on a rampage with impunity— with impunity, which is to say, on the margins of the ethically ordered rest of his life, leaving him clean hands that can stroke a child's head or light the candles on the tree on Christmas Eve. What contents, then, should we use to flesh out a structure for an ethical norm, what should it be aimed at if it is not to lead us into depravity? Does a single true content exist while others are a counterfeit and a fraud? Contrary to all those powerful slogans of historicism, which denies that there are immutable, constant elements, I believe that one such element does exist. Every serious Christian will have no trouble agreeing with me, since the one, eternally binding truth of the Gospels does not permit any deviations or sophistry. I said in my previous letter that I am searching for a reliable foundation apart from any faith, and that I see that foundation in the ethical instinct—or whatever one might like to call it, that it is the sole example in a vortex of dubious things. And now here I am, all confused. How can it be, one might ask, if that same ethical drive without which it is impossible, in general, to build civilization, at one time justifies slavery, then again lauds the burning of sorcerors at the stake or the slaughter of tens of thousands of Albigensians, and on another occasion is perfectly comfortable accepting the extermination of non-German peoples—can one accept that as a higher instance, as a model for deeds and ideas?! It is, perhaps, only an innate drive to assign value, but *how* to make those distinctions remains an open question, and once again we are deprived of any fixed point.

Here we touch upon the fundamental argument that has been going on for centuries in the bosom of Western civilization between the pessimistic and optimistic conceptions of man. Christianity has not looked with confidence upon man's innate capacity to distinguish between good and evil. The virtue of the Stoics, which existed without divine assistance, sinned in Christianity's view by an excess of pride. Human beings' innate inclinations, if not illuminated by the light of grace, could lead, in the opinion of the Church, solely to sin, blindness, and error. In addition, the Western Church looked with a certain amount of disbelief upon the earning of that grace in isolation, upon the settling of accounts between God and a human soul within the privacy conferred by four walls. *Ecclesia* was to be the intermediary, the dispenser of grace by means of the sacraments created for that purpose. And although human reason was not actually surrounded with contempt, reason had always to follow the path of God's law; reason—to use the language of the Church doctors—had to be illuminated by the sun of supernatural knowledge. This lack of confidence in man's possession of common sense, this reliance not on the average person's intuition but on the opinion of *Ecclesiae militantis*, expresses a pessimistic view of human nature as marred by original sin and incapable of distinguishing between good and evil without resorting to extraordinary means. The Renaissance and Reformation were an act of faith in autonomous morality, in the grain of truth within each person; they applauded natural reason. The bonds of the Church organization and the assistance of the sacraments were unnecessary, since each human being possesses a voice that dictates unerringly what he should do and what he should not do. Grace and damnation became a mystery of the human heart, for which no priest can offer relief nor any encyclical simplify the path. That was the germ of faith in man as the judge of his own actions; that is how man grows to colossal proportions: master of his own destiny, answering for it only and exclusively to God. And then along comes that optimist Rousseau, reared in the Protestant spirit, and he proclaims man's natural goodness, paints in the most exuberant colors all the innate drives of the human animal, accusing civilization of perverting them. Next comes the optimist and Protestant Nietzsche, summoning man to total liberation from the chains of "slave morality," inciting him to a transformation of civilization in the spirit of power and health, but not truth, and pronouncing the slogan, "Let truth die, let life triumph!" (And so it did, poor, mad philologist.) Nietzsche is seconded by the Protestant and optimist Gide, his ardent admirer. And then these new men come along, these ultramoderns, these worshippers of the magnificent beast in man, whom we know so well. I have a book by a young Nazi poet, presented to me by the author in 1935. I pick it up and read the dedication: *"Au dessus de la loi le Créateur a posé la vie."* Yes, we know it, that's the way it is. Life is superior to law, life fashions and creates laws for its own purposes, life breaks laws when it needs to, and life is man— magnificent, not answerable to any court of law, free, deriving from himself the rules governing his conduct.

Slow down, slow down. I am too incensed. More than one Catholic writer speaks of Protestantism like this; we need only mention Maritain. This is the way Naphta would have phrased it had his quarrel with Settembrini, inscribed in the pages of Mann's *The Magic Mountain*, flared up again today. Faith in man has had some fine representatives, however, who, wary of Rousseau's and Nietzsche's perverse excesses, were measured in their claims and drew entirely different conclusions from their optimistic conception of man. I need only mention Anglo-Saxon literature as an example. Nevertheless, I must admit that whoever wishes to seek moral authority in man and to base himself on it, whoever believes in man's right to an autonomous resolution of ethical problems, is taking the path of humanism and the Reformation, and not the path of the Catholic Church. The path that leads from Luther to Rosenberg, as you correctly say, is by no means crooked, while Rosenberg is separated from Catholicism by an abyss.

No, I harbor no illusions. All noble humanitarians, debating to the present day the rights of man and of the citizen, are descended from the same spiritual family that the Church has condemned on many occasions, thus giving proof of her wisdom. And just as the germ of monarchism and totalitarianism persists within democracy, so a germ of slavery persists in their appeals to complete freedom of conscience and thought. Man became free, but being free, he created certain historical ideas and bent his neck under the yoke that he himself had created. Soon the idea of self-sufficient humanity took hold. It was contaminated by the corrosive acids of the work of philosophers whose goal it was to prove that "man" is an abstraction, that "Man" with a capital *M* does not exist, that there are only tribes, classes, various civilizations, various laws, and various customs, that history is filled with the struggle of human groups, and that each of them brings along different ethics, different customs, and a different worldview. Like Marx, they yearned to prove that "being defines consciousness," or, as my Nazi poet says, that "the Creator placed life above law." On the heels of this came the necessity to replace the idea of one's fellow man with a narrower idea, the idea of the proletariat or the Aryan, and instead of "do no harm to your fellow man," they began saying "do no harm to your countryman" or "do no harm to a worker." And now, my dear friend, I shall share with you my greatest doubt. Without religious and metaphysical underpinning, the word "man" is too ambiguous a term, is it not? From the moment it is deprived of traits such as an immortal soul and redemption through Christ, does it not disintegrate into a vast number of possibilities, of which some are better, others worse, some deserving of protection and cultivation, and others of absolute extinction? Finally, is it really possible to invent a single ethics, since the daimonion, left to its own resources, turns out to be something like Pythia? His pronouncements can be interpreted any which way, however one wishes—Mr. Goebbels is well aware of this. I am not comforted in the least by the opinions of writers like Huxley. Rolling down a steep slope toward valleys inhabited by the wolves of totalitarianism, along with all of Europe, they seem to be unaware of this, and they mistake a brief period of as yet incompletely disrupted equilibrium between freedom and slavery for a permanent state. I am not comforted by allusions to European tradition; her cart has driven more than once along this rutted path, but she has forgotten the dark moments of the past . . .

And so, what remains is to give up the attempt to discover an ethical authority in man, to shrug one's shoulders in response to the hopelessness of human justifications, and if one is to fight, then to do so only as a member of a threatened nation, only as enemy against enemy! There is something within me that rebels, something that demands that I assess justice and pass judgment on them both, the persecutor and the persecuted, according to a standard different from that of patriotic exaltation.

Allow me to end my letter with this doubt. May it balance out my frequent impulsiveness.

IV

Jerzy Andrzejewski to Czeslaw Milosz

Dear Czeslaw,

I see that this time I have to be more disciplined and restrict the range of my response more narrowly than I did last time. You have helped me to do this by commenting in detail about the meaning of the doubts I expressed so that, going through them one after the other, you could raise new doubts. It turns out that our questions divide and multiply, and the question of an ethical norm in man that we touched upon has many layers surrounding the heart of the matter—that "philosopher's stone" which, once discovered and accepted, was supposed to bind human beings with an immutable law. Allow me to approach this question by a somewhat circuitous route, but without taking my eyes off it. I agree with you when you say in conclusion that you want to judge "according to a standard different from that of patriotic exaltation." It's not that I don't appreciate the values that derive from tradition and national unity. On the contrary, the national tie seems to me to be deeper and more real than class unity, and its ethical, social, and cultural value is, in my opinion, superior to the slogans of those who profess a religion of the proletariat or a religion of the people, when what they mean by that is a single social stratum. We know from experience, after all, how reality begins to darken ominously when the idea of the nation becomes the ultimate proof of value, the highest instance of the ends and means of action. It may well be that today, when nearly 150 years separate us from the philosopher of Jena's *Addresses to the German Nation*,[1] the time is right for penning a new praise of nationalism (yet one more good word that has become saturated with the stench of blood and hatred), praise that an apologist should be able to contain within its proper boundaries. From among the many nineteenth-century historiosophical concepts—including those of Cyprian Norwid and Stanisław Szczepanowski—many, many thoughts could be retrieved that, if resurrected today and expressed with a new word, would resound like the voice of true humanity amid the present cacophony of barbarity. It appears that the belief that only superior truth, immutable and universal, can grant a nation true ethical authority has manifested itself in few nations with as much force as it has in ours. It might be argued that nations that carry this awareness within themselves have also made war, and have legalized, at least in practice, violence, cruelty, and hatred. No doubt. But the France of Saint Louis or Joan of Arc is not the same as the France of Napoleon or Nazi Germans. This difference will be obvious to everyone who is not satisfied with looking at history as a bundle of specific facts. As for me, I would have grave hesitations if anyone observing, for example, the present pogroms against the Jews wanted to find precedents for them in history and, having found them in the Middle Ages, were to place an equal sign between these phenomena. The famous saying of that wise man, Lessing, that "everything has already happened" is by no means obvious. There is a big difference between the pyres with burning witches and heretics and the cellars of the GPU or the Gestapo. I am no enthusiast of the Holy Inquisition, but I would not place its judges in the same row as the judges who pronounce their sentences in the shadow of the swastika. Also, the burning of books branded by the *Index Librorum*

Prohibitorum strikes me as entirely different from the similar fate of books in the square in front of the Berlin Opera. "Sophisms!" you might object. One cannot refuse to accept facts. They speak to us, and the sufferings of the Albigensians slaughtered under the beautiful skies of Provence count just the same as the sufferings of Jews murdered by the Gestapo. The tortures of the Inquisition caused agonies no different from those experienced by Kraków professors in the camp in Oranienburg. What the cause is in whose name someone suffers and is tortured is a matter of secondary importance, making it possible at best to place in a suspect light an idea that not only utilizes similar methods but seeks sanctions and justifications for them. A consistent humanist cannot adopt a different position. But were you never overwhelmed with bitter suspicions, definitely bitter, that that consistent, uncompromising humanitarianism intersects tragically with the truth about life and the truth about man, that it appeals to a man who never existed and does not now exist, and, permit me to prophesy, never will? I am capable of sparking glints of optimism in myself when I think about man and his fate, but I do not find that faint gleam when I look at history. Borrowing the Catholic concept of Grace, I would risk the supposition that if man's personhood can always be found within reach of Grace, the ragged current of history runs very far from it. I do not believe in man's innate goodness, nor in the possibility of the human race's perfection. I do not experience great illusions when I hear voices speaking enthusiastically about the development and progress of civilization. What is much dearer to me is the conviction that man will always be a composite of good and evil, and that to the end of his existence he will love and hate, engender life and murder, build and destroy. That, finally, no social system will remove wrongs, injustice, and violence, and we will never be without worthless people, just as we will never lack saints and heroes. Of course, I recognize the difference between a Hottentot from darkest Africa and a son of so-called good Europe. I've made that point explicitly by refusing to equate an agent of the Gestapo with a judge of the Inquisition. I am convinced that a poet could not say about any contemporary leaders, "The sacred armies, and the godly knight, that the great sepulchre of Christ did free, I sing."[2] I give full due to the weight of objective historical facts, and it is precisely what they say that commands me to take a pessimistic view of the history of humanity. Still, I am convinced that over the course of centuries, the motives and reasons of this same human activity have undergone constant change. While agreeing that man has always been prepared to kill and to hate, I also know that he has done this for ever changing reasons. Sometimes those reasons were high, very high, in the hierarchy of moral concepts; at other times they fell, as they do now, to the lowest depths. The graph of these vacillations, like the graph of a sick man's temperature, shows constant motion, and no human mind can foresee its future fate. One can only confirm that the graph exists, and nothing more. Certainly the totality of concepts that are at the source of human actions do shape history, but they act, as it were, undercover, and are invisible in the objective significance of facts. The humanitarian is right to equate crimes and punishments, to reduce human wrongs and sufferings to a common denominator. Of course, nothing changes in history except for the unrepeatability of facts. The only things that change are what goes on behind the scenes, the strange world in which, throughout the ages, man has been wandering between heaven and hell. And it is only the changeability of intentions, which sometimes commands an inquisitor to burn a heretic at the stake out of concern for his soul's salvation, and sometimes, in the name of the superiority of the German race, makes a contemporary German into a fervent exterminator of "subhumans," as you put it. Only my awareness of the capaciousness of this world behind the scenes protects me from extreme and utter pessimism.

That said, let us return to man. The word "soul" was uttered. You ask: "Without religious and metaphysical underpinning, the word 'man' is too ambiguous a term, is it not? From the moment it is deprived of traits such as an immortal soul and redemption through Christ, does it not disintegrate into a vast number of possibilities, of which some are better, others worse, some deserving of protection and cultivation, and others of absolute extinction?" It appears that we have reached the ultimate level of this ethical dilemma, and that whether the "philosopher's stone" will reveal its shape or whether we will withdraw from it, retracing the steps of arguments made till now, depends on the answer and the consequences that flow from that answer. But here I have to return to the beginning of your letter. One can agree that "doubt is a noble thing," although I would prefer to subtract some of the certainty from that assertion and add some conditions to it. I would be more convinced had I read that "doubt can be a noble thing." Doubt ad infinitum, and also the constancy of a point of view that is characterized by the simultaneous interweaving of doubt and knowledge, do not seem to me to be as noble as I would like either one of them to be for my purposes. Just consider this: if I respond that without religious and metaphysical support, "man" is truly a word that can mean many things; if I then accept a moral law that exists outside of me, eternal and unchanging—where, then, is there room for doubt, if my life and the labor of my intellect are not to become a proverbial crab walk? They are, in the final analysis, questions that demand a clear "yes" or "no" answer. You remember that place in *Demons* where the young Verkhovensky confesses that every moment when he yearns to do something, a voice whispers to him, telling him to do the exact opposite. For his own deep reasons, that reflex fascinated Gide, who did not neglect to comment on it eloquently in his book about Dostoevsky. The perspectives that open up before the permanent coexistence of doubt and knowledge run roughly parallel to the consequences of a duality of desires.

I would not have taken up this question, which you touched upon only in passing, had I not detected in it a fairly universal phenomenon in our times. Is not the impossibility of relying on Truth one of the most tragic breakdowns of contemporary man? Contemporary man can understand Truth with incomparably more ease than he can, without reservation, believe in that Truth. A shadow of doubt never leaves him, even when he confronts values to which, rationally and of necessity, he is ready to lend his unwavering approval. One can say that contemporary man is able to discover the Truth and understand it, but he is unable, does not wish, or is incapable of submitting to that Truth, of coexisting with it in accordance with the laws which that Truth demands. How many people can one meet today, even among the best people, who truly know and understand the Catholic religion in its essence? Such concepts as original sin, Redemption, Grace, eternal damnation, and reward meet with total comprehension in their minds, but they find in their hearts the possibility of satisfying the most vital needs and desires. These people value the universal character of the Church as they should; they are capable of discovering both in strict Church discipline and in the established sacraments and the liturgy that social bond whose equilibrium and harmony with eternal life only the Catholic Church, alone among all Christian churches, has been able to maintain. These people think and speak like Catholics, yet they are not Catholics. If understanding the sacrament of confession leads to the confessional, they will be there. If understanding that the Redeemer is truly present in the white wafer elevated by the sinful hands of a priest permits one to take Communion, they will hear these words above them every day: *"Domine, non sum dignus, ut intres sub tectum meum . . ."* Yet, appreciating as they do the personal and social meaning of religious practices, they do not practice them. Understanding faith, they do not live by faith. Having need of it, they do not live in it. Not being believers, they are also not heretics. Their anxiety, their seeking, characterizes our time more eloquently, perhaps, than fascist jabbering, which—one has to sustain this hope— will ultimately die down and terrify or bemuse future generations as a spectral memory, until a new *führer* or *duce* arranges the masses in ranks with a wave of his hand. Instead, the laicization of religious feelings (because many contemporary people can be called religious laypeople) seems to be a phenomenon that is a hundred times more dangerous, carrying within itself the possibility of infinite variations. The Nazi under his swastika simply lies by telling a lie; the religious layperson frequently lies by speaking the Truth. In his hand the "philosopher's stone" loses its brilliance and slowly changes into an ordinary gray stone. As I mentioned before, without longing for the times of the Inquisition, I regret that no one kills today in the name of his victim's salvation.

Religious laicism is an enormous puzzle. In my previous letter I expressed my reservations in relation to your assertion that Catholicism has become "a desiccated mummy." I still have reservations because I do know true, fervent Catholics, and also—I can admit this to you—because I need to sustain the hope that that position is not yet lost. I also do not think that the gravest danger that threatens Catholicism comes from the inside. In this matter I rely on the wisdom and circumspection of the Church, which in the course of its history has experienced painful breakdowns but has always managed to rise up and renew itself. If a danger is threatening Catholicism now, it is above all an external one—and not at all from the side of militant atheisms or fascisms. An obvious enemy is usually less threatening than a hidden one. The positions from which fascisms and historical materialism do battle with Catholicism are defined, and the lines separating the two sides run along a deep abyss. Meanwhile, those who stand on one side of the barricade beside the Church, sympathizing with it but not belonging to it, are the most dangerous enemies. The Catholic Church resembles a Trojan horse at present, with the one difference that many of today's Agamemnons and his comrades are unaware of the role they are supposed to play. Today's Ulysseses are great friends of Catholic Troy. And they are losing her while standing up in her defense. They kill without always knowing what they are doing. The Church is often denounced for its compromises and the flexibility of its policies by people who attempt to ascribe the distortions of one maneuver or another to the entire institution. Many accusations are undoubtedly justified, because like all human activity, the Church has its own shortcomings. An inclination to compromise is not, in fact, one of its less frequent errors. But it is often forgotten that the Church stoops to compromise only in its earthly sphere of activity. On the other hand, it has always been, and still is, uncompromising toward any attacks against its sacral character. The Pope and the vicars may be dolts from some remote village, but this in no way affects the Church in which the mystic body of Christ lives and from which it radiates. This other, eternal, supernatural Church demands of its sons a faith that is total and unconditional. The sacral character of the Church does not recognize partial Catholicism. Either one is a Catholic or one is not. One must accept everything or reject everything. Today's religious laicism is founded precisely on this not wanting to accept everything. Whose fault is this? I don't wish to speak of guilt here; I don't feel I have the right or the strength to do so. So I shall strive to limit myself to an attempt at what will certainly be an incomplete explanation of the complex causes that are directing today's religious current into channels, that current amid whose eddies and whirlpools people pass from the fertile sacral shore to the barren and sinister secular shore.

1. Nowhere does historicism engender so much desolation as it produces when used as a tool for the study of the history and development of the human religious imagination. I am not speaking, obviously, about historicism that comprehends the development of religion on a plane equal to the development of economic, social, or political systems, making it strictly dependent on those systems. No; I am thinking about a historicism that, approaching religious questions, from the outset posits the existence of a supernatural being, asserting that "scientific studies of the origins of religion, like scientific studies of the origins of life, are condemned from the outset to sterility." This assertion, one of several in the preface to Tadeusz Zieliński's *Religions of the Ancient World*, in no way contradicts the Church's doctrine. Indeed, if we were to limit ourselves to this one example, in Professor Zieliński's multivolume work one can find more than once a tone of profound faith in the supernatural intercession of religious imaginations. It is sufficient, however, to go beyond the Revelation of Christ to discover in the religious systems preceding it an only too obvious kinship of imaginations, similarities of symbols, a thousand connections from which an important fact emerges: every religion is a bond between human content and divine content. Traced back into the ages, it reveals an ever more perfect form of God and an ever higher ethical norm. One more step, and doubt will emerge as to whether the truth enclosed in the Gospels is the ultimate expression of the Revelation of God in man, or whether, as the most perfect achievement until now, it will yield in time to an even more perfect law and an image of God as different from the Christian one as the God of the Holy

Trinity is from Zeus or Amon-Ra. The nineteenth century's yearning for the coming epoch of Paracletus was really the expectation of a new Revelation.

Further consequences: if we recognize as the object of religious feelings the concretization of the Absolute, we will see that over the course of centuries the developmental line of these feelings continually and consistently gives way to dematerialization. The path from the Absolute, located in primitive religions in the forces of nature and in animals, to the Absolute of Christianity, located in the God Man and in a God who thinks in the categories of our thought, is as long as the path that separates the Christian Absolute from the abstract Absolute of contemporary thought. Perhaps the process of the dematerialization of the Absolute that is taking place before our eyes and with our collaboration is like a revolution in the history of humanity, incomparably more fundamental and far-reaching in its consequences than the rise of Christianity. Whatever truths may be said about the superiority of Christian religion over earlier religions, the differences separating the faith of primitive man from the faith of a Christian are less than those separating the Christian religion from the religion of contemporary man. After all, without exception, all beliefs before Christianity imbued the Absolute with characteristics of the human race, and in the final analysis, the Egyptians' Apis and the Greeks' Zeus were, like the Holy Trinity, composed of human elements transferred into the sphere of the Absolute. The Greek gods are also like human beings in the sphere of action, and they share with mortals amorous, maternal, and military vicissitudes. In the sphere of the Absolute in action, Christianity revealed in the figure of Christ the bonds between the Absolute and the human tribe. The Christian God, however, no longer interferes in earthly affairs as matter; he thinks only in human terms, his justice is ideal human justice, his eternity and heaven and hell are the ideal measure of punish-

ment and reward. Church iconography and secular painting
could create, in an entirely responsible way, a material image
of God the Father; they could secure Fra Angelico's vision of
heaven and Signorelli's vision of the resurrection of bodies.
The Divine Comedy could appear and not seem false.

Today, dogmas and eschatological imaginings have been
transformed in most minds into the sphere of abstract, intellectual concepts. The Holy Ghost does not hover with the glow
of a dove as in El Greco's paintings; God the Father emerging
from the clouds of creation does not extend his finger to touch
the hand of Adam, summoned to life; angels in white robes
and golden halos do not stroll in the flower-carpeted meadow
of heaven; and the trumpets of the Last Judgment do not resurrect the dead. I do not anticipate that human thought will be
able to return to materialized religious concepts, unless, perhaps, if nothing at all remains of recent centuries' civiliza-
tional and cultural achievements. Without assuming such a
possibility, one can, rather, expect that the remaining material
religious imaginings, which have been preserved until now
among those who believe in a traditional way, will slowly disappear. The time will come, perhaps, when the abstractness of
ultimate notions will suffice to fulfill man's needs.

Today the situation is far removed from such equilibrium.
We are in the midst of a revolutionary period that belongs to
the past in its demands and to the future in its possibilities.
We are too enmeshed with our culture of more than twenty
centuries to be able to suddenly break with it and stand,
without swaying, on steady legs. The time will come to bid
farewell, and not without regret, to the vanishing throne
of God the Father, the circles of hell, and the Son amid
the angels' trumpets, thunder and lightning accompanying
the judgment of the living and the dead. The loneliness of the
religious layperson is bitter and painful. He keeps turning
around inside the circle of those same concepts that create the

Catholic construct but are stripped of their sacral character. The shadow of mystery and the unknown has thickened and grown dark. Man is losing the ground beneath his feet, and his immortal soul no longer garners the ultimate measure of justice that carries rewards and punishment.

For Conrad, who is a great writer of religious laicism, materialized metaphysical concepts no longer exist. The sign of impenetrable mystery stands on the threshold of the super-terrestrial world. And the only thing that can save man in the darkness are the ideas of duty, responsibility, honor, and loyalty, displayed like Platonic ideals somewhere in the unknown. Some ten years after Conrad, Malraux poses an eloquent question: What shall we do with the soul if there is no grace? When, however, he begins to search for an ethical norm that might give man back his dignity, he discovers it in the secular concept of fraternity. So, again a return to man. And it is yearning, rather than faith and knowledge, that strives for an ethical sanctioning of reliance on a fuzzy, abstract shape of God.

2. Surely you must have had occasion to notice more than once how common a phenomenon is the dissonance between man's worldview and his life in our day, True, this dissonance is as old as the world, but it seems to me that it is particularly sharply drawn at present. People who live according to what they profess are rare. People live worse; they are more cowardly, more impoverished. With every step, their lives give the lie to their words. We are inundated from all directions with unbounded lying, deception, cynicism. I doubt that Diogenes, were he alive today, would want to live in a barrel. I suspect that he would write articles and give speeches on the radio recommending that way of life, but he would live in a luxurious modern villa. Although all contemporary ideologies recommend a life that is difficult, heroic, manly, the ideal to which the majority of our contemporaries aspire, and which they are

achieving in practice, is an easy life. While their ideology proclaims self-abnegation and self-sacrifice, those who believe in it are inclined, rather, to exploit life to the full. With admirable skill, our contemporaries have perfected the ability to keep the left hand in ignorance of what the right hand is doing.

This is too vast a problem for me to submit it to a more detailed examination in the confines of this letter. I would only like to share with you my supposition that this dissonance between worldview and life is not in some degree a consequence (because there are undoubtedly more causes for it) of a secular way of thinking. Did not the dematerialization of such concepts as heaven, hell, the immortal soul, and grace influence the weakening of the ethical instinct even among those who accept these concepts, but only in their abstract, mysterious form? What is there to say here? Dante's hell was much more effective in teaching people to fear punishment than the dematerialized, incomprehensible dimension of punishment that is sketched so vaguely in our minds today. If I remember correctly, Georges Bernanos writes in his *Diary of a Country Priest* that hell is the eternal absence of love. This says a great deal. But years will pass before people begin to tremble from terror before the horror of that vision, before they are able to understand and penetrate it sufficently for it to become as concrete as the flames of the hell they still believe in. A new eschatology is barely emerging; almost no one believes in the old one, and not many people take its requirements seriously. One might say that we are living in a period of the absence of eschatological punishment, a transitional disturbance and disorder of heavenlessness and hell-lessness. That Catholicism is undergoing the most painful losses through this is clear. After all, it makes the most and the hardest demands on man. But Grace and the ethical laws suspended above the human tribe are incapable of responding with force to the powerful temptation of evil. Equilibrium has been lost, perhaps for a long time, for who knows how many generations will pass before the lost souls of immortals will accept a new heaven and a new hell, and Grace will renew its weakened covenant with them.

3. At last, my final observation. I am concerned about the currently common phenomenon of inverting the hierachy of values. Never before in history has the Church received so many offerings as now. It receives them from the left and from the right. The addressees are various and so are the addresses. They are composed in different ways by the right-wing Polish nationalist, the French socialist, the Catholic who is attracted to communism, or the Communist attracted to Catholicism (a rare freak of the interwar era). But for all these subtle differences, a certain kinship unites these religious petitioners: they understand Catholicism as a means, not an end. Despite my revulsion at our homegrown fascism, I realize that many of our young nationalists sincerely consider themselves to be Catholics and see their ideology as a fortification of the Church. I am thinking of their best representatives; I won't speak of those among them, who may very well be in the majority, who *give way to despair with studied cynicism*. But even among the best of them it is easy to see that they are Catholics because Catholicism fits their ideology. They practice it for some of the same reasons that a woman chooses the color of her shoes and hat to match the color of her dress. In their worldview, truth yields to the utility of Truth. It is regarded as Truth because it is useful. A year from now, should the situation demand it, it can stop being Truth, and a different truth will replace it. This is precisely how many Catholics and would-be Catholics think today. Of all the contemporary Ulysseses of Catholic Troy, these seem to me to be the most dangerous. Although often with the best intentions and in accord with their conscience, they do strike, after all, at the most sensitive core of religion, at its superior authority and tran-

scendent quality. Since they are men of action for the most part, fighting for concrete political, social, and economic matters, the worse it is, the greater the possibility of devastation. And should a similar way of thinking become more entrenched and universal as time passes, one day Europe will arrive at the painless death of its religious feelings. If, however, it accepts the existence of a superterrestrial ethical norm, one would have to reject such a possibility. There would be no room for it. After all, that which is independent of man is inseparably connected to his earthly fate and cannot perish, and although sometimes it shines with a great radiance and at other times fades into the faintest shadow of light, it exists at all times, even despite human will, and always carries with it the hope of renewal.

September 1, 1942

V

Czeslaw Milosz to Jerzy Andrzejewski

Dear Jerzy,

The changes in contemporary religion . . . this is an important question, and not only when these changes are being evaluated with the coolness of an investigator, but important for us
(you sense this perfectly) for highly personal reasons. I can say
about myself that having been raised on French literature,
I am marked with that particular affection for *"choses spi-
rituelles"* that is characteristic of it; that even my language
bears the seductive, dangerous stamp of pathos that derives
from an almost excessive respect for spiritual subjects. After
all, there is continually present in my consciousness the opposition *"éternel-temporel,"* which has often exposed me to attacks
by historical materialists, and *temporalité* itself does not disturb me. The path I have followed until now is, I believe, quite
characteristic of many people—from absolute historicism and
Marxist interests toward Catholicism or, rather, toward lay religiosity. It is difficult for me to write about this. I am rather
skeptical of assertions about "the rebirth of Catholicism" in
the interwar period, although the fashion for Catholicism in
scientific and artistic circles testifies to such yearnings, which
are not necessarily deserving of mockery, and I doubt this is
only one more manifestation of "catching up with the West,"[1]
by which I mean "the complete irrationalization of ideas." I

sometimes wonder what form these yearnings might take in the event that Anglo-Saxon culture spreads throughout the world, and whether a different style, a different language, might then be adopted, different from the language and style of Thomas Aquinas or Maritain. As you see, I adopt a dual stance: restraint and caution go hand in hand with my sympathy for and understanding of Catholicism. You yourself have described such a posture as quite widespread; I won't refute that, only I ascribe it not to moral causes (the impossibility of acting, or an inclination for an easy life), but to intellectual causes. Yes, you are a hundred times right when you say that the gradual dematerialization of religious imaginings is much more important *signum temporis* than the howls of various fascisms; it is much more deeply rooted. And it is this that causes the duality; it places in question even the most fervent declarations of the neo-Catholics. I insist that in connection with the progressive retreat of Christian eschatology into a fuzzy, indeterminate sphere, contemporary man's understanding of religion reaches no further than an understanding of Christianity's salvational consequences until now—human, solely human, and all the rest is understood as abstract scaffolding that, although totally deprived of any imaginative content, ensures that the entire construction is harmonious and unified. Commentaries about Catholicism emphasize above all its wisdom, its harmony, the way it soothes all desires of the human heart; and a great deal of attention is paid to the perfect applicability of its dogmas, their perfect interconnectedness and the mathematical precision with which one can derive the foundations of human behavior. That is quite a lot in and of itself, but it is insufficient to awaken faith in the incarnation of God in man, in the body of Christ contained in a wafer baked by human hands, nor in eternal damnation. True, in such a case the Church commands people to practice and pray for the light of faith, teaching that with practice comes a strengthening of

conviction and a state in which things that are initially difficult to comprehend become simple and obvious. That state is
a form of exaltation, a form of good exaltation, since there
are also bad exaltations awakened by Satan, and Satan never
makes more conquests than where man strives for the peaks of
spiritual elevation. That is what the Church teaches, and if
I were capable of doing what I understand it to be teaching, I
would submit to that rigor. I confess that there were periods in
my life when I acted like that. At present I certainly cannot
achieve this. Why? It is because of shyness and prudence,
which one can analyze only in the course of confessions and
self-observation. It's just that I detect a fear both of the artificiality of imposing such states on myself and of the state itself,
which is so difficult to define and to name. Fear of artificiality
equals fear of falling into falsehood. I have seen people who
struggled heroically with their skepticism, imposing religious
obligations on themselves in the name of a deep conviction
that the indecision into which such a weak and industrious
mind falls does not embolden him to break free of the burden
of rules supported by the authority of the Church. I say that I
have known people, although I might have said I knew myself.
But this struggle with pride was marked by all the attributes of
pride. There was something pharisaical that could be glimpsed
behind these efforts to show oneself as sufficiently humble,
and therefore fully deserving of discovering truth, while millions live in the darkness of disbelief. I have detected in this
the ache of ambition, the desire to elevate oneself by the possession of knowledge, and when my lips said, "I believe," my
conscience, obeying its own thought, insisted, "I don't know."
As a result, this entire operation carried out on oneself by
Catholic intellectuals seemed quite close to other operations of
contemporary man, in which the same "will to believe" is repeated. The final, Catholic phase of Stanisław Brzozowski, that
ambassador of pragmatism (although he himself denied it) on

Polish soil, would probably confirm my diagnosis of the origin of attempts like these. Great respect for action—internal action in this case—and less respect for truth. The recognition of the fundamental unknowability of truth by purely intellectual power and faith, such as it is, in the *"élément obscur,"* in the hidden corners of the human soul, which are closer to Mystery than intellect is. But these are precisely initial tendencies of the very suspect arationality of our time, and I am not surprised that those who were raised on William James, Blondel, or Freud are attempting to renew Grace, since it acts within the closed, gloomy regions of the "underground I." Still, I fear that by acting that way, they will not resurrect Rome, but rather will create something that is called Catholicism, but whose dimensions are no greater than the "art of the subconscious" or the philosophy of action and power that derive from similar sources. Perhaps it is only a new Trojan horse, closely related to the Modernism condemned by the Church. Catholic teaching about the grace of faith yields here, perhaps, to a growing interpretation—to the best of my knowledge, it arose in an era when the intellectual element in man was not surrounded with such contempt as it is today, and the intellectual path to faith had nothing improbable in it. To make the state of Grace into a sudden blow, a sudden illumination, entirely separate from a condition of normal thinking—is that not too daring a step? I said a while ago that the state in which one suddenly begins to believe is recognized by the Church as a state of good exaltation. I misspoke. This is not true. The Church is afraid of exaltation, even the very best sort. It is we who have grown accustomed to counting on the sudden opening of a locked gate, the sudden leap from darkness into light. I am as afraid of such states as of the artificiality that precedes it. As a poet, I have often experienced a powerful, overwhelming inspiration (I am not afraid of that word), and as a man, various types of exaltation. I know it is good as long as the winged creature who carries us away into a land of intense feelings has a strong bit in its mouth. There is a boundary that one must not cross if one does not want to taste disillusionment and repugnance. But the worst are those noble states of exaltation, that pseudo-grace to which we are urged by certain individuals who modestly call it submissiveness of thought and who promise that while we practice it, faith will descend on us as a state separate from what we were previously. Like everything that arises from the sphere of inner darknesses—this exaltation has my "I" as its subject—my own knowledge, goodness, humility, my own bestowing of gifts, become the cause of my tender emotional state and crocodile tears. Never are so many evil deeds and errors committed as in exaltation over one's own nobility or one's own calling. Tartuffe is not a simple, easily comprehended figure.

Someone will surely remark that false grace has nothing in common with true grace. Yet it seems to me that where the grace of faith is understood as an internal revolution, as the overturning of habits of thought that one has held until now, falsehood will be exceptionally difficult, if not impossible, to avoid. I do not know what the Catholic Church says about this. If it distrusts sudden conversions and epiphanies, all the better for it. I know that waiting for faith that may come at the cost of clear and plainly delimited contours of thought is too close to certain contemporary and compromised efforts. During the two interwar decades many people became convinced that they had to be Communists and, doing violence to their doubts, "joined the ranks." Others, chasing after a "worldview," stifled their common sense with a mixture of Thomas Aquinas and theoreticians of imperialism and fascism. People were consumed by a rage to denounce their own thought, a blind drive to subordinate and discipline themselves—which is, perhaps, understandable as a reaction to the excessively liberal nineteenth century, but which projected a quite pitiful image.

As you see, I don't place a very high value on faith that develops apart from thought or in defiance of thought. Blind faith deserves respect. But voluntarily blinded faith does not inspire admiration in me. If religion is to grow and become stronger, and not to dry out slowly and painfully, it can probably achieve this only by imparting to religious concepts a content that can be understood by contemporary man. You propose that it will be that same eschatology, but totally dematerialized, and that that will suffice. Perhaps. In any case, this can be accomplished only through intellectual effort, and not through voluntary stupefaction. *"Credo quia absurdum"* is a beautiful confession when it fills in the gaps of understanding, but it is dangerous when it is placed on a banner as the chief slogan. Too many elements of religion have become absurd for contemporary man to make use of programmatic absurdity without disturbing the equilibrium of the human psyche. This does not mean (as was recently proclaimed) that religion is old-fashioned, and that man has defeated it, having moved from the age of infancy to the age of maturity. I am even prepared to agree with some Catholic philosophers when they argue, for example, that all nineteenth-century thought is a coarse misunderstanding and that the fault lies entirely on the side of the sterile, mechanized imagination of our epoch, that there is in this the most ordinary spiritual deformation. But it is difficult to dream of a return to past periods of history; we should chalk up fantasies about "a new Middle Ages" to the account of all the bluster that is dressed up today in beautiful words. Perhaps it may yet happen that a great collective surge of mental power and a total transformation of the intellectual atmosphere will take place, which will remove today's impenetrable borders and open our eyes to many new and, in fact, ancient truths, depriving them of absurdity. Certain signs appear to point to this.

The situation of people such as you and I is dreadful:

they are exposed to accusations of "mysticism," "idealism"—
without gaining any profit, any strength or support from the
gravity of a defined faith. The historical materialists are offended by our reluctant attitude toward historicism and the
opposition *temporel-éternel*. They, who perceive all attempts at
discovering immutable, constant elements that do not submit
to the changes of history as loathsome irrationalism and mysticism (they hurl such epithets at virtually the entire history of
philosophy from Plato to Husserl), are unsparing in their efforts at unmasking us and, using us as their example, demonstrating the hopelessness of the position of Western thought.
Despite these attacks, I feel a great deal of sympathy for them.
Marxism, having chosen for itself the role of gravedigger, has
played that role quite well. Thanks to its courageous and brutal
criticism, many sacred cows have revealed what goes on behind
the scenes, which, in my opinion, did not, after all, touch the
few truly sacred things but, on the contrary, lent them even
greater value.

Since we are talking about this, I must digress a bit and
touch on the field of art. Not that I have a great desire to dis-
course on questions of aesthetics. But nowhere else does the
"spirit of the epoch" appear so distinctly as in works of art:
they become a storehouse of the trademark pulsations of the
collective atmosphere, and if one wants to become acquainted
with them, one cannot avoid certain observations about the
sphere of artistry which is, as people used to say, detached
from life.

Indeed, the development of contemporary art (it has become customary to use this term to define the period more or
less from Impressionism in art and from Rimbaud and Mallarmé in poetry) provides us with many instructive examples.
It is characterized (speaking in very general terms) by a great
blossoming of, if not metaphysical, then at least mystical interests, which coincides most peculiarly with a progressive secu-

larization of religious feelings. I sense that I am treading upon quaggy ground; this is a vast theme for a longer essay, which I still hope to write. I shall summarize what I would like to demonstrate in it, using, of course, numerous quotations and similar ballast. No, I shall not summarize, I shall drop several terms, several names; let them suffice for a wise head. Claudel was right to a certain extent when he called Rimbaud a religious poet. There is mystical material in him, a desire for the decomposition of matter (*"par le dérèglement de tous les sens"*) that is perhaps close to the Impressionists' predatory attitude toward matter. Mallarmé loosening the logic of language and replacing it with a suggestion or mood. Half-crazy Lautréamont, the patron of the Surrealists, writing hyperrationally, hyperlogically, gushing a stream of often incomprehensible images. As for poetry and painting that is closer to us in time—isn't art that which appeals not to the rational part of the human soul, but to that "something," to the "I of the depths" that is supposedly connected to Being (with a capital *B*), Mystery (with a capital *M*), and so forth? The theorists have introduced never-before-known definitions. Never before did anyone teach that art provides a bond with "the metaphysical umbilicus of existence" (unless it was Plotinus!). Bremond charmingly, though vaguely and deceptively, defends "pure poetry" as a mystical revelation related to prayer. Here in Poland, Stanisław Ignacy Witkiewicz constructs a theory of art as "the sense of the Strangeness of Existence," stemming from metaphysical insatiability. Enough examples for now. We can already see in them a shared aspiration to be liberated from the constraints imposed by so often maligned common sense, a hunt for the mysterious core of human existence, which is unknowable and alien to consciousness. That is what I am aiming for. I aim to comprehend the mentality of a religious layperson that is expressed in these artistic currents. It is characterized by seeking a substitute, seeking understanding for the needs that images of heaven, hell, and purgatory no longer satisfy. There is no point in denying it, this art is our spiritual fatherland, too. Many of our friends believed that by deconstructing words, colors, shapes, and connecting them in new ways, they stood on the border of the unknowable and were able to penetrate it; that inspiration is a form of ecstasy enabling union with the very root of being. Perhaps I, too, believed in this a little. I assume, however, that art does not reach beyond the boundaries of the knowable and does not rise to any heights that are inaccessible to thought. That it only enlarges the boundaries of the knowable, and that "the sense of the Strangeness of Existence" is a powerful spur to a multifaceted knowing of the world, and no more than that. That inspiration is, after all, intensified curiosity and a heightened consciousness of intellectual proportions, and not a primal shudder, that "metaphysical shudder" of Witkiewicz—since the furthest that shudder could have led to is an inarticulate mumbling. I respect Conrad because, having arrived at the boundary of the dark sea of mysteries surrounding human life, he did not attempt to fly across that boundary on wings of ecstasy, nor did he pretend that he knew something that he did not really know. I also believe that there is no potential for revelation concealed in man's hyperconscious depths, and that if one peers down into that well in the hope of catching a glimpse of a sorceror's power, one will see only the reflection of one's own face. So I am grateful to the Marxists for their attack on our spiritual fatherland and the mentality of the religious layperson. Our paths diverge, however, at a certain point. Unlike them, I will not deny the existence of metaphysical inclinations in human nature, nor take umbrage at a certain type of intellectual intuition that is capable of discovering constant values and a permanently binding order of human actions. If seeking a loosely defined absolute *"par le dérèglement de tous les sens"* is a hopeless amusement, one cannot agree that when our gaze directs

us toward the world and summons all our powers of consciousness to help us, bringing them to the highest intensity, that this
effort is fruitless. According to the Marxists, it is capable of discerning the law of development. I think it is capable of something greater: it can also embrace principles and values, and
acknowledge the superiority of some of them over others.

In my previous letter I expressed my doubts about whether
an ethical sense, deprived of metaphysical support and grounding, won't lead us astray. I confess that I am in no condition to
answer this decisively. It is civilization's great dilemma, too
great for me to dare to unravel it. The one thing I can do is to
express the hope that the activity of the human mind will not
leave the ethical intercessor defenseless, handed over as prey to
collective insanity, but rather that, extracting from it certain
general indications of the direction to proceed in, will repay it
with appropriate motivation. Will that be a metaphysical foundation? Perhaps. Max Scheler has gotten me all confused; un-
fortunately, his weak side is that he belongs to the family of
German philosophers, and they are great, masked prevarica-
tors, and it is best not to trust their good intentions.

Yes, despite everything, I think that the impossibility of
remaining a Catholic need not thrust us into the embrace of
historicism and a general distrust of eternal values. And that
the condemnation of various metaphysical urges does not contradict what everyone clearly senses: the existence of that great
expanse of darkness that surrounds us, that spreads out not
only beyond us but inside us, too. But truth does not depend on
these dark regions, and there is no point in seeking revelation
there. Probably it also does not depend entirely on human reason, as Descartes argued, yet we have to keep trying to achieve
it with constant attention to sufficient clarity and evidence,
without acquiescing, as we do today, to the widespread cult of
the absurd, even if it is supposedly positive and worthy of our
respect. And if these two rivers are different——the river of

Catholicism and the river of humanism—I see that I appear to be floating down the latter. But I have some slight hope that they are only two branches of a single stream and that they may yet meet. Contemporary worshippers of the deed do not contribute to such a meeting, those who say in December, "After the first of January, I shall be a Catholic," and in February, "After the first of March, I shall be a National Socialist . . ." I could pose a modest question: "What is the source of everything I proclaim? Where does that ardent defense of eternal values come from, that intellectualism, and that aversion to even the best feelings? Is it that by spending the war years thinking about things, I have suddenly and spontaneously arrived at a wisdom that alters many of my previous views? Did my intuition, with no outside assistance, discern the slender path of truth in the thicket of true knowledge?"

Here I yield to people who are fascinated by history. If that is how it happened, then I must ascribe it to the collective current that has enveloped me. The moment is unique. In every book that I take up, the same slogan calls out to me, which I would not have heard if the surrounding reality were different. I read reference books, poetry, novels, and in their margins, in the writing of human stupidity, cowardice, and cruelty, an eloquent commentator ponders, makes notes, inserts red exclamation points and periods. Probably you, too, will not ignore that commentator.

VI

Jerzy Andrzejewski to Czeslaw Milosz

Dear Czeslaw,

When talk turns to so-called fundamental issues like God, ethical norms, eternity, conscience, and so forth, I sometimes detect in myself a reflexive impatience. It is not so disturbing as to make it impossible for me to conduct a discussion; it is sufficiently strong, however, for me not to feel a certain—let me put it in general terms—falseness in speculation of this sort. This, it seems, is because I am not a typical intellectual. To avoid misunderstanding, let me state from the outset that I consider the typical intellectual to be a person who considers the cognitive work of the mind to be a value sufficient in and of itself. I admit that a similar attitude toward life, even were it replete with the most voracious yearning for knowledge, could not satisfy me personally nor inspire total respect were I to detect it in other people. Fundamentally, I am too little an intellectual. I am not exaggerating when I say that the so-called orderly, decent, comparatively wise, life of the ordinary man inspires me to greater respect than the most perceptive observations of a powerful mind deriving a subtly constructed worldview from mysterious interconnections. Don't misunderstand me. I am as distant from the cult of the "ordinary man" as from contempt for, or at least underappreciation of, the human mind as an instrument of cognition. Also, the posture that would strive to limit to a minimum the sense of a worldview in man's life, replacing it with a superior sense of life's practical realization, is equally alien to me. You will deduce that I am not enthusiastic about pragmatism and its consequences. Yet I assure you that I, too, when I undertake cognitive tourism and see others engaged in this industrious and (no irony intended) praiseworthy mountain climbing, am always overwhelmed by a certain anxiety, or, as I said, impatience—what to call it is of no consequence.

This reaction of mine is nothing specific; on the contrary, I find some primitive characteristics in it; I might even risk saying that they are quite universal. There is nothing elitist in it; one can find it among people of the most varied levels and worldviews. I notice it when a so-called intellectual or semi-intellectual grumbles about an extortionist doctor; when a peasant hurls a dirty word at a parish priest who is living with his housekeeper; when an intellectual wrinkles his face with disgust hearing about a socialist activist, for example, who is entangled in suspect financial transactions with capitalist sharks. I believe that a large pinch of salt and a healthy ethical sense lie at the root of these reactions, even if they are often too trivial and inclined toward drawing very general conclusions. This opposition to the falsehood revealed in a contradiction between the obligations of a particular individual and what that individual represents in actuality is more often instinctive than conceived within a framework of rational rules; this reflex of disdain, reluctance, distrust, irony, and even hatred seems to me to be sufficiently characteristic and significant for its implications to merge into intellectual considerations.

I am not suspicious by nature, but the suspicion often besieges me that a cognitive stance toward life and events is connected very subtly with those character traits that might be better defined by such broad concepts as egoism and egocentrism. I do not insist that it has to be this way; to do so would make no sense. But it seems to me that this is frequently the case. There is a kind of mean-spirited paradox here in that a cognitive stance arising from an interest in existence manages, by thrusting existence into the sphere of conceptual schemas, to somehow distance the observer from existence itself, although no—distance is not the right word, it would be more accurate to say that this stance takes one beyond existence, not destroying, perhaps, but certainly loosening the elementary ties that bind a person to other human beings. Individuals who are gifted with a strong social instinct are inclined to treat the reality of closed monasteries as a shallow, empty, easy, useless, if not to say parasitical, existence. An opinion like that is alien to me, distant. However, I place a higher value on Brother Albert's rule than on the rules of the Cistercians, and Francis of Assisi awakens more sympathy in me than does Simon the Stylite or the Eastern desert anchorites. I would also prefer (if it is permissible to express such a desire) that Saint Anthony had resisted temptations among people rather than in the desert. I am not trying to determine which is easier and which is more difficult. I think that that would be the same as trying to walk in someone else's shoes, and it is inappropriate to pronounce too categorically and eagerly, from the outside, on the possibilities and correctness of another's way of life. I am expressing only my own personal preferences. But I realize that on the basis of these confessions, someone might take me for a proponent of action. And that person would be right, although not entirely so. It's true, I place a very high value on objective action, but that does not mean that I would embrace action for action's sake, constant movement, being endlessly unsatiated with reality, or seeking, under cover of the most various sublimations, ever newer stimuli and false consolations. Often, a position of this sort evolves to inflict violent gashes in the brilliance of great slogans and dazzling signs. So much the worse.

Writing about corrupt religiosity, you correctly remarked that "Never are so many evil deeds and errors committed as in exaltation over one's own nobility or one's own calling." Personally, I am irritated and disturbed by the blithe energy with which some people move through their days, some of them like scurrying ants, immersed up to their necks in the minutiae of daily life, and others, who are more refined, seeking the most effective means of satisfying their lofty ambitions. One can always find in the hearts or minds of such individuals a painful scar that they themselves are often unaware of, or, if they recognize it, they try to heal it, to bind it with movement, shouting, bah—even with sacrifice and dedication. Oh yes, the sphere of human activity can provoke a good deal of wariness and doubt. But let us leave these dark depths; there is too much to say about them. You will see that the territory in which the shades of Rastignac, Julien Sorel, the younger Verkhovensky, and Almayer stumble about is not the sphere that I would want to contrast with an intellectual cognitive position. If one could throw that sorrowful realm onto a scale, it would certainly pitch violently downward. Allow me to make a certain personal confession at this point. When I consider my own life, I see myself first as a boy, then as a very restless youth, rocked back and forth between extreme opposites. I don't think I am falsifying my image when I say that it was precisely in that chaotic, passionate sampling of opposites that I found meaning in my own life and in existence in general. Ah, those anxieties, that blind, greedy restlessness. And now . . . I would be lying if I wanted to convince you that I have achieved equilibrium and imposed order on my many contradictory elements. No. Sometimes I even doubt that I will ever achieve that. I am not convinced that internal *classicism* is a condition that is capable of subjective confirmation and ultimate subjective approbation. Who knows if that state you described in one of your previous letters as "wisdom" is not, to our dying day, like the horizon,

which constantly disappears into the distance before the eyes
of the traveler. I think that one can bow one's head before
another person's classicism, but one cannot make that same
gesture before oneself.

But I am interested in something else. Perhaps my ener-
getic distancing myself from the thirties, perhaps the combination of wartime experiences, perhaps both the one and the
other, and also additional factors, have caused a certain displacement of desires in me over the last few years. To be sure,
I am still tempted to immerse myself in contradictions, but
now only as forbidden fruit. Most likely, I will never beat that
temptation to a pulp. But perhaps that is exactly what the difference between youth and maturity is based on—that imperceptible "hint of a shadow," that while youth tastes temptation
greedily and without scruples, in maturity one first enters the
circle of true temptations. In youth, one does what one wants
to; at least, one is poised to act that way. Maturity, in contrast, is
deprived of that rapacious freedom; it understands the illusori-
ness of apparent human freedoms and, struggling to give them
up, accepts regulations and laws. Truly, only he who knows the
power of prohibitions understands the power that tempts one
to defy them and cast them off. So much is said about the
temptations of youth! That is a misunderstanding. Youth only
succumbs to temptation. Youth is not an equal partner. It is
weaker. Temptations don't have to reach a man's depths and
scream in order to be victorious. A superficial whisper is all
they need. They keep their reserves on hand for later.

If I can speak, then, of a change in myself, it is only in the
sense of the displacement of my internal evaluation of myself.
Bearing within myself many contradictions, I do not praise
them. Not being a classical man, I accept that type of person.
I shall try to explain briefly what I mean by such a definition.
The term "classical" is not meant to signify here an attempt at
making connections with those periods of history that we are

accustomed to call classical. I use this concept in the sense in which we often speak of a work of art—that it is classical. *The Odyssey* and *Antigone* are classical, but so, too, are *Pan Tadeusz* and *Madame Bovary*. As you see, I am not interested in content, but in measure, in the proportion and harmony of the content. The concept of "classical man," although it is undoubtedly derived from the spirit of the ancient world, seems to me to be universal and alive in every age. Today, however, we may have moved further away from this concept than ever before. We are all lacking in equilibrium; there is a lack of clearly delineated hierarchies of values; the proportions of our internal and social lives are subject to constant shocks and displacements. We are fluid, we are hazy, the boundaries of reality within which we move are as uncertain and impermanent as the borders between nations.

At some time, years from now, the literature of our time will surely become a moving document of that lost human equilibrium. It is difficult to speak of a type of man created by the art of the past several decades, because the entire effort of that literature was moving in the direction of differentiating human individuals. So one can speak only of a certain general cognitive stance, about the position literature adopted in relation to man. This is one of the characteristic features that appears in innumerable novels, from Proust to Huxley—a striving to portray a true man, described in detail and against the broadest possible experience. Writers have striven to plumb man to his depths, seemingly believing that they could succeed with the help of subtle psychological analysis. Today one can say with almost total certainty that the attempt did not succeed. From the pages of contemporary literature emerges a man whose dark depths certainly interest us, but who also disturbs and disorients us to the same degree. It seems to me that finding one's way through the dark thicket of instincts, yearnings, desires, and contradictory reflexes that are revealed through miscroscopic examination exceeds man's possibilities. At the same time, the most subtle psychological analysis is capable of encompassing in its magnifying glass only one moment in time. The image that we receive as a result of these presentations is not truer than the image that arises in our imagination when we wish to encompass a vast, mysteriously constructed landscape with the help of a field glass that magnifies only fragments of it. We shall have to rely on reconstructing that landscape, but we will never encompass it in a single moment and in its entirety. Man, as he has been constructed by the literature of psychological inquiry, passes before us in the shape of a series of fragments. His entirety remains inaccessible to us. I believe that this is also because there is a great chasm between thinking about man and that which man is in essence. What we call classical art only thought about man; contemporary psychological literature strives to know man. Every classicism has consciously simplified and construed man, subordinating individuality to such intellectual concepts as pride, miserliness, heroism, love, ambition. After all, it was only thanks to such an approach that Macbeth, Molière's miser, El Cid, Romeo and Juliet, Père Goriot, Sorel, and Jim could be born. It turns out that in literature, it is precisely the striving for realistic truth and verisimilitude that can create falseness, whereas falsified man is often real. Applying the criteria of verisimilitude, ninety percent of the great literary figures are depicted only in fragments. Can you imagine El Cid meditating like Joyce's Bloom in the w.c.? Faust embroiled in the delirium of Witkiewicz's characters, or Antigone declaiming her famous role under the direction of Stanisław Maria Jankowski, the nationalist author of *Sword Against Sword?* Yet it is precisely El Cid, Faust, and Antigone who satisfy our need to see man whole: this Cid who cannot sit on a close stool; Faust, who is not permitted to get the hiccups in Margaret's presence; and Antigone, who cannot fend off persistent associations between her thoughts and her memories. We are not satisfied, on the other hand, by Hela Bertz from Witkiewicz's *Farewell to Autumn*, Gide's Eduard, or Mann's Hans Castorp, nor by a crowd of other characters, those shadows illuminated by the misleading glow of analysis. That is what I am aiming at. I want to emphasize how very significant the element of conscious selection and construction is in man's existence. It seems to me that one cannot exist as a complete self. It is necessary to select; to discard something, to accept something else. The parable about the eye of the needle suspends a particularly eloquent accent mark over contemporary man. Few of us would be capable of passing through that eye; we are too fat, too inflated. We could benefit from an inner fast, restraining ourselves from consuming everything that life brings us and that we offer ourselves.

Expending one's energy with the aim of maintaining equilibrium between thinking and action seems to me to be one of the disciplines that the individual must impose upon himself, especially today, when, faced with the monstrousness of life, it is so easy either to flee to the sphere of intellectual decisions or to blindly hurl oneself into the whirlwind of action. Both postures, even if they represent the best measures in their range of choices, seem incapable of creating foundations for harmonious and orderly existence. When I speak of "classical man," I have in mind a man who could manage to act consistently and tenaciously according to the claims of his intellect, and to affirm through his own existence those values that, in his mind and heart, he acknowledges to be values. I am absolutely convinced that even the best idea will not return dignity and proper respect to human relations if it does not pursue dignity and affirm human deeds, starting with the smallest kindnesses of an ordinary day. This is surely not the last time that humanity will experience days as dark as ours today. Hatred and contempt will undoubtedly destroy many more cities, and a great deal of blood will flow because of their blows in centuries to come. I have no illusions. So if one can yearn for something, it would be for a time of even temporary renewal, of being lifted up out of the misery and sordidness in which we wallow today. I know that even then, in that time of escape, people will suffer, murder, and hate. But may those voices of unchanging evil not be the loudest, may their darkness not cover everything, may the pure tone of love arise even briefly above this saddest of all worlds, so that we, too, after so many years, can breathe more freely, and so that those who will live in the future can, in a moment of loss like ours today, renew their hope, turning their eyes toward that streak of light among the nights. I confess that I would be happy if in my lifetime I could hear those yearning voices in the company of those who are dearest to me. I know that whether the earth moves forward or not also depends upon us. On me, on you, on everyone alive. Our relation to the present reality must be different than it was toward the world of the two interwar decades. That was the world of our first youth, the world we found; it wasn't our hands that pushed it toward catastrophe. Today is different. Without false shame we must say that, in some respect, this obligates us.

Perhaps I have written rather chaotically about this. Forgive me. Time feels extraordinarily heavy, airless. I find it difficult to concentrate and to focus my thoughts on what I am aiming at. A few days ago we entered the fourth year of this war. It is as beautiful and sunny now as it was during that first autumn. Again there is the dull throbbing of the bombers overhead at night; again terror is driving thousands of people from their besieged city. But how different "now" is! Three years of such times means something. Three years is not such a long time in one's memories, but so very long when one lives through that time day by day.

Dear Czeslaw, I have to confess to you that sometimes, when it was very difficult for me, when my personal affairs were also too painful and the world in which we live was casting up so much evil and suffering, I experienced moments of doubt as to whether all this, we ourselves and life—whether, in general, this has any meaning. It seems that these doubts no longer assail me. If I have derived from these last years some enduring knowledge, it is, first and foremost, a profound conviction, belief, and knowledge simultaneously, that everything that happens, everything without exception, has its own meaning. If I were to be asked what meaning there is in the death of a young, wonderfully promising lad tortured in the Gestapo's cellars; what is the meaning of human sufferings that no words can express; what is the meaning of a thousand things whose dread slices into our hearts, the meaning of the spilled blood of innocents, the meaning of the torment of children and of mothers bereft of their children, I would not be able to answer. But I know that a meaning exists, that it is circulating among us like an invisible spirit, and everything, every tear and every drop of blood, is filled with its uncomprehended breath. Less and less frequently I catch myself in a direct, reflexive reaction when I suddenly come face-to-face with an event whose purpose seems impossible to grasp, so incompatible does it seem with a sense of justice that one cries out, "That makes no sense!" I cannot fathom the meaning of the world, but I understand that this meaning exists.

It is only this conviction, held in spite of these times that contradict reason, that lends a higher sanction to my existence. For I know that my life, like the existence of all people, has its unique and unrepeatable meaning, its purpose in the general framework of the world. I am absolutely convinced that every person possesses a certain assigned role and is conceived of as a particular, defined being. Tragedy begins only with the failure to fulfill one's meaning, with a person's deviation from his proper path, with the awakening of gnawing desires that cannot be satisfied by the limitedness of nature and whose insatiability so exceeds human possibilities. This is exactly how I imagine original sin: a lack of humility toward oneself, the desire to become someone other than it is possible to be, the impossibility of satiating oneself through one's own limitedness, the inability to accept oneself and to understand that it is precisely within defined boundaries that true and important meaning is contained, even though it may differ so greatly from one human being to another. I do not know if even one man exists on this earth who is free of this tragedy. It is, apparently, universal and will always exist. I think that man is predetermined, but I see man's free will in that it depends on us to decipher the contents of our predestination, to understand it, to accept it, and to fulfill it. To be able to bear the burden of one's limitedness and smallness wisely—who can say if this is not more difficult than to bear greatness. You remember Norwid: "For I end where my possibility is."

Recently I have given a lot of thought to the expression of the commandment in the Gospels about loving one's neighbor: "Love thy neighbor as thyself." Have you noticed with what unequal force the history of Christianity has emphasized the first part of that law, since love of self has not hung over people with equal violence? One might say that to love oneself is to be self-satisfied. But that's not it. Such love seems to me to be a consistent internal disposition that allows me to understand that my individuality is a creative act, a unique value, whose measure, whatever it may be, larger or smaller, only I can bring to fruition. Pride, arrogance, one's own egoistic love, command us to seek expression for our individuality above our place in life and above our possibilities. We measure ourselves by the measure of other people's achievements. We wish for gratification, which might be called social. At the same time, the *habitus* of true self-love finds gratification in a higher order, arising as it does from embracing the harmony of all existence, not from its individual fragments. Every person strives to discover the meaning of his existence, even those who are unaware of it. But a person who seeks only social satiation, which is verifiable, strives for this by erasing the most glorious image of himself in order to strongly accentuate that meaning in his own consciousness and in the consciousness of his contemporaries, and also of those who will live after him. Certainly a whisper will not reach the ears of future generations; still, in the system of all human existence, beyond the order of time and space that encloses our existence from birth to death, even the softest whisper may resound with the force of a great summons. True love of self relinquishes awareness of the essential meaning of one's own existence. It commands man to fulfill his social destiny, lending a shade of mystery to the final goal. This is wise love, because it is reconciled with life in time and in space. It is also submissive love, because it understands life as duty, as command, without attempting to penetrate its ultimate purpose. Finally, it is trusting, because it carries within itself faith and hope that the command that has been given to me is just and purposeful. Finally, it unites with all people in a dual fraternity: earthly travail and the harmony that binds the contradictions of the world with incomprehensible links, injustice and sacrifice, suffering and violence, destruction and the springtime sowing of grain. You ask me what bond exists between the objective measure of "classical man" and my subjective faith, whether they are not two currents of thought that simply flow past each other. I personally think that that is not so. I believe that only from the moment of accepting life and one's own existence can one speak about constructing reality and oneself. It is like the first step on a road down which one is led by the need for order. I am concerned with a fundamental attitude toward life. Today, too, when, among so much devastation, faith in existence itself has fallen victim to weakness, restoring power to that position of accepting life would not strike me as a mere truism. I also think that

certain moral disciplines flow from that position if one can define respect for another person and consciousness of human
solidarity as a concept of an ethical norm. I think it can be. I
also think that this measure of both human thought and of a
human deed that is worthy of it can serve as a foundation.

VII

Czeslaw Milosz to Jerzy Andrzejewski

Dear Jerzy,

I was taken aback and somewhat disconcerted by your last statement, so I have to stray from thinking about the doubts that assail me, stop tooting my own intellectual horn for a while, and enter into a more direct conversation. You sneaked up on me and suddenly questioned whether all this mental tightrope walking is meaningful in some way; you assure me, instead, that it is of little use for one's health and even destructive if engaged in excessively. That it moves one away from existence, or perhaps carries one beyond existence. You also make intellectualism responsible for the excessive analysis of man in the literature of the last few decades—analysis that, as we know, instead of depicting man fully, eclipsed him and surrounded him with a fog of insinuations. You also assure me that unlike conscious or unconscious fascists, you are not proposing praise of action as the opposite of intellect; on the contrary, you call for an equal balance of these elements.

Very well. Let us consider this calmly, although I am already in a rage. Oh, don't think anything bad, it's the rage of a chess player or a lawyer, because I like "the blow of words and the fire of arguments." You yearn for equilibrium between thought and deed? I do, too. You think that the world will not move if each of us, by word and deed, does not make it happen? I think so, too. You put forward the ideal of classical man; you would like to be that classical man! I would, too. And so would everyone, because who can resist the temptation of that little word "classical"? The problem is that all of this amounts to a reasonable and beautiful "in order to." But having uttered in one breath a lot of "in order tos," one comes up against a wall that blocks one's way. And the wall is "how." How to revive classical man? How to get rid of the growths that have so painfully deformed his features? There is no other way; one must try to cross over the wall, but that, alas, requires the intellectual mountain climbing that you so dislike . . . Perhaps you see other means. Perhaps you believe in "let us live decently," "do in your own little circle what God's spirit commands," "have a heart and look into a heart"—and think that will suffice. I treat these maxims without any irony; on the contrary. But a light tremor runs down my back when I hear them, because they remind me of something. Oh yes, there was a time in our history: it was when rival currents of thought were swirling around in the West, when here in Poland newspapers that were published with the aim of building up noble families counseled distrust of the immoral West. Who cares what that Hegel thinks up, who cares about those Frenchmen and Englishmen . . . old Polish virtue is better. Midgets' distrust of the Babylon of ideas. Then, betraying the creative ferments of positivism, Sienkiewicz exploited this splendidly: all deliberations, the arguments of philosophers, debates—they're all foolishness, "but Saint Peter's basilica rules the world." No, I do not assume that your intentions were similar to this. So you have to go about things differently. According to you, equilibrium is threatened by a cognitive stance that, pushing toward ever deeper analysis, deconstructs man into little pieces and then does not know what to do with those pieces. Am I right? You prescribe an internal fast, restraining oneself from that dangerous game. Terrific. But I am afraid that there is a

simplification concealed within this, and my pettifogging eloquence will strive to reveal what kind it is—even if only in
part.

For several decades now, the world has lived under the sign
of anti-intellectualism. This is textbook knowledge, almost a
truism. Officially, this wave started at the very beginning of
the nineteenth century as a reaction against the spirit of positivism, but it was building up much earlier, and it is amusing
to recall that more or less with the appearance of the steam
engine and mechanized textile manufacturing, the first voices
expressing dislike of reason as the highest arbiter of right
were raised. If we can understand through intellectualism the
direction that detects the highest and most important element
of human nature in consciousness, then we are living now in a
time when the opposite tendency is celebrating its triumphs.
By opposing the will, instinct, even the subconscious to consciousness; by teaching the primacy of the deed over knowledge, writers prepared the soil for the great philosophies that
are recognized by masses of people and whose contents are
blind faith in the biological drive, in the voice of blood and
race, in the infallibility and accuracy of animal appetites—all
of which does not lead, as we know, to the awakening of respect for intellectual values. Development followed two paths.
On the one hand, observing man as a biological creature, it was
discovered that what moves him above all are drives, reflexes,
instincts, and that consciousness, therefore, is a kind of superstructure above a tangle of the most various urges and desires
that dictate their laws to it. On the other hand, looking at man
as a social creature, those inflows and outflows of collective
battles and hatreds whose goals are symbolized in money were
emphasized; these collective storms and pressures shape the
consciousness alike of entire classes and individual people, and
consciousness descends to the level of a tool.

One way or another, the role of consciousness is very modest. To assert that we are threatened today by danger on the part of intellect, that we dispose of too extensive an intellectual apparatus, seems quite bold, if not too bold. Pushed to the end of the line, prohibited from passing judgment about the most important matters in life, it has made peace with its role as a subaltern and given up on its potentialities. Taking into consideration the enormity of the cultural changes that demand intellectual ordering, during which intellect has been largely silent, it is no longer "intellect," but a mere "intellectling," wagging its tail before the new powers that the biology or sociology it created talk about. In almost every field we are witnesses of its resignation. It does not trust itself. It is not courageous. It is no longer tempted to renew the Cartesian effort to spin the silken threads of truth out of itself. It has changed into an author of pedantic notes, into someone who rummages in archives; it amasses facts, takes notes, not daring to yearn for something greater than an archivist's position.

But perhaps that is not what you had in mind when you spoke about intellectualism? Intellectualism can also be the name for a certain stance toward life, a certain fondness for observation that is understood as an end in itself, a certain monastic regime of mental exercises. An intellectual is interested above all in the mutual bonds between phenomena; he delights in plunging into that garden filled with fantastic flowers; he seeks relationships, classifies them, shouts *eureka* when he succeeds at making some new and striking connection. He is less concerned with ultimate results; it's the activity itself that he is passionate about. Curiosity replaces all other passions in him. He looks at society, at man, as an immense test tube: he doesn't worry about what man *ought* to be like; his entire ambition is to discover what he *is*. As in a game of hide-and-seek, I call out "hot," and it seems that we are close to the heart of the matter. Allow me just a tiny change in terminology. Let us call this man an observer in the broad sense of the term.

"Intellectual"—it's too fluid, too ambiguous a word, and it's not clear if it is being used as the history of philosophy once used it or as Goebbels did when he said, "When I hear the word intellectual, I reach for my revolver." The observing, analytical position is highly valued in certain periods; it becomes a common ideal. In other periods it serves as a *bête noire* and meets with all sorts of rebukes, losing all dignity in the eyes of public opinion. Recently it has been doing badly. The ideal of the active life is far more attractive to the masses; and in the circles of highly educated humanists, knowledge "as such," that doesn't aim at producing outcomes to improve the world, no longer meets with such a warm welcome.

Using contemporary literature as an example, you pointed out the barrenness of analysis that deforms man more than it teaches us to measure him by his proper measure. I agree with you on this point one hundred percent. It is a theme I care about deeply; it touches me to the quick. Several months ago I wrote about this, and although it is not polite to do so, I will pull it out of the drawer and copy from my manuscript:

Several decades ago a revolution in knowledge took place that may be called *the destruction of substance.* The classical understanding of man, developed under the influence of Christianity, demanded that we see in him a subject that undergoes no changes throughout his life that would reach to his very essence. The human soul, passing through layers of sin and virtue, maintained its identity and after death stood before the Creator, who looked in his great ledger—under the entry for last and first name—for the headings "credits" and "debits," and meted out justice. The human soul was substance, the entire universe was composed of substances, of definite entities that could be named, which possessed enduring life until the moment when time would be fulfilled and the hand of God would take back their names and put an end to their time. Like the planet Venus, like the North Star, the soul of every man shone in space like one of the infinite number of things with which the sky and earth are filled. Such a concept constructed an immutable base for each human soul, and a single thread bound all the stages of man into a single whole, running not only through childhood, maturity, and old age, but also through his posthumous existence. The new discoverers opined: "That thread is an illusion." So the atom of individuality was smashed. In place of a statue whose individual parts could be distinguished and named—seeing in it reason, will, feeling, transgression, virtue—there appeared a multicolored plasma of reflexes and reactions, something like Pavlov's dog. All monumentalism in treating the human figure became impossible, because it rests above all on choice, as you correctly say, on a certain fragmentary nature, on underlining the most important, general outlines of form. If everything is equally important, if everything is placed on the same plane (with a slight disinclination for "pure" consciousness), one cannot speak of establishing a hierarchical order, any such efforts would verge on artificiality. Alas, striving to portray "natural man," they achieved an outcome that was entirely contrary to their intentions. Naturalness turned out to be more artificial than the former schemes. And the next question, "What now?" stimulated a desire to turn back. Does the analytical, observing position bear responsibility for this state of things? Without a doubt. It arose under the influence of the flowering of scientific methods, where it is entirely appropriate. But soon it achieved a terrifying universality. It was transformed into a means of experiencing life; it excluded entirely the position of the moralist and seeker of ethical reforms. In Balzac one can still see the abrasive encounters of these two positions, although already with a significant dominance of cool, merciless objectivity. In Stendhal, Flaubert, and Zola we can follow the increasingly bold movement away from any assessment based on values, a naturalist's cruel attitude toward phenomena, beyond all hope, beyond all desire that things might be different from what they are. At the same time, there is a certain disdain, the aristocratic distancing of the observer. His penetrating gaze elevates him above the human ant heap, frees him from worries about goals that may be good for other mortals, but not for him; his goal is to observe, only to observe. It is to the credit of Russian literature that one must state that it never succumbed to this inclination toward total objectivity. Man as an ethical value remained its central aspiration, in Tolstoy, in Dostoevsky, not to mention lesser figures. Thanks to this, Russian literature is a great debate that develops around the question: How should one live? In the meantime, in the West the process of analysis developed at a dizzying pace. At first the results were splendid, and our knowledge about man was enriched by valuable experiments. But obviously there exists a boundary that may not be crossed with impunity. Striving for an ever more thorough understanding of the motives for human activity, the observers stumbled upon huge layers of mystery, the super- and also subrational sphere.

It turned out that the thinking being who had been taken to be man in his entirety is like the tip of an iceberg; it is an almost insignificant part; the rest is hidden beneath the surface of the sea. So they began soundings, dives, probes, experiments. It turned out, furthermore, that intellect is not at all the best means for creating Truth. Because we are always dependent on the grace or lack of grace of those animal instincts that inhabit us, intellect too often leads us into error, enacting all sorts of comedies. And it is heavy, a crudely hewn weapon. In order to reach those deep, irrational layers, we must extract ourselves from under its police control and allow our underground voices to speak. The quintessence of analysis is the automatic registration of internal states, as in Joyce or the surrealists. It came to pass. The position of observer contradicted itself. The serpent bit its own tail; the circle closed.

Intellect arrived at the condemnation of intellect, which was greeted with a howl of joy by proponents of the superman. For nothing guarantees such freedom as the rupture of trust in rationally ascertainable truth. Then the genius of the race can speak out, not caring that its speech sounds like the war cry of Papuans. Indeed, we are at a turning point. We distinctly feel that it is time to look at man differently, that historical accidents while trampling human existence into a pulp are at the same time raising up a monumental form, and perhaps a Sophoclean or a Shakespearean hero is closer to us than the hero of Joyce or Proust. It may not be an accident that our letters revolve around ethical issues. We are more concerned with the meaning of human actions than with their mechanism, and we are slowly arriving at the conclusion that just as the most detailed analysis of a work of art does not illuminate even a drop of its puzzling genius, detailed rummaging about in the motives and causes of action does not advance by even one step our knowledge about the ultimate result, about the world which is more fully and perfectly expressed through the elementary oppositions of beauty and ugliness, good and evil. Is it, however, possible to go back, to impose a kind of censorship on oneself and activate an ideal of spiritual divinity, such as blessed are the poor in spirit? No, I don't think that is possible. It is possible to erase the achievements of a particular period, but probably only the way the English Puritans did in 1641, or the Nazis in 1933, but even that is not permanent. A complication once begun will not die out on its own; it is not a blackboard that one can run an eraser over and it's ready to be written on again. Well, perhaps—but under one condition: that that passion for observation will be defeated by an equally penetrating passion that will assign to the activity of the human mind a new goal that is no less seductive. Notice that the passion for analysis was directed almost exclusively toward psychological investigations. The deterioration and decrepitude of the psychological novel appears to indicate that a new field of investigation is opening up before us, which has until now been left unplowed. It is certain that the evolving and continually improving sense of community life weighed heavily in this. But this field is above all the sphere of values in and of themselves, the sphere of hierarchy, which, for the observer inclined toward naturalistic explanations, signified nothing, absolutely nothing. Were I to insist that I know precisely what it is I want, I would have to pick up someone else's pen and cite authors who have managed to convince me. I prefer not to do so.

It is unbelievably strange how collective currents penetrate a particular individual's mentality; strange how new, at first timid, thoughts of a couple of philosophers originally find only a weak echo and then are disseminated. At first they are like single drops of mercury that run around in the dust of long-held habits. The entire system of thought continues as it has existed, but now it is disturbed, filled with anxiety and contradictions. That, it seems to me, is what—if I may use such a vague term—our generation's state of mind was like. We set off on a journey more or less loaded down with our inheritance of pragmatism, psychoanalysis, and many similar plagues, but the glimmerings of other desires, other yearnings, shone through that thick layer. For example, the problem of free will lost its vitality; it melted away, sharing the fate of so many other problems humanity has forgotten about. We can count this as very instructive. Suddenly we ceased to be interested in whether and how our deeds are predetermined, and we entered a land of ultimate decisions, naked, opposed to the background from which they grew. Similarly, the disturbing question—Could our consciousness just be a screen on which libido projects its simian capers?—just faded away. Having long given ourselves over to the study of the cells and tissues of a plant, we suddenly slapped our foreheads and understood that we had inappropriately neglected the color and the scent of its flower—inappropriately, because our knowledge of the structure of the calyx, the corona, the anthers, and the stamen need not make us less sensitive to the beauty of the whole. This whole also has its mysteries of symmetry, color, line. Pure human consciousness or human action can be looked at as a construct that is, perhaps, artificially limited, excised from the chain of determinants; but precisely because of this, it is raised up to the rank of phenomena that are worthy of study and not just of investigations into their origins, their genealogy.

By no means does all of this amount to some sort of anti-intellectualism. On the contrary, retreating from the path on which it has erased itself, intellect turns toward its proper field; it strives to give back to truth the position it has squandered.

"Nonsense," scream the Marxists. "We know what you are talking about. You are right that intellect has contradicted itself. Fascism is only a practical solution, the sole solution left to a Europe corroded by irrationality and mysticism. But what you are recommending . . . why, that is just the gibberish of philosophers like Husserl, Scheler, and company; it is the line of German idealism, and we know where that leads. 'Absolute truth!' What the devil is that? A pathetic search for a life raft in a return to some Platonic idea, to long-since buried, empty words. It's like the rewarming of Thomas Aquinas by Catholics in the hope that it will help their religion, which is suffering from senility. There is something even more mundane concealed behind this: looking all around for permanent, immutable elements, these people yearn to instill in us the conviction that the world has been standing still since the beginning of time, that cataclysms and revolutions roll over it like floodwaters but the earth and man on earth undergo no changes, that the selfsame proportions of good and evil exist now as they did in the time of Cain and Abel. Furthermore, that therefore the idea of a new structure that might do away with injustice and hatred is only the raving of maniacs. We know that calm sorrow of idealists! In the face of bloody events they maintain the calm of wise men. Let humanity clamor. There is nothing to do. If their own nation lifts its hand to commit a crime, they praise quietly. Because the immutable ideal of good is one thing, but the demands of life are something else again. 'One has to live,' they say, like a noble, melancholy pickpocket as he inserts his fingers into your pocket."

Let the Marxists scream. A debate with them would go too far. I am satisfied with sketching contradictions; a stroll through the garden where "pro" and "contra" grow side by side suffices for me. That is why I am much more of an observer or, as you would say, an intellectualist, than a proponent of solutions. And although my position is characterized by a healthy dose of ethical evaluation, I would not be capable of renouncing it in favor of the position of a moralist, which is your tendency. I could not, because it is not clear to me how to achieve equilibrium. I see before all of us, before our whole coming era (assuming it would be one great darkness in which wild hordes wander aimlessly), enormous cognitive work, and I confess, asking you to keep this private, that I believe in a new humanism more than in a new Middle Ages. Whoever wishes to be a moralist must be prepared to write a phenomenology of evil, of evil in its pure state, or of cruelty, or mass insanity. Exhorting people to become good is not going to help here; it will be necessary to show them that he who oversteps an imperceptible boundary, who justifies evil in whatever form, is in a pact without knowing it. Evil has become complicated, it has become more clever and sly, and he who wants to confront it must arm himself with equivalent perspicacity. It is possible that even the best ethical canon will not suffice now, when, for example, the commandment "thou shalt not kill" demands extensive commentary because we know that killing is not limited to the body; one can also kill spiritually, which was an alien concept for the creators of the Ten Commandments. You seem to believe that a sense of the immutable meaning of our deeds, a sense, in general, of the meaning of existence, offers the key to internal equilibrium and teaches the true value of human affairs. That would be a kind of intuition that reaches to the very essence of life. My dear friend, I would very much like this to serve as some kind of foundation. But I would never have written that I know the meaning of existence and that I am not assailed by doubts. I would be afraid to. I would be afraid of delusions such as intuitive certainty carries with it. I would be afraid of the hypocrisy that lies in wait for those who assert that the light has descended onto them. How often faith is only masked self-adoration. I have lived through many revelations, and the conclusion I draw does not necessarily redound to the benefit of those brief states when earth and heaven appear to us in the glow of perfect harmony. I do not trust myself; in general, I do not trust man. He is too often led into temptation. Too often he mistakes the fire of his own desires for the star that leads to Bethlehem. This does not mean that I don't feel, somewhere deep inside myself, my own calling, that small portion of work that I must carry out as long as I am alive. *"Mais ce sont là les choses—dont le nom n'est ni son si silence,"* as the poet says. Words—round, beautiful words—often lead us farther than we might wish to go. Transported by their rhythm, we utter incantations and prayers whose contents are beyond our experience. Frequently, where it is a matter of giving expression to weighty, ultimate matters such as predestination, death, the meaning of existence, words are like a cloak made of heavy brocade—stiff, formal—which, instead of accommodating the movement of the human form, conceal and stiffen it. It is very difficult to choose a different garment in such matters; habit makes us adopt an anointed, priestly tone. And that is why I value intellectualism, which rends that coarse, gilt fabric with ceaseless liveliness of thought, always seeking new definitions that are as precise as can be, worrying about elasticity, about the garment's adhering to our form. It encourages us to doubt. And doubt rips many a tirade in two, destroys it, gives us a new race to run. Even if one does not have what it takes to be an original thinker, if one has only the powers of an intelligent tourist in the countries of thought—still, the effort pays for itself. For a writer, this is labor that is necessary for health. Since you love Stendhal, I remind you that when the model style in France was Chateaubriand's well-rounded, monotonously moving prose, someone appeared who disdained easy charm and the falsity of the romantic lexicon and took the stiff, attentive language of the legal codes as his model. That someone was Henri Beyle—Stendhal. Just as he had predicted, he began to be read only after 1880, and today *The Charterhouse of Parma* has lost none of its fascination, whereas *Atala* and *René* bring to mind dried flowers in one's great-grandmother's book. Because Beyle had a "violent and poisonous" mind; because he was a rationalist and a skeptic. Which I note not because I take precision and stiffness as a model (I am incapable of that) but to offer an example of the saving results of intellectualism for breaking down conventions.

VIII

Jerzy Andrzejewski to Czeslaw Milosz

Dear Czeslaw,

It seems to me that our last two letters are talking past each other to a certain extent, and that they are bringing in more marginal issues than essential, positive formulations. Perhaps I am somewhat to blame for this, because I started using very general concepts; perhaps part of the blame also falls on you, who so love "the blow of words and the fire of arguments." Most likely, both the one and the other. But taking a broader view, I suspect that some part of our talking past each other, a certain vagueness about our conclusions when we ought to be stating how much two times two is—in a word, a certain helpless, cautious, doubtful attitude when our questions are weighing on us with ever-increasing force and insistence—isn't this all a particularly characteristic feature, not so much of our era as of a certain type of people who are caught in this era? If we are to understand each other with the help of such broad concepts as good and evil, then we will certainly agree that evil brings us a reality that is incomparably more clearly crystallized than good. It is more aggressive and combative, better fortified in its positions. Good displays a much blurrier profile; to put it more precisely, many of those who yearn for the restoration of human order speak about this more vaguely, with less precision, than those who thought up the concentration camps and the mass slaughter of defeated peoples. I am thinking of those people who, like you and me, do not feel at home with the concepts of dogma or in the ranks of religious orthodoxy. The very qualities of mind of these people and the kind of emotions they have condemn them (and there are many of them) to a certain piecemeal quality in their worldviews, often to many contradictions, many hesitations, and to ever so many difficulties.

I recognize all this, but as a painful burden and lack, not as a position and method. Meanwhile, your intellectualism or, as you call it, position as an observer often strikes me as the anxiety of a man who, running through a room that is crammed with furniture, cannot choose a place to sit down, because he understands that not a single piece can be relied on. You are even inclined to go further, because, should you chance to take a seat during this wandering in some attractive, thoroughly comfortable armchair and experience so-called "good feelings," your anxiety and your distrust would immediately make you leap up. You write that you are afraid of hypocrisy, which "lies in wait for those who assert that the light has descended onto them." You suggest that "often faith is only masked self-adoration." Finally, you admit that you do not trust yourself, nor man in general. Consequently, distrusting and suspicious, you look closely at everyone who might sit down beside you, even on the edge of his chair. Now you are going to shout that this is misrepresentation, that it's not fair.

My friend, since on the evidence of my previous letter you took me to be an anti-intellectualist in general, although I clearly defined what type of intellectual position I want to oppose, and in addition ascribed to me a few other thoughts that I did not express at all—for example, when you suggested that I said I know the meaning of existence—to avoid further misunderstandings, don't suspect me of nurturing a contemptuous or belittling attitude toward intellectual anxiety. I carry that anxiety in myself, too, and I know how many of our contemporaries share a similar anxiety. But don't insist that I approve of this position, nor try to convince yourself that it is sufficient. I don't understand why you introduce so much passion, such "pettifogging" passion as you yourself say, in pursuing so-called "good feelings" (doing this, to be sure, with generalizations), and do not show the same passion when you survey the concealed aspects of the position that hesitates before respect and before basing itself on certain values.

You say that "sketching contradictions" is enough for you, that "a stroll through the garden where 'pro' and 'contra' grow side by side" is sufficient. Do you think that taking such a stroll excludes the possibility of a skeptical glance behind the scenes? Does a man who is unable to sit down not deserve just as much attentive observation as one who is seated or about to sit? If you have come to the point of not believing in and not trusting man, then you must be consistent, and not say yes at times, no at others. If you don't trust yourself when you are seated, than don't trust yourself when you are walking.

You condemn, and rightly so, our homegrown nineteenth-century anti-intellectualism, which scornfully and indifferently passed over the work of Western minds, but tell me whether, concealed in the position of an observer, which you admit to and which you propose to maintain, isn't there also the flaw of a certain aloofness, a self-ostracism not just from the problems of the day but from life itself? As far as I'm concerned, Sienkiewicz deserted with his vision of Saint Peter's basilica ruling the world; but believe me, I detect an element of desertion, of dry abstraction when you portray yourself as a wanderer among contemporary "pros" and "contras." I am not saying that this is an easy position. It is difficult, I appreciate that, but despite the passionate tone in which you sometimes speak, the position of "observer," such as you define it, strikes me as somehow crippled, stripped of an essential embrace of man's fate. I'm sorry; that is how I perceive it.

My previous letter had a modest goal. I wanted to emphasize that contemporary man will never move out of his present misery and confusion if he does not make the effort to support the work of his intellect, his cognitive and value-assigning work, with action focused on achieving equilibrium between the spheres of thinking and of acting. You responded that you yearn for the same thing, but at the edge of that pious yearning you see a wall, and that wall is the question of how to get there. Obviously that is a question that can be posed always and everywhere, parading it on a leash to the end of one's life. I do not feel strong enough to create a new Ten Commandments. I imagine, if you were to hear something as generic and peremptory as "love thy neighbor as thyself," you would ask, "How can that be done?" At the end of your letter you return to the same doubt, and you say that how to achieve equilibrium is not clear to you. Thus you place a question mark over the entire subject of the possibility of even a temporary restoration of man. I don't know if you are doing this consciously or unconsciously, but you are leading yourself into a blind alley, you observer of "pro" and "contra," who can counter the intellect's darkness only with "I don't know."

But you defend intellectualism and the position of the observer very effectively, evoking all the devastation and depravity created by contemporary irrational tendencies. You make it clear that by according intellect permanent and peremptory sanction, returning superiority and dignity to it, you stand in opposition simultaneously to contemporary barbarism and all the murky irrationalisms that summon people to the myth of race, nation, or class. You are right to do so. But . . . Yes, there is a but. Insofar as I understand you, you are inclined to profess that a sphere of extra-human reality, a metaphysical sphere, does exist. Nevertheless, discerning the vagueness of that metaphysical sphere, you find no support in it that is sufficiently trustworthy, or capable of satisfying you. And since man is inclined to hypocrisy, and nowhere is it easier to achieve false sublimation than in the sphere of metaphysical experiences, you therefore are suspicious of all attempts at resolving man's problems on the plane of religion. The problem of an ethical standard—eternal and supernatural, or changeable and historic—remains unresolved in your view. Innate tendencies and needs incline you to the former, but intellectual exertion commands you to doubt. Finally, striving to discover a new, permanent ethical norm, you find a cognitive instrument instead. This is the intellect. The demands of that intellect incline you, in turn, to adopt the position of the observer of "pro" and "contra."

Intellectualism understood in that way does not seem to be a position whose roots and most essential motivation can be distinguished in any way from the many contemporary irrationalisms that you have condemned. Both positions, though they appeal to different human elements, inhere powerfully and decisively in the traditional thinking of modern times during which man has been construed as an autonomic value. Since the end of the Middle Ages, from the moment the concept of man as tied to supernatural existence began to crumble, down to our time of multiple isms, one immutable motif has been threaded through all the various currents of the Renaissance, Reformation, Cartesianism, Enlightenment, Romantic philosophy, materialism, fascism, totalitarianisms, and rationalisms: a naturalistic concept of man. Probing somewhat deeper than appearances would suggest, your humanistic intellectualism, fascist nationalisms, and Stalinist materialism all revolve within the same circle of naturalistic man separated from his supernatural intercessor.

[It is unclear if the letter ended at this point.—*Czeslaw Milosz's note*]

IX

Czeslaw Milosz to Jerzy Andrzejewski

My dear friend,

I think that we ought to focus on outlining our positions, and as soon as these positions emerge clearly, there will be no point in multiplying casuistic arguments, to which, mea culpa, I am even more inclined than you. Now I would like to engage in some digressions that although they may appear to be at a remove from our main theme, will add a good deal of clarity. Recently I have spent a lot of time pondering what might be called, metaphorically, the river of history. There are certainly moments in history when the river flows lazily and with dignity, or at least that is how it appears to human eyes. There are other times when, as is happening today, its current is accelerated. What especially fascinates me is not only that which grabs our attention by its enormity, not just the collapse and birth of powers, armies, states, dictatorships. More than what takes place on an immense scale, it's the small reflections that fascinate me, the wrinkles of the tiny, just-born waves, the first gentle breezes, the outlines of not yet filled-out shapes. Matters that have matured sufficiently to become historical fact are more or less in the past, even if they have affected us so profoundly that we, together with them, are turning into the past. But there are other things whose strength rests on their not yet existing; in a moment they will emerge from darkness, from chaos, just as soon as they appear on the shadowy boundaries of our perceptual field. It's a dark thing, this becoming. Uttering that word, I see, as surely every person does, the time that I have lived through. I see the dances, fashions, fleeting and local fame, fleeting collective passions. I see the faces of friends no longer alive. I remember the fervor with which they defended certain slogans that had already become part of the distant past for me, but not for them—for them there will remain forever the final boundary, the last card signed by death. Fulfillment, transience . . . All the metaphysical strangeness of time. But that is not what I wanted to speak about. Astonishment in the face of the transitory, like all the deepest astonishments in relation to life, does not lend itself to contemplation—it belongs, rather, to an ur-form of art or religion—and I suspect that this can be revealed only obliquely, only between the lines; quite likely, what we call the individuality of the artist is not a proper means of living through time. Here I want to impose limits on myself and to stop to consider only one variety of becoming. How fashions and intellectual habits come into being—that is what I would call it.

It is easier to express an opinion about this when one looks backward; historians of literature and customs do this when they demonstrate how one current is transformed into another without anyone having noticed; how the *preambula* of the second are already contained in the first; how, in the space of a couple of generations, taste, mores, and even man's imagination of what he himself is can change. Once he imagines that man is romantic, sensitive, impulsive, that he suffers from unhappy love, from the baseness of the world, he imagines this, and in fact he does suffer, he does endure and despair. At other times he considers himself to be sober, ironic; he likes to contain everything in rational formulas and, convinced of this and not another type of his nature, he transforms himself into the image and likeness of this image of himself. After all, the thousands of men and women who walk the streets of today's cities are, considering the matter physiologically, specimens of the same species that just a hundred years ago, in the Romantic era, fainted at every amorous emotion and poured forth a stream of tears. Young men who today trade in gold or are engaged in conspiratorial work are the same people who in Paul de Kock's day would have wandered among ruins (artificial ones, not like the real ones now) and sent up sighs to the moon. And the SS men who order Jews they shoot to do knee bends while they insert new clips into their guns are the same as those German youths who under the influence of *The Sorrows of Young Werther* ran into fields and woods to commit suicide from sorrow over the imperfection of the world. What point is there in speaking here about race or heritage? Man is a being who is susceptible to autosuggestion; perhaps that is the *differentia specifica* of the species.

I said that it is easier, when one looks backward, to opine on the changes in man's mentality and the changes in his nature that follow from this. But after all, aside from great variations and great changes, there are also small changes from day to day. A plant swells, puts out leaves, blooms, bears fruit, and a passerby is apt to notice this; but is he not aware of the changes taking place from minute to minute, is he not cognizant of its growth, hardening, decay? Locked in this great laboratory of time between 1939 and 1942, at times I would have liked to be an investigator, at other times to be a secret observer. And that is why I say that in the river of history I seek the small, as yet unhatched forms. That is why shocking political news and an ordinary detail of life in Warsaw have almost the same significance for me: conversations while waiting in line; educated women with sacks of potatoes on their back; the cut of overcoats made from army blankets; and the story going around in which a white airplane appeared over the Żoliborz district and the Pope leaned out of it and yelled to the people working in their garden plots: "Keep digging, keep digging, just hang on till springtime." This rapid decline in the continent's standard of living to the level of revolutionary Russia, the disappearance of social hierarchies, the difference of that which sustains and defines hierarchies: elegant clothing, abrupt shifts in fashion, snobbery—what an image for the observer! And at the same time, from minute to minute, the proportion of human imaginings is changing. Isn't it always astonishing that certain tendencies to look at phenomena one way and not another arise spontaneously, flood in from many directions? People who are unacquainted with each other notice that even in the most difficult problems, similar solutions will come to mind, that they respond similarly to certain books and individuals; a wave of enthusiasm flows through them for Norwid, for example, or for the unmasking of German philosophy. The rise of convictions is similar to the rise of rumors: a rumor takes hold and spreads, thanks to its having landed on soil that is the same for all those who hear it, prepared in just the same way. The greatest absurdity will not elicit any hesitations, because it is the same color, the same temperature as the minds of those who swallow it.

Convictions are adopted in a somewhat more complicated manner, that is certain. I am just as certain that our knowledge about the rise of collective judgments is more than pitiful. Mutual ties, the whole psychological osmosis, elude our attention. Causes and results create a single braid of interwoven threads, branches, offshoots. But it would not be impossible to identify and name at least a few of these threads. Let us take an example—the most trivial, the most trite. Every evening a great number of Warsaw's inhabitants sit down with their English-language textbooks. This is a true collective mania, a collective addiction. Anyone who understands how significant knowing one, and not some other, language is for the nuances of mentality will ponder this seriously. In recent years Polish intellectual circles remained under the spell of French or German, and I would not be far from the truth were I to insist that one can define and classify a person with a great deal of accuracy on the basis of which language, other than Polish, he does his basic reading in. Or rather, we could, if we had more perfect tools. The study of English makes it possible to get acquainted with authors who touch upon (more or less) themes that are very close to the concerns of contemporary man; it is mainly curiosity that directs one to those authors. The reflections of Anglo-Saxon authors differ significantly from similar reflections among the French or the Germans; there are differences of nuance, differences of tradition, differences of historical conditions. So, doesn't an intelligent reader, entering the world of Anglo-Saxon intellectual tradition and bringing with him his own anxieties and questions, yield to a certain "makeover"? Isn't some new ground created for his future agreement with readers like him? I repeat: this example is simplified and one-sided; it represents only one of a great number of links that are—I won't prejudge—either lasting or merely temporary.

I agree that we have very limited means for grasping the formation of popular opinion as it is crystallizing, but I still insist that contemporary man, even if only hazily, senses the dependence of his convictions on the ebbs and flows of the collective spirit; that he ascribes to them relative rather than unconditional authority; that he measures them more by their relation to the convictions of his milieu than to so-called eternal and absolute truth. We think historically, and there is nothing we can do about that. It is appropriate and useful that historicism elicits objections and provides occasion for many rebukes, for its dangers are many. Nevertheless, we are so marked by historical and social thinking that the sphere of impersonal and superhuman truth appears to us as an excessively cold and inhospitable space. Even in the condemnation of historicism, certain historical illuminations, certain powerfully pragmatic justifications for this condemnation, are concealed. And if we agree that the disappearance of criteria of truth other than the criterion of utility leads humanity to terrible catastrophes, this still does not mean that we are capable of seeking truth by any means other than our experience of social life. Our "eternal truth" rests on the comparison between experiences of a higher order and experiences of a lower order, on the recognition of a tradition that acknowledges the superiority of good over evil and is founded on a certain ethical empiricism. I believe that one should not underestimate this developmental line whose representatives are various utilitarians and pragmatists. Nietzsche mocked the English historians of ethics who, having discarded the Christian concept of the Divinity, were not courageous enough to break with Christian morality. He called them ninnies. He was one who dared, and he wanted others, too, to dare to cross the boundaries sanctified by the tradition of Christianity. This expresses the difference between the "anti-Platonism" of the Anglo-Saxon pragmatists and continental "anti-Platonism." Nietzsche's present-day reader is inclined to recognize those "ninnies" as right, since audacity of thought is not always a guarantee of truth. Respect for *common sense* has its virtues, too; it also has a disinclination for continual revolutions, for continual overturning of the ladder of values. Blessed is conventionality, blessed is the shame of "those who think decently"; after all, were it not for them, it would be difficult to believe in civilization . . .

Now I will return to the matter of intellectualism that we discussed in our earlier letters. Defending it, I sought a place for it in the system of components we could use to create those timid outlines of tomorrow. This is how I relate to my own convictions: I try to distinguish in them those threads that bind me to the group, though it is a small one, of people who think as I do. In other words, I do not value complete isolation or complete audacity; rather, while maintaining my isolation, I believe that somewhere there are brother minds and that there will be more of them—in a word, that by saying something, I am connected with the development of things that are still shrouded in mist but are slowly gaining in strength. (Such a faith is good medicine. Who, after all, will guarantee that I am not an epigone of a dying world? To which I reply: even were it so, dying out also has its own development, its own ascending motion, and it is not for me to judge the ultimate outcome.) If, despite all the quite universal complaints, I still find positive aspects in intellectualism, this is because I see around us processes that in one form or another lead to it and can justify its existence.

Undoubtedly, so-called intellectualism is, at the same time, a rather definite ethical position. When someone says "intellectualist," he pictures to himself a room filled with books and a man with white, delicate hands sitting in an armchair and bent over a manuscript. The armchair is a boat on which the man floats away from "the miserable cacophony of the quotidian" into the realm of pure thought. In our time, people argued a lot about the rights and obligations of the *clerc*. In this sense, "*clerc*-ism" and intellectualism are two names for the same subject. It is a question of a certain disinterested mentality, gazing from a distance at human passions and struggles, to which is contrasted an ideal far removed from the practice of everyday life. *Clerc*-ism sustained a significant blow during the last couple of decades. The transformation of entire classes and nations into armies at war with each other left little occasion for remaining on the sidelines. Even the most aristocratic minds found themselves "in the eye of the cyclone," and had to align themselves with one side or the other. The disdain of the general public began to pursue those who still pretended that nothing had changed and that they were free to remain in the wise man's hideout.

Nonetheless, it seems to me that the sentence imposed by political events on "intellectualists" does not preclude a finding in their favor. On the contrary, the obligations they have taken upon themselves have cleansed intellectualism of many faults—above all, of the sin of fleeing from reality. There was too much avoidance of inconveniences in them, too much self-protection in "safe" spheres. If, during the first world war, many of the *clercs* looked at the mutual slaughtering of the European nations as a pitiful spectacle that was unnecessary and meaningless from the point of view of reason, during this second world war they have had to admit that this is for the highest stakes, that it concerns their own "to be or not to be," and thus it is by no means a topic for pacifist novels. This is one example. Their posture in relation to other "arch-human" quarrels also took a similar turn. The "intellectualist" started wearing a uniform and medals; not long ago, he was still floating on the broad waters of various sympathies and sampling various dishes to see which one he would select. Today he is (because he must be) an antifascist and, with few exceptions, an anti-Stalinist; he knows the regrettable consequences of liberal democracy and seeks new means of planning, free of the stupidity and criminality of totalism. Thus he has entered the sphere of practice and ceased being Gulliver among the Lilliputians; on the contrary, he has recognized the importance of the Lilliputians' worries. Has he thereby betrayed his calling? I don't think so, not if he has preserved some of his fundamental virtues, such as: aversion for hasty solutions, capacity for admitting ignorance, and respect for visions of what might be the best relations among peoples.

Still, if in periods like the present, what is demanded is the greatest speed in decision making, as well as the ability to cut through Gordian knots with one blow, stubbornness, and rejection of doubts (these often have a smell of defeatism about them)—if in such conditions there is room for people of a certain type, then can one proclaim (and not only theoretically, but on the basis of experience) that a collective atmosphere is appearing that is favorable for them?

If the rhythm of enthusiasms and boredoms and the intertwining of action and reaction are not an illusion, then one may answer the question in the affirmative. The venting of irrational urges and slogans, that whole fantastical collection of realia over which even the leaders of states with millions of citizens had lost power—all this elicits boredom now and a disinclination for extreme solutions, and following upon that is a yearning for moderation, clarity, and even coolness. The loss of faith in spontaneity, so evident in art in recent years (art is the most sensitive of manometers), would confirm my suppositions. Obviously these changes can encompass very few circles of especially sensitive people and either become the beginning of a new way of life or remain only an underground current that will surface very slowly, after all cataclysms have been shunted aside and extinguished. Furthermore, intellectualism does not seem to be possible as a style for the masses; they will always live by "spontaneous" passions, and that is one of the quite threatening and probably incurable diseases of a system based on regimes of denunciation (tyranny, naturally, is one such system). Intellectualism, however, can soften the absurdity of collective urges, giving them a more noble direction; it can undertake education. We have seen with our own eyes the kind of results that an education based on letting the passions "hang out" can lead to. It is not my field, but everyone must admit that a total lack of education (in the broadest sense), such as can be observed in Europe in the last half century, must be ascribed to the cult of "spontaneity" (Freud made that perfectly clear). Here I should say that just a few days ago I read a pamphlet by Bogdan Suchodolski about Irving Babbitt, and I promise myself much pleasure from reading books by that American philosopher. It is very invigorating to happen upon an intellectual movement to which one has matured internally during wartime (it is no accident that before the war I passed by a type of Babbitt humanism without paying it any attention). The idea of restraint and moderation, the distinction between the natural sphere and the exclusively human sphere, that great act of returning dignity to man after so much blundering in the forest of instincts—"How beautiful the world is!" one would like to cry out. "How valuable is an existence that affords an occasion for intellectual meetings and in which we always find what we have matured to." You accused me of being content just to stroll among various questions and of being more concerned with posing them than resolving them. I am not surprised by that rebuke. People are thirsting for prescriptions and models, today more than ever before. "Dynamic" ideas such as racism or Marxism have made us accustomed to boldness and outrageous demands. I even know people who insist that the present period is the twilight of civilization, primarily because it lacks the red dawn of mass movements such as socialism, or a vision of revolution that existed in the past era. Don't you think, though, that the spirit in which questions are asked is more important than universal answers? If we work in a certain spirit, in a certain atmosphere, then even answers that are remote from each other will possess a profound bond that unites them into one. And the point is precisely in that bond; the future depends on its coming into being.

You may well remark that in this slighting of conclusions

there is a tendency to play around, to escape, a sort of slipperiness that is concerned with always ensuring that one has a way out—that this is a position characterized by an excess of *désintéressement* and a distancing from human fortunes, from the very ones that demand the swiftest sorting out.

I would agree with that opinion if someone were able to convince me that it is useful to make an effort to enclose life in a certain number of formulas, formulas such as those the nineteenth century appreciated: the struggle for life, the selection of species, adaptation, class warfare, libido, and so on. For only with the help of similar formulas are vehement arguments possible, such as, for example, those engaged in by youth during the period of Positivism. As for me, I value highly our incapacity for principles. We are living in a different climate; we realize that what is most important is the way of life that derives from our method of thinking (or that precedes it—it's all the same). We are more humble toward the earth, and we know that no scientific discovery will change the thoughts that man in his isolation has dreamed up over millenia, pondering time, the changing order of things, and death. The spirit and intentions with which men arrived at such thoughts influenced their color, their satiation, their connection with everyday events. Indifference, if it really existed, would be a serious rebuke. I think, though, that the current of history holds us so tightly in its embrace that even the greatest loners have to pay a sizable tax to the so-called demands of the moment. Silences, blank spots, question marks, are all oarlocks—to continue using water metaphors—that hamper us in handling the oars; if it were not for them, we would flee too quickly, losing sight entirely of the shores on which the statues of ancient leaders and sages shine. It was they who taught us contemplation of human nature by comparing many pros with many contras, by placing circles around the perhaps unreachable point of per-

fect truth. There is no need to rush. When one is thirty, one is
not obliged to possess a so-called "complete worldview" (from
the moment a worldview is completed, it is dead, it is pure ver-
bal exercise). One is, however, obligated to walk along a particular line of life, to work at completing tasks in a prescribed
direction.

How can I state this more effectively? Because I don't write
clearly. The point is that when we have become accustomed to
looking at our creative work, at our thought, at our faith as a
particular *modus* (understanding that in some forty or fifty
years an entirely different *modus* may be operating), our concern is that the *modus* of our era should not cause man's de-
generation, should not turn him into a beast or a jester. The
modus of the Decadents (Stanisław Przybyszewski, for example, or Wacław Berent's novel *Rotten Wood*) was offensive; the
modus of the Romantics often reminded one of cardboard
Gothic palaces. And our *modus*? It has no name yet, and we
don't know where it begins. In truth, we ought to take care not
only about what we are cutting out, but also what material we
are cutting from. This fumbling along the cloth with our fingers as we seek to detect the bumps, softness, drape of the material—that is the indecision that you accuse me of. But there
is already a choice in this indecision. It is expressed by empha-
sizing certain aspects of man and skipping over others, by the
set of names I have cited and the aggregate of my sympathies
and aversions.

Please don't understand me to be preaching universal relativism and involuntary submission to historical mutability. No.
I strongly believe that there are epochs and people to whom it
is granted to come very close to the mystery of man, to look
him right in the eye. There are other epochs that blunder
around somewhere far away, or like blind men who, stroking
the elephant's trunk, insist that the entire elephant is long and
thin like a snake. To take in the actual *modus* that is accessible

to us and close to enduring human truth—that would be no small thing. Are there signs of this? Whoever believes in the purification of mankind through suffering and blood will answer yes. And he who believes that man is worn down by cruelty and freedom of instincts will also answer yes.

THE LEGEND OF THE WILL

1. All my comments on *ressentiment* draw upon M. Scheler, *L'homme du ressentiment* (Paris: Gallimard, 1933).
2. Zdziechowski, *Pesymizm, romantyzm*, vol. 1.
3. See Charles Andler, *Les précurseurs de Nietzsche*. Paris, 1920.
4. See Alain [Emile Auguste Chartier], *Stendhal* (Paris: Editions Rieder, 1935).

ABSOLUTE FREEDOM

1. Letter to Elsie E. Pell, quoted after E. E. Pell, *A. Gide—L'évolution de sa pensée religieuse*. Grenoble, 1935.
2. Ibid.
3. "*Subliminal self*" in English in the original. [Translator's note]
4. A. Fouillée, "Etude sur August Comte," *Revue des Deux-Mondes*, 1895. Cited by Gide in *Nietzsche*.
5. Stanisław Brzozowski, "Pragmatyzm i materializm dziejowy" [Pragmatism and Historical Materialism] in *Idee. Wstęp do filozofii dojrzałości dziejowej* [Ideas: An Introduction to the Philosophy of Historical Maturity]. Lwów, 1910.
6. Ibid.
7. Ibid.

BEYOND TRUTH AND FALSEHOOD

1. J. Huizinga, "*Incertitudes*," *essai de diagnostic du mal dont souffre notre temps*. Translated from the Dutch by J. Roebroek. (Paris: S. J. Librairie de Médicis, 1939).
2. Ibid.
3. Ibid.

ZDZIECHOWSKI'S RELIGIOSITY

1. M. Zdziechowski, *Europa, Rosja, Azja. Szkice polityczno-literackie* [Europe, Russia, Asia: Political-Literary Essays]. Wilno, 1922.

Notes to the Essays

THE LEGEND OF THE ISLAND

1. Marian Zdziechowski, *Pesymizm, romantyzm a podstawy chrześcijaństwa* [Pessimism, Romanticism, and the Foundations of Christianity], vol. 1 (Kraków, 1915).
2. Hippolyte Taine, referring to Robinson Crusoe in his *Histoire de la littérature anglaise* (1883), confesses: *"Parmi les hasards de la toute-puissante nature, dans ce grand roulis incertain, un Français, un homme élevé comme nous, se croiserait les bras d'un air morne, en stoïcien, ou attendrait en epicurien le retour de la gaieté physique."* (Amid the perils of all-powerful nature, a Frenchman, an educated man like us, would cross his arms with a mournful air, stoically, or would await in epicurean fashion the return of physical joy.)

THE LEGEND OF THE MONSTER CITY

1. "The heroes of *The Iliad* don't even reach your heels, Vautrin, Rastignac, Birotteau—and you, Fontanarès, who did not hesitate to confess publicly your pain concealed beneath the convulsive mourning frock coat that we all wear; and you, oh, Honoré de Balzac, the most heroic, unique, romantic, the most poetic of all the characters whom you delivered from your own breast." Charles Baudelaire, *Le salon de 1846*.
2. Roger Caillois, *Le mythe et l'homme* (Paris: Gallimard, 1938).
3. Ponson du Terrail, *Le club des valets de coeur*, cited by Caillois, op. cit.
4. Charles Baudelaire, *Constantin Guys—Peintre de la vie moderne*, 1859.

LETTER ESSAYS *(from the Publisher)*

The second half of the book is composed of letter essays by Czeslaw Milosz and Jerzy Andrzejewski that also date from that period and touch upon related themes. Czeslaw Milosz published letters I through IV in 1990 in *Tygodnik Literacki* [Literary Weekly] (Warsaw), adding a short introduction:

> For a long time I opposed publication of these letters. I was convinced by those who argued for their archival value, since there are few testimonies about people's state of mind during the time of the German occupation.
>
> Obviously, the letters were not sent by post. Jerzy Andrzejewski and I lived at opposite ends of Warsaw—at the very end of Aleje Niepodległości and in Bielany. We would meet in Śródmieście, in the city center, often at the Aria or the Actresses' Café on Mazowiecka Street. Andrzej Panufnik and Witold Lutosławski performed on two pianos in that coffeehouse, and for a time the bartender was our friend, the film director Antoni Bohdziewicz. If I am not mistaken, it was there that we were sworn in by Wacław Zagórski as members of the socialist organization Freedom.

of Hitlerism was terrible not only because of the crimes that were committed, but also because millions of Germans were forged into one by a faith that seemed completely absurd to people outside the magic circle in which the Germans, acting upon one another, were creating that faith. That is to say, this was a typical example of the mythologizing of reality, and it prompted the suspicion that the modern history of the European soul was rich with such deceptive imaginings of man about himself, collectively held, and emanating one from the other by way of a path of fancy-dress logic. I probably erred in seeking a sacrificial lamb, but that is not important; what is important is the need that impelled me to do so. Hitlerism belonged in every possible way to the climate, aura, or structure—whatever we may wish to call it—of the interwar period, and a large number of threads linked it with the tendencies that emerged in a different system, while they, in turn, had their own past. I therefore ascribed responsibility not only to the myth of blood and soil, not only to the myth of race, but also to the cult of life, instinct, blind vitalism; that is, my enemy was natural man. It was only superficially a matter of ideas that had been disrupted. In essence, I was carrying out, indirectly, an accounting with prewar *"ideolo"* (as the poet Julian Tuwim called it), for occupied Warsaw, after all, was its living continuation. For me, that had all come to an end, and conversations with the poets of the nationalist grouping Art and the People, who were ten years younger than I, could not be successful, since they did not understand that it had ended. But I was also compelled by a much more private need; there is a reason why there is so much about religious problems in these essays. A born intuitionist, I had to worry when I turned against those varieties of intuitionism that I suspected of collaborating in the transformation of so-called European culture into a fata morgana, into a realm of deception whose consequences I had experienced on my own skin, as we say. In other words, this was the task: to submit what is dear to us to a critical test so that it would remain standing only if it could manage to withstand the test.

An overly ambitious plan, an impossible plan, which is why even if the individual essays are not foolish, the link leading from one to the other does not come across clearly and is somewhat capricious, poetic. So perhaps it is good that this book never appeared as a whole.

Poland after his death, if I am not mistaken—appeared immediately after the war in *Nowa Polska* [New Poland], which was edited in London by Antoni Słonimski, and then in the commemorative volume *Stanisław Ignacy Witkiewicz, Człowiek i twórca* [Stanisław Ignacy Witkiewicz: The Man and His Work] (Warsaw, 1957).

Why did I write the book at the time? (1) Because of the German bomb in September that landed in the wing of the Staszic Palace that housed the Instytut Français. Its rich collection lay in piles mixed with rubble. The books were slowly cleaned and transferred to the University Library. For a while I was hired to do this for a bowl of soup, to tell the truth, because my daily wage was pennies. And it was those French books, set aside if the author or title struck my fancy, that provided the first impulse. (2) Out of the need to save myself. It was an attempt at autotherapy according to the following prescription: if everything inside you is agitation, hatred, and despair, write measured, perfectly calm sentences; turn yourself into a disembodied creature observing your carnal self and current events from a great distance. I am not going to insist that this prescription can be used at all times, but it was of help to me then.

What do I think now about this never published book? Is it good? Yes and no. Its shortcomings were more or less apparent to me even then. I quote from the preface: "History's violent leap and the sense that there is much to be done evoke a desire to be rid of old habits and illusions." Man "must attempt to recognize and explain the phenomena that shock him. Burdened by obsolete methods of thought and style, his attempts will be in vain ten times in a row. On the eleventh try, he will achieve what he aimed for. What number attempt these essays are, the author, obviously, does not know." Today I confront these texts as something that has no relationship to me, that is in the past, but admittedly with a certain respect for the intellect that mastered such a backbreaking task in the conditions of that time. There is a great deal of prewar influence in them. It is somewhat too literary; there is too much of the essay writer in it, so that the preface describes it perfectly: "Certain *i*'s are not dotted. In some cases there is more irresolution than certainty. In this sense, the book is an expression of dark times in which any thorough accomplishment is a virtually impossible task. The book's value, then, is based instead on its being something of an intellectual memoir."

Today I would say "a memoir from a period of delayed maturity." Because all the obsessions and themes that appear under my pen later are already present here. This is what it was like, more or less. The phenomenon

Notes to the 1996 Polish Edition

ESSAYS FROM THE OCCUPATION *(Publisher's Note)*

The essays included in this book arose as a unified work more than fifty years ago in Warsaw. Four of them (half, that is) have been published by Czeslaw Milosz elsewhere: the essay on Stanisław Ignacy Witkiewicz appeared in 1957 in a book of reminiscences devoted to that artist; the author included the other three —"The Legend of the Island," "The Legend of the Monster City," and "Zdziechowski's Religiosity"—in *Prywatne obowiązki* [Private Obligations] (1972). At the time, he added a brief introduction to them. We append it below in its entirety.

WARSAW ESSAYS *(Czeslaw Milosz)*

The three essays printed here for the first time were written in 1942 (the third, at the beginning of 1943) in Warsaw. They survived, and I have them in front of me: the paper is yellowed, crumbling; it will disintegrate at any moment. They are from a book in which I attempted to answer for myself the question: Why did the European spirit succumb to such a devastating fiasco? The entire collection was purchased by a publisher who was collecting manuscripts for postwar publication, and the purchase price supported me for quite a while, along with the money I earned from work commissioned by the underground theatrical organization, i.e., by Edmund Wierciński, and by Oficyna Polska, Zenon Skierski's underground publishing house. Individual chapters were read at meetings of various discussion groups. One chapter, about Witkiewicz—the first essay written about him in

2. D. Parodi, "Le problème religieux," *Revue de métaphysique et de morale*, 1913.

3. Ibid.

4. Ibid.

5. Ibid.

6. Zdziechowski, *Pesymizm, romantyzm*, vol. 1.

7. M. Zdziechowski, *O okrucieństwie* [On Cruelty]. Kraków, 1928.

8. J. Baudouin de Courtenay, *Mój stosunek do Kościoła* [My Attitude Toward the Church]. Warsaw, 1927.

9. Ibid.

10. Ibid.

11. Zdziechowski, *Pesymizm, romantyzm*, vol. 1.

12. Ibid.

13. Zdziechowski, *Europa, Rosja, Azja*.

14. Paraphrased in Zdziechowski, *Pesymizm, romantyzm*, vol. 1.

15. B. Jasinowski, *Wschodnie chrześcijaństwo a Rosja* [Eastern Christianity and Russia]. Wilno, 1933.

16. Zdziechowski, *Europa, Rosja, Azja*.

17. Ibid.

18. M. Zdziechowski, *Pestis perniciosissima*. Warsaw, 1905.

THE BOUNDARIES OF ART

1. John Sparrow, *Sense and Poetry: Essays on the Place of Meaning in Contemporary Verse*. London, 1934, p. 42.

2. Ibid., p. 65

3. Henri Bremond, *Histoire littéraire du sentiment religieux en France depuis la fin des guerres de religion jusqu'à nos jours*. Paris, 1916–33.

4. Henri Bremond, *Prière et poésie* (Paris: B. Grasset, 1926).

5. Edgar Allan Poe, "The Poetic Principle," *Essays and Reviews* (New York: The Library of America, 1984), pp. 92–93.

6. Ibid., p. 77.

7. Poe, "The Philosophy of Composition," *Essays and Reviews*, p. 17.

LETTER IV: ANDRZEJEWSKI TO MILOSZ, SEPTEMBER 1, 1942

1. The reference is to Johann Gottlieb Fichte, *Reden an die deutsche Nation*, 1807–08.
2. Torquato Tasso, *Gerusalemme liberata*. Trans. Edward Fairfax. The Online Medieval and Classical Library. http://sunsite.berkeley. edu/OMACL/Tasso/.

LETTER V: MILOSZ TO ANDRZEJEWSKI

1. In Russian in the original: *dognivaniia Zapada*.

Czeslaw Milosz was born in Szetejnie, Lithuania, in 1911. A witness to the devastation of Lithuania and Poland by the Nazi and Stalinist tides, he survived World War II in German-occupied Warsaw with his wife, Janina, publishing in the underground press. After the war he was stationed as a cultural attaché from Poland in New York, Washington, and Paris; he defected to France in 1951. In 1960 he accepted a position at the University of California at Berkeley. He was awarded the Nobel Prize in Literature in 1980. He died in Kraków, Poland, in August 2004. *Legends of Modernity* brings together essays and letters written during the war years 1942–1943.